URBAN SPRAWL

A Reference Handbook

Other Titles in ABC-CLIO's
CONTEMPORARY
WORLD ISSUES
Series

Books in the Contemporary World Issues series address vital issues in today's society such as terrorism, sexual harassment, homelessness, AIDS, gambling, animal rights, and air pollution. Written by professional writers, scholars, and nonacademic experts, these books are authoritative, clearly written, up-to-date, and objective. They provide a good starting point for research by high school and college students, scholars, and general readers, as well as by legislators, businesspeople, activists, and others.

Each book, carefully organized and easy to use, contains an overview of the subject; a detailed chronology; biographical sketches; facts and data and/or documents and other primary-source material; a directory of organizations and agencies; annotated lists of print and nonprint resources; a glossary; and an index.

Readers of books in the Contemporary World Issues series will find the information they need in order to better understand the social, political, environmental, and economic issues facing the world today.

URBAN SPRAWL
A Reference Handbook

Donald C. Williams

**CONTEMPORARY
WORLD ISSUES**

ABC-CLIO

Santa Barbara, California
Denver, Colorado
Oxford, England

Library of Congress Cataloging-in-Publication Data

Williams, Donald C.
  Urban sprawl : a reference handbook / Donald C. Williams.
    p.   cm. — (Contemporary world issues)
Includes bibliographical references and index.
  ISBN 1-57607-225-8
  1. Cities and towns—United States—Growth. 2. City planning—United States—History. 3. Land use—United States—History.
I. Title. II. Series.
  HT384.U5 W55 2000
  307.76'0973—dc21   00-011033

06 05 04 03 02 01 00   10 9 8 7 6 5 4 3 2 1

ABC-CLIO, Inc.
130 Cremona Drive, P.O. Box 1911
Santa Barbara, California 93116-1911

This book is printed on acid-free paper ∞.
Manufactured in the United States of America

I dedicate this book to my wife of fifteen years,
Audrey Wong Williams.
It is her unstinting support and faith in me
that has made this work possible.

Contents

Preface

The United States of America is in the midst of an unrivaled economic boom that has brought record rates of growth and employment as the country enters the new millennium. Even as this prosperity continues, however, many residents of metropolitan areas are experiencing the effects of growing pains that detract from their own quality of life. Some contend that every metropolitan area seems to be on the way to becoming its own worst nightmare, with bad-air alerts, traffic gridlock, loss of open space and recreational areas, racial and ethnic tensions on the rise, and a huge gulf between rich and poor.

Although these problems have long been the subject of public attention, only in recent years has a connection been made with prevailing patterns of urban development popularly called sprawl. This has taken shape in the form of low-density housing subdivisions, office parks, and commercial strip and mall development and has led to more cars on inadequate roads, increased utility costs, the decline of once vibrant inner cities, and the loss of a sense of community. Suburban sprawl also threatens the nation's capacity to maintain a viable agricultural sector and protect its environmental quality.

A growing number of planning professionals and environmentalists are calling for an overhaul of existing land development rules to make them more flexible and sensitive to the changing needs of communities. They advocate the increased use of urban growth boundaries, higher densities in residential zoning ordinances, better mass transit systems such as light rail lines, more affordable housing, and redevelopment of brownfields and neglected inner-city neighborhoods, as well as more tax incentives for conservation easements, local land trusts, and the greater use of technology to map natural systems and determine the effects on them of different land uses. From a political stand-point they argue that land use planning powers should be shifted to regional and statewide authorities.

On the other hand, free market advocates, often representing the real estate, home-building, and financial communities, respond that such policies invite too much governmental control into private sector decision making, distorting markets in harmful ways. Some even claim that the kinds of policies advocated by planners would only serve to exacerbate existing problems, rather than contribute toward solutions to our urban dilemmas. Too much regulation, it is said, will threaten the high standard of living enjoyed by Americans and hinder the functioning of our economic growth machine.

This book presupposes that its readers know little to nothing about the subject of urban sprawl. With this in mind, it is designed to serve as a launching pad for those seeking more information. It helps to define exactly what the phenomenon of urban sprawl is all about, why it has become a hot public issue, and points individuals toward resources that will be useful in gaining a better perspective on it. I trust that those who are more intimately familiar with the subject and its controversial attributes, particularly activists from both sides of the debate, will still find much utility in the large compilation of resources contained within.

Chapter 1 provides a general introduction to the subject of urban sprawl in the United States and is highly recommended to all who are new to this subject. It helps to provide background context by describing the historical development of this urban development pattern over the past century. It also examines policy solutions that have been devised over the past thirty years, reviews debates from competing political positions, and highlights issues that merit further study in the future.

Chapter 2 contains a chronology that highlights key urban development patterns as well as land use policy initiatives that have evolved over the previous century.

Chapter 3 consists of biographical sketches of some personalities who have articulated a wide variety of viewpoints on the subject of sprawl.

Chapters 4 and 5 are designed to give those interested in the facts more ground to stand upon. Chapter 4 presents a number of the key questions being raised in the current debate over urban sprawl, followed by charts and quotations from leading authorities that respond to these issues from different perspectives. Chapter 5 provides an overview of relevant laws and policy proposals that have been considered at the state and federal level. Both of these chapters should provide a much-needed empirical basis for those developing policy positions and opinions on this vital and pressing issue.

Chapter 6 offers the reader a comprehensive listing of advocacy groups that are involved with many different aspects of urban development policy, planning, property rights, and environmentalism. It also lists those federal and state agencies that administer programs directly dealing with sprawl.

Chapter 7 contains a select bibliography of books and reports dealing with urban sprawl, while Chapter 8 contains a similar list of nonprint sources.

A glossary of terms commonly used in both scholarly and public debates surrounding this issue has also been included as a ready reference for those who are new to the subject.

Donald C. Williams

1

Introduction

I. Background to the Current Crisis: Land Resources and Public Policy in America

The United States of America has long celebrated its productive farms, ranches, and natural beauty in song and verse. In recent decades though, newly built housing subdivisions, suburban office complexes, shopping malls, and accompanying traffic jams along congested highway corridors and side streets have become as commonplace as white farm houses, red barns, and verdant fields and forests once were. Translated into more emotional terms, America is presently experiencing an unprecedented loss of "open space"—productive crop and pasture lands, along with forest woodlands, fragile wetlands, and other natural wildlife habitats.

These trends show no sign of abating any time soon, as Americans continue to move out to new homes and shopping centers on the fringes of metropolitan areas. Even in areas of the country that have seen less dramatic population growth, outward urban expansion into rural areas—a phenomenon known as sprawl—has proceeded at a tremendous pace without letup. For example, in just the six years between 1990 and 1996, Little Rock, Arkansas, witnessed almost a doubling of its urban area from 109 to 199 square miles, even though its overall population was nearly flat during that time period. Akron, Ohio, experienced a slight population increase of 3.5 percent, while its urban metropolitan area grew by 65 percent. High-growth regions of the Sunbelt states have seen even greater increases in land area. For example, the Austin, Texas, region experienced a 50 percent population increase between 1990 and 1996, while expanding its metropolitan area some 160 percent into surrounding land (Brown 1998).

To most Americans, there is nothing particularly unusual about the sight of new houses under construction and shopping malls and office park developments quickly going up around them. Many eagerly seek out such places for new homes, shopping locales, and business opportunities. In the eyes of critics, however, this kind of real estate development represents nothing less than a tragically underrecognized "silent crisis" in which Americans are rapidly squandering their finite land resources at rates that are simply not sustainable. Neither are they desirable for the greater good of future generations. Chastising a decision-making process mostly under the authority of local government officials, they are calling for an end to uncoordinated, sprawling development patterns and a shift toward public control through planning institutions that function at the regional and state level. Might such controls, however, put a damper on business expansion, job growth, and long cherished personal freedoms, as opponents fear? An increasingly heated debate is presently under way between advocates of private property rights and government regulation that has moved from local to state and even federal political arenas over the past decade.

Historic Evolution of Urban Land Use in America

Why has urban development in the United States followed such sprawling patterns, and what is it about these land use patterns that creates problems for society? In many respects, present day urban development patterns are merely an outgrowth of trends set in motion over the previous 200 years. A closer look at these past developments is needed to fully comprehend the current debate over sprawl.

The wide open expanses of wilderness of the New World invited much profitable speculation in land for many early settlers from Europe. From the very beginning though, there were countervailing forces at work. The notion of treating land as a marketable commodity was incompatible with the preexisting Native American system of land use, which was largely based on rights of universal access and subsistence needs. Aside from these claims, often forgotten are contrary forces that were at work among the settlers themselves. European settlers brought with them a long tradition of city planning that dated back to medieval communities in which municipal corporations possessed the independent authority to own and dispose of all vacant lands. With the blessing of the crown and colonial governors, much of the early municipal development of colonial North America was surprisingly orderly in the design of residential street grids, open public spaces, public buildings, and market places (Cronon 1983).

After the American Revolution, these traditions began to recede. Urban areas had become politically subordinate to their respective state governments, which now had enormous political clout under the new federal Constitution. Counties were given more authority to act as agents of state government in many aspects of land use policy, while municipalities and towns were restricted to only those powers granted to them under state charters or legislative enactments. As a consequence cities no longer possessed any clear authority to control, let alone direct, the development of land within and beyond their boundaries.

The frontier now began to be developed by private land companies that purchased huge tracts, surveyed them, and then sold them off quickly to private citizens. With so much money to be made in speculation and sales, there was little support for restrictive land controls in the thousands of new settlements that were founded in quick succession in the decades that followed. Many early towns were actually planned on the basis of traditional grid designs reminiscent of colonial America, but a combination of rampant speculation and minimal government regulatory restrictions quickly reduced such orderly patterns into jumbles of crowded, noisy streets where residences were mixed with shops, taverns, mills, tenements, tanneries, and the like.

It was out of the chaos of these nascent cities that a renewed demand for more orderly growth eventually returned to the political sphere. The rise of the industrial city in the latter half of the nineteenth century attracted tens of thousands of people to urban centers, seeking employment in the new factories, mills, and foundries. Most were crowded into hastily constructed multistory tenements that grew up around the factory sites. Streets became congested and dirty, and the odor of raw sewage and pall of coal smoke spewing out from factory chimneys rendered city life uncomfortable and hazardous. Disreputable realtors subdivided lots, sold what they could, and moved on.

Ill-equipped city governments found themselves facing the need to provide order in the midst of this urban chaos. The public was demanding a better quality of urban life, access to clean water, waste disposal, sewage treatment, public education, adequate transportation, and gas and electric power, along with other municipal services. Political pressure was soon brought to bear on state legislatures to enhance the independent authority of cities to govern land use and economic development.

By the last two decades of the nineteenth century, cities like New York and Chicago were enacting building codes and making use of professional design standards to realign streets and construct new sewage systems, water treatment plants, and other services. City governments also began to develop the first land use zoning systems at this time as well. Their intention was to use the power of regulation to delimit the locations of industrial, commercial, and residential land uses to predesignated zones. This would enhance public welfare, stabilize property values, and better control the future spatial development of the community.

A number of legal challenges were brought to these changes, mostly by urban development interests that feared such laws were threatening their property rights. In 1926, however, the U.S. Supreme Court upheld the legality of this type of zoning in *Euclid v. Ambler Realty* (272 U.S. 365 [1926]), and soon thereafter model zoning codes were being promoted by reformers all across the country. State after state passed enabling acts permitting their municipalities to engage in planning. Some, like New Jersey and Massachusetts, even made it mandatory. Public officials subsequently went to work drawing up master street plans, adopting official maps, and enacting zoning codes to enforce their new regulations. Henceforth, future urban land use patterns would be indelibly influenced by the guiding hand of locally elected or appointed planning commissions and zoning boards.

Another significant response to the declining quality of life in major urban centers was the gradual expansion of residential settlement outward into suburbs. Until the arrival of the electric streetcar, the residents of cities were largely confined to living within distances of their workplaces that could be reached either by a horse-drawn cab or by foot. Although some outer suburbs had developed just after the Civil War, most of these were refuges for the rich, who did not have to worry about a daily commute to the city center. Trains and streetcars enabled many more people to escape the crowded and dirty city for the bucolic life of the suburbs. Real estate developers quickly saw the market potential, and began to buy up thousands of acres along the new rail lines so that they could construct modestly priced housing, most of which was built on uniformly narrow lots within an easy walk of the streetcar line. Advertising made much of the tree-shaded streets, broad open lawns, and leisurely pace of life in a setting where traditionally only the elite could have resided. Suburbs not only represented a place to live, they embodied a "romanticized and idealized image of nature and of the role of the family in such an idyllic setting . . . the humane alternative to the dehumanizing aspects of the city" (Paton 1995, 68).

With the growing popularity of the automobile by the 1920s, there was no longer any need to stay close to the streetcar lines. Urban development patterns consequently began to spread out even more widely than before. The compact retail sales and business areas of the pre-1920 era, clustered around the railroad terminals and trolley stops, now began to relocate along busy streets and highway intersections to capture the attention of automobile-bound commuters. This outward progression was enormously costly, especially as residents were now expecting well-surfaced roads, along with sewers, public water, gas, and other amenities. The only way this more diffuse development could be affordable to home owners was for local governments to underwrite these costs out of general property taxes under the assumption that roads benefited everyone and that urban growth would naturally raise property taxes. State money was also available, as was federal funding after 1916 through grants to state highway programs.

Some of these early suburbs were absorbed by the older cities as each grew ineluctably toward the other over the ensuing decades. Many more suburbs sought to protect and preserve the perceived sanctity that their quiet, orderly suburban havens provided. They vigorously opposed urban annexation, hoping to keep out the noise, pollution, immigrant populations, and corrupt governmental institutions that they associated with the big city. By the turn of the twentieth century state governments routinely granted independent recognition to these politically influential communities as distinct municipal corporations. Once this status was gained studies show that these suburbs quickly made use of their new zoning powers to adopt ordinances intended to exclude "undesirable" development such as low-income apartments and factories (Haar and Kayden 1989).

The Great Depression and World War II provided only a temporary lull in these trends, and urban patterns now were firmly established throughout the United States. In fact, plans were under way to encourage urban growth even while most governmental efforts were concentrated on winning the war. This arose from concerns in the Roosevelt administration about the inadequacy of decent housing for many Americans, which was becoming increasingly apparent. The 1940 census had revealed that one out of every eight urban dwellings had no indoor bathing or plumbing facilities, and one out of every seven had no running water or plumbing of any kind. In addition, the nation faced a shortage of over seven million urban housing units by 1945. Subsequent state and federal policies were designed to address these shortages, as well as satisfy demand that had built up over the previous fifteen years.

Most important were the generous mortgage insurance and loan programs that received a big boost toward the end of the war under the auspices of the Federal Housing Agency (FHA) and Veterans Administration (VA). The FHA provided federal guarantees to private mortgage lenders, lowering the minimum down payment to just 10 percent for home buyers, and lengthening repayment periods to twenty to thirty years. The VA offered low-interest mortgages with no down payment required at all of qualified veterans. The federal tax code was also modified at this time to permit mortgage interest payments to be tax deductible. Other federal and state subsidies existed as well. Funding became widely available for the construction of new regional airports, interstate highways, and tax-exempt bonds for the construction of schools, water treatment plants, and other public utilities. Low federal tax rates on automotive fuel also contributed to this development. Thanks to these programs, millions of young families had the wherewithal to leave cramped apartments and duplex houses in older residential neighborhoods and seek out new single-family dwellings in the suburbs. Historian Kenneth Jackson points to popular media programs and advertising on television as also playing a significant part in heightening the prestige of the suburban lifestyle among the upwardly mobile middle class (Jackson 1985).

All of these forces worked to generate a massive expansion of suburban growth after 1945. The census of 1950 indicated that 84.5 million out of 151 million Americans were living in metropolitan areas. The greatest share of this growth was in the direction of suburban communities, which had grown by 35 percent since 1940, while central cities increased by only 13 percent during this time. By 1960 two-thirds of the increase in twenty-eight million people recorded by the census were living in suburbs, which now had a total of sixty million residents compared to just forty-five million in the cities.

Urban development patterns would henceforth be guided very much by the preferences of suburban residents. Most pronounced in these communities was the use of restrictive zoning ordinances designed to shield these suburbs from the real or imagined evils of the older industrial city. Typically, this included minimum lot area requirements of one-half to one acre or more; minimum floor areas that would preclude less than substantial construction; and prohibitions on an array of multifamily housing that would effectively deny entry to any who could not afford to purchase a detached, single-family residence. Over time, Eugene Lewis contends, central cities became surrounded by a suburban wall of exclusionary zoning that effectively denied entry to lower-income groups, many of which comprised racial and ethnic minorities. This trend was reinforced by official FHA policy, which for many years endorsed restrictive covenants on deeds that prohibited property from being sold to nonwhites. FHA loan officers were also prohibited from approving loans that would upset the racial composition of neighborhoods. The tens of thousands of black migrants that poured into the booming cities during the 1940s and 1950s were steered into crowded, deteriorating ghettos, where they were later to be joined by equally large numbers of Hispanics from Puerto Rico, Mexico, and elsewhere (Lewis 1973).

By the latter half of the 1950s another trend saw retail businesses moving out of older city centers and into these outer suburbs. Drawn by newly constructed highways, subsidized public utilities, low taxes, and, of course, a huge market of well-to-do suburban residents, retail store owners found a much more amenable climate to do business. Some sought to relocate in strip plazas that provided them with highly visible locations lining the main travel corridors out of the city. Others were attracted to new shopping mall sites, especially those located near the intersection of radial and concentric perimeter highways. With acres of parking lots and easy access in and out via the automobile, suburban consumers saw little reason to look elsewhere to satisfy their shopping needs. A variation on the suburban mall, the "big box" discount chain, also grew rapidly at the confluence of major metropolitan travel routes.

This outward development pattern even affected the industrial base of America's major urban centers, which had historically served as the mainstay of economic growth and job opportunity. Factories, mills, stockyards, and manufacturing enterprises sought out locations on the urban fringe where taxes were low and land was cheap, or moved out even further to rural areas in the southern states. Warehouses followed as well. Thanks to the fast-moving highways, distribution enterprises were finding that they could more easily move freight by tractor trailers directly to strategically placed warehouses on the periphery of metropolitan areas. There, goods could be broken down into smaller lots for local delivery in the surrounding suburbs. In many cases this progression was openly encouraged by cash-strapped suburban local governments. They offered generous property tax breaks, cheap utility rates, and municipal bonding for roads and other services expressly for the purpose of attracting such employers to their communities.

The progressive disinvestment in America's inner cities was compounded by internal forces working against urban revival. Lacking a sound tax base due to the loss of large employers and a deteriorating urban infrastructure, these areas became afflicted with high rates of joblessness, crime, drug addiction, inadequate housing, and social distress. These problems in turn triggered a growing set of demands on existing city services that were difficult to meet by beleaguered city officials. Inner-ring governments had nowhere else to turn but to existing businesses, which were taxed at even higher rates. Today, even with substantial federal and state subsidies providing funds for economic development assistance, public housing, city welfare services, and education, the greener pastures in the outer-ring suburbs always seem to look a lot better. With much open land available for rock-bottom prices on the urban perimeter, safer streets, better schools, and the rest, the advantages are obvious for both downtown businesses and upwardly mobile city residents.

All of this meant that, in a remarkably short period of time, the older downtowns of America lost their monopoly position as the regional centers of choice for entertainment, commerce, trade, and industry. At best, they were just one of several business districts now in competition with newly fashionable suburban shopping centers and office parks that constituted entirely separate "edge cities" (Garreau 1991).

City mayors did not go down without a fight. Supported by those businesses that chose to remain downtown and real estate owners who had suffered big losses, they vigorously pursued federal and state assistance to save their cities through redevelopment. Rather than fight the trend toward flight, the strategy they sought was designed to accommodate suburbanites by making older downtowns more easily accessible to the automobile. These plans commonly began with massive clearance projects that entailed the demolition of older, run-down apartment blocks and dilapidated housing. This was followed by urban renewal projects that sought to reinvigorate the city with high-rise buildings, indoor shopping malls, and entertainment centers—along with spacious parking lots throughout the city center. Inner-belt freeways were built at the periphery of the downtown redevelopment zones, with radial linkages leading out to the suburbs so that the middle class and wealthy could quickly move to and from their places of residence. Meanwhile, many of the poor displaced by these projects ended up in poorly conceived high-rise apartment projects, or were shunted into already overcrowded housing elsewhere. The number of displaced people has never been fully accounted. One study showed that a total of 335,000 homes of low-income Americans were razed in just one decade, most without receiving any compensation (Hanson 1986).

The legacy of this development has been the curious juxtaposition of glittering downtown business and shopping districts surrounded by a succession of concentric urban rings. The most immediate ring consists of impoverished lower-income neighborhoods, followed by outer rings of sprawling middle- and upper-income communities. Yet even more distant in this sprawling pattern are the newly developing peripheral rings that are the preserve of the upwardly mobile and well-to-do. Those residing in the innermost ring find themselves locked in a cycle of poverty that is worsened by the lack of readily available employment opportunities and feelings of isolation and hopelessness. Trends in places like Minneapolis–St. Paul over the past thirty years indicate that these serious social and economic problems have spread from inner-ring city neighborhoods to adjacent middle-income rings as public and private investment continues to follow development further out into the periphery (Orfield 1997).

By the late 1960s and early 1970s urban development patterns of this nature were coming under increasingly critical scrutiny. The most pressing complaints about sprawl came from two political movements that shared little in common at the time: affordable housing advocates who operated from a base among minority residents in the inner cities, and environmental organizations that mostly drew their support from affluent urban and suburban residents.

Although the 1970 census showed that more Americans than ever were moving to the suburbs, lower-income families, particularly racial and ethnic minorities, were not generally well represented in this outward movement. Part of the reason for this rising disparity had to do with economics. Those with low incomes or who were dependent upon welfare subsidies, regardless of race or ethnicity, simply could not afford to join their more well-off neighbors in moving out to the suburbs. Housing prices and transportation costs were beyond what these people could afford based on meager incomes. Exclusionary zoning practices in the suburbs were also to blame, as these ensured that affordable housing would not be available outside the inner cities anyway.

Complaints about the inequality of this situation came to a head in 1975 when the National Association for the Advancement of Colored People (NAACP) brought suit against the township of Mount Laurel, New Jersey. The case faulted local zoning for the way it deliberately excluded housing opportunities for low- and moderate-income families. The New Jersey Supreme Court decided in favor of the plaintiffs, ordering Mount Laurel to revise its zoning to correct these inequities and setting the precedent for affirmative, inclusionary land use obligations among local governments throughout the state.

Although other states adopted somewhat similar fair housing laws, the potential impact of these policies was watered down in a subsequent case decided by the U.S. Supreme Court in 1978. In *Village of Arlington Heights v. Metropolitan Housing Development Corp.* the Court ruled that such laws have a bearing only if there is proof of intent to discriminate through exclusionary ordinances—an evidentiary threshold that has been difficult to meet. The fair housing agenda has also been deflected by countervailing political forces in the suburbs. Fueled by fears generated by school busing mandates, a striking number of suburban communities have stood firmly by their right to home rule, even going so far as to pass referenda against the provision of public housing, and low-income and multifamily housing in direct defiance of state mandates. Facing this kind of steadfast opposition, inner-city activists and their allies have shifted their attention to redeveloping existing minority neighborhoods where they have a natural political base, rather than trying to break into the white majority suburbs.

The other major force at work equally critical of urban sprawl development emerged from the nascent environmental movement. Alarmed by the rapid loss of natural habitats and threat of extinction to hundreds of species, environmental activists sought to use local planning and zoning codes to restrict further development, especially in sensitive wetland areas. Proposals ranged from stopping all further development (no growth), to simply placing restrictions that would slow down the process (slow growth). Environmentalists, many of whom were affluent suburban residents, were able to find natural allies among fellow home owners concerned about rising property taxes and the loss of scenic open space in their communities.

In 1971 the city of Petaluma, California, adopted the first significant local growth management policy in response to these sentiments. It imposed a quota of no more than 500 new building permits per year as a means to halt the pace of new development. The policy was upheld in federal court in *Construction Industry Association of Sonoma County v. City of Petaluma* (522 F2nd 897 [1975]). It was found that the concept of public welfare is sufficiently broad to uphold the desire to preserve small-town character, open spaces, low-density populations, and orderly growth. Another key case in New York at this time challenged the right of the city of Ramapo to impose a zoning ordinance that made issuance of a development permit contingent on the presence of public utilities, drainage, road access, and other public services. The state appeals court ruled in 1972 that this community had the right to determine the pace of its own development in order to better manage its own fiscal resources. Rutherford Platt argues that both cases set important precedents for future growth management legislation at the local and state levels that began to appear at this time (Platt 1996).

The Contemporary Phenomenon of Urban Sprawl: Costs and Consequences

Sprawl patterns of urbanization have continued throughout the past two decades of the twentieth century, slowing down only moderately during periods of economic recession. Since 1980 suburban population has grown ten times faster than central-city populations in larger metropolitan areas, averaging a net gain of between 2.4 and 2.9 million per year between 1988 and 1996. Almost 80 percent of Americans today live in metropolitan areas, and of these, a growing proportion—now well over 60 percent— reside outside of central cities in suburbs. Even so, the highest rates of urban growth today are found in the most distant fringes of metropolitan areas. Dubbed "exurbs," these are typically unincorporated rural areas that can be as much as forty miles or more from a central city. The long daily commutes for these exurban residents has helped to push motor vehicle use from one to two trillion miles on average per year between 1970 and 1990. As more Americans move to the suburbs, the more dependent they become on their automobiles to travel to work, for shopping, school, and virtually every other activity (Benfield et al. 1999, 6).

These trends have had a dramatic impact on the land. Between 1960 and 1990 the amount of developed land in large urban areas of the United States more than doubled, while population grew by less than half this rate. This can be seen throughout the country in greater or lesser degrees, with high-growth poles like Los Angeles, Seattle, Denver, and Atlanta witnessing an expansion of their physical sizes from 80 to 100 percent. As mentioned above, these trends are also evident even in regions of slower population growth and economic contraction. New York City's population grew by only 8 percent, but its area grew 65 percent during this time. Similarly, Chicago's population increased only 4 percent, but the city experienced some 46 percent growth in physical size. The Cleveland area actually lost population by 11 percent, yet still expanded its land size by 33 percent.

The expansion of urban development ever further out into the fringes of metropolitan areas has brought mixed results for the country. On the positive side, these trends represent an unprecedented boom in the suburban real estate market that has lasted for several decades, most especially in high-growth regions like the Southeast, Mountain States, and West Coast. Those who have taken risks by purchasing farmlands and undeveloped woodlands on the periphery of metropolitan areas have reaped enormous returns on their investments more often than not. So too have home builders, developers, and real estate sales agents who have catered to the large market for spacious homes situated in exclusive, large-lot subdivisions or larger multiacre estate lots. They have fulfilled the dreams of many Americans who are searching for an escape from the poverty, crime, underperforming schools, pollution, and other associated problems of older cities and inner-ring suburbs. Commercial developers have filled another important market niche by locating large shopping malls, office complexes, gas stations, and strip developments within easy commutes of these suburban areas. Elected legislators, board members, and executives representing these localities also have gained much by taking the credit for delivering millions of dollars in federal and state taxpayer subsidies to their suburban constituents in the form of new highways, freeway interchanges, schools, and utilities that make it all possible.

The development of such large amounts of open space has also attracted backlash against sprawl among a diverse array of critics. Among them are farmland preservationists at the American Farmland Trust (American Farmland Trust 1994), who point to the rapid loss of productive farmland that has accompanied urban sprawl. National statistics do indeed confirm a dramatic loss in farmlands during the second half of the twentieth century. Although rates vary tremendously from one state to another, federal statistics analyzed by Staley show that land in farms dropped from 1.2 billion acres in 1950 to just 968 million by 1997, a 20 percent decline. The most dramatic losses occurred during the 1960s, when 7.3 million acres of farmland went of out production on average each year. Since then an average of 6.3 million acres were lost yearly in the 1970s, 5.2 million in the 1980s, and in the first half of the 1990s 2.6 million acres per year (Staley 1999, 17–18). Although these figures suggest rates of decline have been slowing, the ongoing loss of such large quantities of open land represents a major challenge for preservation advocates.

Given the relatively flat, open, and well-drained nature of cultivated and pasture lands, it is not surprising that real estate developers view this land as being the most readily suited for their projects. In turn the amount of profit to be gained by farmers selling off lands is well above what prevailing commodity prices offer, should this land remain in agricultural use. High estate taxes also make the transfer of such land from one generation to another unviable, as do rising property taxes that often accompany the encroachment of housing subdivisions and strip developments located within the proximity of a growing metropolitan region. With the average age of the American farmer surpassing fifty, and record numbers of farms being sold off to developers each year, some analysts now question the very survival of farming in certain sections of the country (Daniels and Bowers 1997).

Such dramatic losses have dire consequences for a significant portion of rural populations that depend on agriculture for their economic well-being. This includes farming families, creditors, seed companies, tractor suppliers, and related businesses that represent the traditional mainstay of many local economies. Once a critical mass of farmers abandons the land, the entire web of support for agriculture quickly diminishes. As one study concludes, "[t]he more farmers in an area that leave farming, the harder they make it on the remaining farmers to survive. Farm support businesses have fewer customers, and are more likely to shut down. The farther farmers have to travel for feed, seed, fertilizer, machinery and marketing services, the more difficult farming becomes" (Daniels 1999, 215).

Farmland losses are especially severe in those regions of the country where soils are richest and most productive. This land, classified by the U.S. Department of Agriculture (USDA) with its highest rating, presently composes about 50 percent of all land under production in the United States, and accounts for 56 percent of gross agricultural sales, 86 percent of fruits and vegetables, 80 percent of dairy production, and 45 percent of meat and poultry production. At present, one important study has shown that 372 of the nation's 640 leading agricultural counties—all of which have this USDA soil designation—are either within or adjacent to major metropolitan areas (American Farmland Trust 1994). As these lands fall out of production the increasingly intensive use of irrigation, chemical fertilizers, and pesticides on remaining lands raises concerns about environmental damage, as well as a long-term loss in soil nutrient quality.

Environmentalists remind us that the loss of vast tracts of open space also marks the destruction of life-sustaining wildlife habitats. The most serious threats come through the loss of wetland, woodland, and prairie environments that provide for the year-round needs of many threatened species. Even when sprawl leaves patches of green in between subdivisions and shopping plazas, studies show that it contributes to habitat fragmentation that disrupts migratory corridors and breeding patterns (Nature Conservancy 1998). Preservationists are quick to point out that farmlands, while certainly not benign to wildlife, do provide habitat for grassland species as well as migratory birds after harvests are over or while land is temporarily lying fallow.

Water supplies necessary to sustain wetlands are also threatened due to the need to pull from already overtaxed aquifers in many parts of the country the water necessary to sustain urban development. More serious still are dramatically high levels of nonpoint-source pollution that is derived from yard pesticides, fertilizers, nondegradable debris, and other assorted suburban contaminant wastes that flow uninhibited through street sewers directly into local lakes, rivers, and estuaries. Additional harm comes through thermal pollution, which results from water being heated on paved surfaces before funneling downstream into wetlands. Warmer water fosters algae growth, which in turn leads to a loss of life-sustaining oxygen. Recent research reviewed by F. Kaid Benfield demonstrates that when a region reaches a point at which just 10 percent of its surface consists of impervious surfaces, considerable wildlife losses occur due to this hazard. Finally, sprawl-induced automobile traffic also contributes a growing amount of carbon emissions into the atmosphere, leading to higher smog counts in large metropolitan areas, as well as the serious threat of long-term global warming (Benfield et al. 1999).

Environmental degradation also has increased the likelihood of human harm from natural hazards. In the past three decades, scientists have accumulated considerable evidence pointing to the vital role that natural wetlands and riverine systems play in channeling, absorbing, and purifying large amounts of rain and snowmelt that otherwise quickly accumulate into flood conditions for surrounding areas. Recent evidence also indicates that woodlands, rangelands, and even cultivated farmlands also contribute to mitigating such threats to human settlement. Large sections of paved surfaces—especially the huge multiacre parking lots that commonly surround shopping centers—have just the opposite effect. Impermeable surfaces like pavement and large, flat rooftops of stores eliminate the natural absorptive capacity of the soil to minimize the effect of precipitation. Building on slopes, ledges, and inappropriate soils further worsens flooding, erosion conditions, and in the worst cases, fosters dangerous mudslides. Critics like Jonathan Barnett charge that the cumulative impact of these pressures can be devastating to human communities. "Once whole regions are regraded, paved, and channeled, there is a high risk of undesirable environmental change: flooding, soil erosion, greater temperature extremes, falling water tables, contaminated aquifers" (Barnett 1995, 6).

A growing level of dissatisfaction about sprawl is also emerging from the very people who have chosen to reside in suburban fringe areas. Part of this resentment comes from rising tax rates. As more and more residential housing is constructed in remaining open space, local governments find it necessary to raise the property tax burden on existing home owners and businesses to accommodate the need for expansion of schools, roads, water and sewage lines, and electrical utilities, along with public safety services like police, fire, and emergency medical care.

Many suburban residents complain of a decline in the quality of life that initially drew them to purchase a home in such localities. Each additional housing and commercial development brings more traffic, turning connector roads and local highway systems into overcrowded nightmares of endless stops and starts. Residents also become dismayed when once pristine open spaces gradually fill in with yet more sprawl.

The quality of life for these suburban residents is also deeply affected by the design features of the subdivisions that they inhabit. In the pursuit of privacy, single-family units are usually spread apart by large lots along winding roads that often lack even a sidewalk to connect them. Houses are positioned along with shrubs and trees in a manner designed to minimize contact between residences. Potential outdoor gathering points that might bring neighbors together, such as porches and sun decks, are universally located in the rear of homes, facing empty back-yards. Other places that could engender casual association with neighbors such as stores, restaurants, parks, and schools are situ-ated far out of walking or even bicycle distance. Moreover, the high cost of housing and lack of available mass transportation to lower-income communities ensures that such residents also rarely interact with people who come from different ethnic, racial, and economic classes. Decades after civil rights laws were put on the books, the outer-ring suburbs remain among the most racially segregated areas of the country.

Critics like Neal Peirce even contend that the design of these communities leads to social stress, purposelessness, and even acts of civic disengagement and violence. Citing the troubling oc-currence of school shootings around the country in suburban communities like Littleton, Colorado, as a reflection of this over-riding sense of alienation, he has written that "Littleton reminds us that we need to tame and convert the soulless sameness of classic modern suburbia, to retrofit all our communities to be more special, welcoming places. The shootings are a reminder that it's only by getting to know each other in real streets and stores, parks, and public places, that we have a chance to be a truly democratic—and safe—society" (Peirce 1999).

II. Making Better Use of the Land: The Debate over Controlling Urban Sprawl

The controversial side effects of urban sprawl have been recog-nized for over thirty years by professional planners and policy experts. Yet to most Americans, these debates have seemed far from their immediate concerns. Only when they hear about plans for a large new apartment complex, a landfill, or roadway in their neighborhoods do they become active and involved. This section provides an overview of various policy strategies for containing sprawl, describing programs in some detail, as well as the de-bates that have been sparked by them.

Containing Sprawl through Local Zoning

Communities experiencing rapid rates of urban sprawl have found themselves overwhelmed by the enormous fiscal burdens created by new development occurring around them. Each new home and business has to be served with public water, sewage connections, and access roads, as well as police and fire protection. Unfortunately, the anticipated tax revenues rarely are found adequate to cover these costs, especially when development pressures from neighboring jurisdictions compound the impact on local services. Faced with pressing financial concerns, local governments have two options: raising property taxes, or making use of growth management tools that are designed to mitigate the impact of future development. Given the general public disposition against higher taxes, it is not surprising that growth management has become a politically popular alternative for ιnunicipal and county governments around the United States since the decade of the 1970s. What forms of growth management have been adopted by local governments, and how effective have they been in containing sprawl?

Local governments can utilize a variety of instruments to better manage sprawl-induced growth patterns. The imposition of large minimum lot sizes, frontage requirements, and bans on multifamily dwellings in local zoning codes can have the impact of limiting the number of newcomers into an established community. However, as was noted earlier, these restrictions have not stood up well in the courts. Douglas Porter also points out that they are typically opposed by real estate companies and developers because they can substantially limit their investment options and financial returns (Porter 1997).

An alternative is to shift costs for infrastructure to developers. Revenue gained from impact fees can be used to defray the costs of extending public infrastructure to new projects. Performance bonds are a similar means of covering infrastructure costs. These require developers to provide a lump sum up front at the beginning of a project that is sufficient to cover the cost of all public infrastructural improvements. Once the project is completed, the local government reimburses the developer, provided all of the specified components are properly in place. Incentives are sometimes incorporated into these agreements to award developers with density bonuses, more flexible design, and more expeditious processing of approvals should they comply with community growth-management objectives.

Other instruments are designed to compel developers to work within a more forward-looking community vision that has been laid out in a comprehensive plan. Such plans can determine exactly what kind of growth a community desires, how it is to be paid for, and where it should be located. To ensure compliance with these plans, periodic project reviews can be mandated. These allow local planning boards to rate the acceptability of a project according to a predetermined point system based on features of the plan. Urban growth boundaries can be incorporated into these plans as well. These are typically created through the purchase or donation of open lands for park development or conservation purposes. The metropolitan areas of Portland (Oregon), Minneapolis–St. Paul, and San Francisco have all established greenbelts as part of a larger regional comprehensive plan adopted by contiguous local governments.

No solid consensus today exists that local growth management laws actually achieve the goals intended. Property rights advocates contend that restrictive laws like these cause more harm than good by distorting the otherwise rational decisions made by consumers and producers in the real estate market. Restrictions have the effect of causing the cost of housing in newly developing areas to go up, thereby limiting the choices of lower-income home buyers seeking to move out to the suburbs. They also punish existing landholders unfairly by placing restrictions on their range of options, an especially unjust outcome for those individuals who had made their investment in land long before the regulations were adopted (Staley and Scarlett 1997).

Moreover, critics like Anthony Downs argue that these measures have done little to stem the tide of urban sprawl anyway. In fact, they charge, in some cases they even make it worse. Government efforts that circumvent the local real estate market merely encourage so-called leapfrog development. This occurs when developers who encounter an overly restrictive regulatory environment in one town simply move out to the next community, worsening the problem of suburban sprawl in the long run. Leapfrog development has serious ramifications for all neighboring communities, even those seeking to limit growth. Facing fierce competition for new sources of tax revenue from neighboring communities that seem to be permitting more development brings pressure on elected officials to relinquish development controls. With the need to build new schools and roads and expand other essential services, local officials find it difficult to resist the temptation to avoid compliance with comprehensive plans in the hope that it will raise more tax revenues (Downs 1994).

Critics also challenge the notion that all forms of urban sprawl development are inherently costly to suburban communities. Although most studies have confirmed that residential development fails to generate sufficient tax revenues to cover services adequately, especially in its beginning phases, other types of development do provide a positive balance. Commercial and industrial property development has been shown to be the most cost effective use for land, costing a community an average of just twenty-nine cents in exchange for each dollar that is returned to the citizens in the form of wages and tax gains (Staley 1999).

Statewide Prescriptions for Sprawl

Over the previous twenty years, the inadequacies of local growth management controls have led advocates to call for greater state-level involvement in combating sprawl. The logic behind this strategy is compelling. According to John DeGrove, state agencies are in a better position to regulate the impact of sprawl on regional transportation networks and environmental quality because problems like traffic congestion, air pollution, and water runoff extend far beyond local boundaries. They also possess the legal reach to sort out complicated political and economic issues that are generally beyond the ability of limited jurisdictions. States further possess the financial leverage and constitutional authority to get results. They can offer either inducements or mandates requiring local governments to develop land use plans (DeGrove 1992).

For several decades efforts have been underway in all fifty states to advance more comprehensive land use planning and growth management at the regional and local levels. Between 1971 and 1974 Oregon, Vermont, and Florida embraced statewide planning laws, following in the footsteps of Hawaii, where these concepts had been on the books since 1961. California and North Carolina also adopted strict land use laws, but these were designed to apply only to their coastal areas. Colorado also undertook limited state oversight in areas deemed to be of statewide importance.

Of all these early initiatives the most ambitious antisprawl strategy was attempted in Oregon. Although it still reserved zoning and planning for its local governments, it required that each community have a comprehensive plan in place that established growth boundaries and adhered to statewide goals. State agencies were given substantial regulatory powers to write and enforce rules and oversee the approval process of local plans. Although this strategy has not been without its critics, Oregon was able to bring together an initiative that overcame longstanding concerns about balancing state priorities with local oversight and local implementation (Abbott, Howe, and Adler 1994).

The momentum toward further state involvement abated as opposition mounted in the mid-1970s against what were seen as unprecedented and even unconstitutional state incursions on local authority. Some of this opposition stemmed from worries that state governments would override local zoning that prohibited unwanted facilities, such as power plants, prisons, trash incinerators, or wastewater treatment plants. The movement also diminished as development pressures abated due to high interest rates, inflation, and energy concerns. Still, even those states that did not opt for statewide growth management reforms did pass a multitude of laws that focused on either specific geographic areas or specific land use issues, such as farmland preservation, coastal zone management, flood plain regulation, housing, and solid waste disposal. It should also be noted that in the absence of state-administered remedies, several powerful regional planning institutions also came into effect at this time, including the San Francisco Bay Conservation and Development Commission, the Cape Cod Commission, and the Pinelands Commission in New Jersey.

When development pressures again resumed after the economic recessions of both the early 1980s and 1990s, additional waves of growth management laws came into existence around the country. Eight states adopted growth management laws of varying magnitude and scope between 1984 and 1991. Florida led this trend with a series of tough growth laws adopted in 1985. The primary instrument in Florida became the principle of concurrency, which was required in all mandated local comprehensive plans. Under this concept new development is not permitted by the state unless local plans demonstrate that the utilities, transportation, and other public infrastructural facilities are present or fully funded in time for projects to be completed. In 1986 New Jersey created a state planning commission to formulate a statewide development plan. Local governments henceforth were encouraged to develop their own growth management plans in conformity with the state plan through a negotiated cross-acceptance process. In New England Maine, Vermont, and

Rhode Island all followed suit in 1988 by mandating that their local governments adopt plans consistent with a statewide growth plan. This was particularly significant in Vermont, which already had in place nine regional planning agencies to review and permit developments of significant regional impact. Georgia, Washington, and Maryland enacted similar state laws in 1989, 1991, and 1992 respectively. Although these latter cases differ in details, most require consistency between local plans and state growth management goals and often insert county or regional planning agencies as a new force for managing growth.

New initiatives again came on to the scene in the late 1990s in several states as growth pressures renewed. Maryland adopted a "Smart Growth" law in 1997 that channels all future state financial subsidies to areas of the state that are best suited for it. Zones designated by county governments as Priority Funding Areas are targeted for state subsidies, while rural areas are set aside for open space preservation. Tennessee adopted a law in 1998 requiring its counties and municipal governments to develop comprehensive plans with urban growth boundaries in place. Once these are drawn up, state funding is relegated to designated growth areas within these boundaries. Other states simply sought to aggressively increase their commitment to open space preservation in 1998. New Jersey approved a measure to spend $1 billion over ten years to preserve half of the state's remaining open space, while Arizona pledged an unprecedented $220 million for the same purpose while also tightening local planning requirements.

Are statewide prescriptions for sprawl the answer? Any measures designed to bring state agencies into local land use decisions are sure to invite contentious politics, especially in those states with a strong tradition of local home rule. Resentment often runs high when state bureaucrats are given unprecedented new responsibilities that mandate local compliance. Debates over land use are complicated by a mix of groups representing real estate, banking, commercial development, farming, property rights, and environmental interests, many of which have close ties to and receive assistance from much larger national counterparts that see these state arenas as just one more battleground in a larger national effort.

Opponents contend that state involvement in planning constitutes an unwarranted degree of interference in the local land use decision-making process. It invites outside actors that include regional and state planning officials, environmental activists, and state courts that do not hesitate to insert their own political agendas into a process that some feel is better left to those who will have to live with the consequences. However carefully statewide programs are implemented, local chambers of commerce, builders, and realtors contend that local autonomy will suffer. The transfer of planning functions to regional and state agencies has also reportedly brought charges of political favoritism (Burchell 1993).

It is for these reasons that many of the mandated components of state growth management planning have been deliberately underfunded or their implementation has been delayed. In the case of Maine the legislature completely withdrew its previous commitment to mandatory planning mechanisms a year after their adoption as a result of a backlash orchestrated by a variety of commercial interests and citizens' groups that feared losing local autonomy.

Is more sound planning really the answer to containing sprawl? The effectiveness of comprehensive land use planning, whether prescribed by the state or not, has long been in question. Citing decades of past experience with master plans, critic James DeLong contends that these rarely correlate with reality, and are more often ignored in the breach than followed by local planning boards and zoning authorities. When considering the provisions of these plans, elected officials who oversee the process are more often swayed by political loyalties and neighborhood vetoes than the principles of sound planning (DeLong 1997).

Saving Rural Lands from Urban Sprawl

Farmland that lies at the periphery of most established urban areas is extremely vulnerable to development. Once urban development begins to creep into a previously rural area, property valuations rise, triggering a hike in taxes for farmers who are already struggling to maintain their operations in the face of sagging commodity prices and stiff global competition. Even those who persevere must endure growing traffic congestion and complaints from transplanted urbanites about the dust and odors raised by their operations, and the pesticides they use on their fields. Is there any policy strategy that could possibly slow down this trend? Are such measures really worthwhile?

Farmland preservationists argue that some policy instruments do exist that can help, especially because farms provide such a worthy asset to communities. Beyond the visible appeal of rustic scenes associated with agriculture and ongoing support among agribusinesses, farms on average draw just thirty-one cents in public spending for every dollar they return to the local economy. Bolstered by growing public concern around the country, a number of policy strategies have been tried by state governments since the mid-1970s.

The primary reason why farms are being sold for development has to do with the potential return these sales have for landowners. Why would any farmer want to continue to work the land for a return of $2,000 to $3,000 per acre when a real estate developer will pay him or her $20,000 to $30,000 per acre? The only way to offset these market pressures is to employ either disincentives to potential developers, or incentives to farmers to remain on the land.

Disincentives include any policy that discourages real estate developers, potential home buyers, or business owners from locating in an area that has been set aside for agricultural uses. Agricultural zoning is one way to send this message. Local officials are authorized in virtually all states to designate particular areas in their communities as restricted to farm-related uses, combined with large minimum lot sizes of thirty, fifty, or even more acres. Typically, these designations also include a significant setback around farm operations to act as a buffer zone between the farm and surrounding urban lands. Although effective in the short run, there is no guarantee that this zoning will remain in place for a long period. Eventually, many farmers seek to relinquish their protected status, because zoning does not in any way enhance the existing market values of their land.

Another disincentive to sprawl are right-to-farm laws, which presently exist in forty-seven states. These laws legitimize the practice of farming in an area by providing legal protection against nuisance suits that involve standard farming practices. The message sent by local authorities is that nearby home owners must put up with the discomforts of farming or leave the area. As with agricultural zoning, however, this instrument also does nothing about rising property values, tax rates, and market forces that render farming increasingly unprofitable.

Incentive policies seek to provide a financial gain to those farmers who choose to keep their land in production. One type of incentive offered by all fifty states addresses the problem of rapidly rising property taxes that accompany urban development. To keep farms operating, a preferential property tax assessment is levied that greatly reduces state and local taxation. As long as farmers keep their land in production, they continue to enjoy lower taxes. Although this may be welcome relief, the amount saved in taxes is usually not offset by the large sums offered by developers. Tax breaks also do not guarantee that the land will be held as open space in perpetuity. They may even be part of a deliberate strategy by farmers who are seeking a tax break until the right price comes along.

Far more effective incentives have been state and local programs that give farmers the opportunity to reap the full market value of their land while remaining in full production. Fourteen states have enacted purchase of development rights (PDR) programs to accomplish land preservation through this kind of logic. These programs offer farmers the opportunity to receive a one-time cash payment (often accompanied by preferential tax inducements) for the full assessed market value of their farms in return for a permanent pledge to keep their land in agricultural uses. In effect, the government purchases the development rights by means of a conservation easement that is affixed to the deed for the land. Although not required to do so, it is hoped that the farmers will use much of their financial gain to reinvest in their farms to keep them competitive, either by upgrading farm equipment or paying down related debts. Should a farmer decide to sell his or her land, it must remain in agricultural production by whoever takes it over, or it will revert to local authorities, who then maintain it as open space.

A variation on this same theme are transfer of development rights (TDR) programs. This instrument differs in that it includes incentives for potential real estate developers to locate their projects in already existing urban areas. Under TDR programs, a local government issues development credits to local farmers equal to the value of their assessed land. The farmer then offers these for sale to developers. Once sufficient credits are in hand, developers are permitted to begin their projects in growth zones previously set aside for high-density urban uses. The advantage of these programs is that they enhance the capacity and clout of local government planning efforts by accomplishing the twin goals of preserving open space and funneling new development into appropriate areas. Tom Daniels suggests that these programs work best in those communities where concerted efforts have been made to develop comprehensive plans for future land use, otherwise land is preserved in isolated patches where open space is much less appreciated (Daniels 1999).

Incentive policies also exist under the direction of private nonprofit conservation land trusts. Some work to save agricultural lands, but many others are driven by a commitment to environmental protection, devoting their financial resources to preserving vulnerable wetlands, wildlife habitat, shorelines, scenic views, and even historic properties. Although these organizations trace their origins back to the nineteenth century, they have proliferated since 1976 when the federal tax code explicitly allowed land trust donations to be deductible. Since 1985 the number of private trusts has doubled to over 1,100 located in all fifty states and Puerto Rico. A variation on this theme are community land trusts, which are active in lower-income rural areas and offer residents a lifetime, inheritable lease in return for their willingness to work the land.

Open space preservation has sparked a heated debate in recent years. Although all sides have acknowledged that record numbers of farms and farmlands have been disappearing over the previous three decades, critics argue that this is not occurring primarily as a result of cities crowding out agricultural production. Recent research points to urban encroachment as being responsible for only 25 to 35 percent of farmland losses. Other factors are also at work that tend to hit smaller farmers particularly hard. These include changes in the global structure of agricultural markets that have brought stagnant commodity prices, growing costs of technology and other inputs, and the emergence of large-scale corporate farming interests that have driven down production costs around the country. The precise accounting of farmland losses over time is further muddled by federal programs that in the past have paid farmers to take crops out of production as a means for stimulating prices (Staley 1999).

Even with the loss of record amounts of prime farmlands, critics also dispute the contention that this threatens an impending national food crisis. The U.S. Department of Agriculture's index of national farm output, which measures total agricultural production, increased 47.9 percent between 1970 and 1993. Total farm income increased by 63 percent from 1980 to 1994 as well (U.S. Bureau of Economic Analysis 1998). These gains are largely due to advances in productivity derived from better harvesting techniques, and inputs that include more intensive irrigation usage, higher-yield seed varieties, enhancements in fertilizer, pesticides, and other technological gains, along with improved distribution and storage.

Opponents like Samuel Staley cite national statistics demonstrating that more open space has been protected in the last three decades than was lost to urban fringe development. Between

1982 and 1992, conservation programs of all types led to a 35.8 percent increase, while developed land increased by only 14 percent. Presently, more than a third of the total land area of the United States is under public ownership or private conservation easements, and is therefore largely closed to future urban development (U.S. Department of Agriculture 1998). United States Department of Agriculture statistics demonstrate that upwards of 95 percent of the total land area in the United States remains rural—either as forest, desert, cropland, or pasture—and less than 5 percent of all land is devoted to urban uses. Individual states do vary tremendously, with some having between 25 and 35 percent of total land area urbanized, but the national state-by-state average remains just 5.2 percent (Staley 1999).

Fighting Sprawl by Reclaiming Central Cities

Another policy strategy for fighting the outward progression of sprawl development is to refocus public and private investment on deteriorating downtown districts and adjacent inner-ring suburbs. For decades, private investment in housing and business expansion in the suburbs have fueled the outward movement of sprawl, while inner-city communities stagnate. The hope is to reverse the forces that are pushing money and jobs out of central cities. Is there any policy short of a miracle that could reverse this trend? Policy recommendations differ markedly.

To planners and urban reformers like Jonathan Barnett who are seeking inner-city revival, the answer is infill development. After thirty to forty years of steady decline, most inner cities have a large supply of old mills, factory buildings, and warehouses lying vacant. The neglect shown toward these under-utilized resources is a tragic oversight in the eyes of these reformers. Many are aesthetically beautiful brick structures that are well served by water, sewer, gas, and electric utilities, not to mention excellent high-speed road and rail networks. They also benefit from a centralized location in the midst of very large population concentrations. Adjacent residential neighborhoods are also filled with a modestly skilled but willing labor pool that is supplemented by a steady stream of eager foreign immigrants looking for job opportunities (Barnett 1995).

With relatively little investment many of these buildings can be converted over to new uses that fill underserved market niches in downtown economies. Experience has shown that a variety of alternatives are possible. Some might serve as incubators for new high-technology industries, manufacturing businesses, and even craft workers and artists. Others can be refurbished to provide loft apartments for people who work in the downtown area and wish to avoid long commutes out to the suburbs. Restored buildings have been acquired by community organizations and converted to low-income apartments or congregate housing for the elderly. Restaurants, small shops, and up-scale commercial establishments can also be relocated into these buildings, often tastefully coordinated with other redeveloped properties in adjacent neighborhoods. Because most of these older cities are situated along major waterways, a logical connection can be made with waterfront development and accompanying park lands. Advocates claim that removing physical causes of urban blight can also be critical in reviving these neighborhoods, as most have a high concentration of railroad tracks, power lines, highway overpasses, viaducts, and exposed electrical transformers (Moe and Wilkie 1997).

One major barrier to infill development in every older community is the presence of toxic waste contamination in abandoned industrial sites, known as brownfields. A 1998 survey of 180 older cities sponsored by the U.S. Conference of Mayors found that more than 178,000 acres of inactive brownfields were reported within the boundaries of these communities—an area equivalent to the combined total of land occupied by Atlanta, Seattle, and San Francisco. The survey also found that should these sites be properly cleaned up and developed, it would add additional tax revenues of between $955 million and $2.7 billion annually, along with 675,000 more jobs for inner-city workers (U.S. Conference of Mayors 1999). The major hurdle blocking such promising development is strict environmental rules imposed by stringent state and federal standards. Only in the last several years has the federal government begun to work with state agencies to modify existing environmental regulations and offer extra grant funds targeting cleanup efforts in these neglected sites.

Urban advocates further contend that inner-city revival will never occur without the presence of a good quality rapid transit system that links its residents to the outer rings of the metropolitan area. Otherwise, the shortage of low-wage labor in the suburbs and overabundance of unemployed workers in the inner city will be difficult to overcome. Highways that open access to the urban periphery provide little assistance to residents of the inner core who cannot afford to purchase the automobiles that make such a daily commute possible. Existing urban bus systems often do not reach many distant suburban locales, because many have population densities that do not justify full-service transit. For these reasons, high-speed light rail lines have been championed by David Rusk and other advocates as a much-needed improvement in facilitating the movement of commuters both into and out of large metropolitan areas (Rusk 1993).

Critics question the assumption that high rates of urban development on the metropolitan fringe constitute the fundamental root of the problem. They argue instead that ill-advised policies pursued by big city governments in tandem with state and federal subsidies are to blame for the exodus of jobs, businesses, and residents. The real problems lie closer to home in the form of excessive rates of taxation and inefficient and overstaffed city government departments that fail to administer schools competently, respond inadequately to rampant criminal misconduct, and engage in corrupt enforcement of housing and building regulations. Flawed public welfare policies that provide no stimulus to work are also a factor as well in these analyses. The fact that large numbers of upwardly mobile middle- and upper-income citizens are fleeing the city for life in the suburbs is a completely rational act, they contend, given the many pressures involved. The rising number of ethnic and racial minorities who are choosing to reside in outer-ring suburbs is cited as evidence that this calculation is not entirely motivated by racial considerations.

The answer is not better-planned cities, critics contend, but cities that are freed of heavy-handed governmental control and subject more to market forces. To this end, they call for policy prescriptions that are designed to spark competition and innovation in the delivery of urban services. They also hope to free up land resources by reforming zoning laws that are full of restrictive regulatory entanglements. This would create an environment that would encourage investment and entrepreneurial activity, while reducing the influence of political calculations. Public subsidies for transit systems are viewed as wasteful and costly to the taxpayer, especially in an era when people prefer automobile travel and long commutes to their homes in the suburbs. Free market advocates therefore seek to privatize these services and permit the private sector to better meet the needs of consumers (Savas 1987; Shaw and Utt 2000).

Improving Life in the Suburbs

Suburban development patterns have placed millions of Americans in low-density subdivisions that are far removed from work, shopping, school, recreation, and other amenities. This necessitates long commutes by car that waste energy and keep people apart from those who reside in their own neighborhoods. Is there any policy strategy that could restore a sense of community in existing and new suburbs?

Zoning controls contribute to sprawl by mandating that all the components of human settlement be strictly separated. Places of employment, whether heavily polluting industry or much more benign office complexes are rigidly separated from residential localities. Neighborhoods are separated by mandatory lot sizes, and so on. Much of this separation is based on priorities dating back to the early decades of the twentieth century, when residential areas needed to be protected from unregulated industrial enterprises. In more recent decades, separation continues to be based on the assumptions that all people prefer automobile transportation and have a natural disinclination against high-density housing. Citing a litany of ills created by land use practices in suburban areas, James Kunstler argues that "zoning destroys the bonds of communities and, ultimately, whole cultures" (Kunstler 1996, 125).

Discontent with suburban development patterns has led to a new approach known as neotraditional planning. The New Urbanists who advocate this strategy share a conviction that planners and architects should follow an imperative to build community, and in the process, completely rethink and refashion existing zoning controls and outmoded urban planning concepts. The form of development they hope to create possesses many attributes common to town planning before the era of automobile dependence, which ended by the late 1940s. Key to these designs are much higher housing densities and more compact buildings that place both residences and commercial buildings within easy walking distance. Often cited in these designs is the "quarter-mile standard," which is seen to be the maximum distance that the average person will walk in order to get to important local destinations on a routine basis. Where this design principle is in operation, an entire array of shopping needs, professional services, dining, as well as visiting with friends, can and should be undertaken without the need for a car and its associated costly transportation infrastructure. Smaller streets organized into more compact grid patterns and allowance for on-street parking help to slow traffic down, making the streets safer for pedestrians.

Parallel parking is encouraged, except under the most extraordinary circumstances, because this provides both a protective barrier for pedestrians and often eliminates the need for parking lots, which in and of themselves are extremely destructive to the social fabric. This kind of transit-oriented planning then makes energy-efficient bus and light rail commuter lines more easily accessible to the public.

New Urbanists like Peter Calthorpe and Philip Langdon claim that tighter community bonds are encouraged by these designs, which function to bring people out of their homes and closer together through daily face-to-face interaction. This can be achieved by making room for multiple-use development, which allows larger family-size homes to be located adjacent to more affordable multifamily homes and even apartments located over garages. Smaller yards and front porches bring people physically closer to their neighbors, as well as to passersby on the sidewalks and streets. Commercial districts, parks, schools, libraries, and other public facilities are important gathering points for community interaction, and are therefore located within close proximity of residences as well (Calthorpe 1993; Langdon 1995).

A greater sense of community is promoted in these developments because people are more likely to see and interact with one another than in large-lot subdivisions. All classes of citizens are brought together and given equal access to the civic, commercial, and cultural institutions of the community. Because people of very different backgrounds come into close proximity on a regular basis, tolerance and mutual respect are likely to be cultivated. It also assists law enforcement efforts, because residents are more likely to be aware of activities in their neighborhood. A further benefit of more compact housing is that it reduces the need for further development on the urban fringes, thereby protecting open space.

The New Urbanist critique of suburban living and prescriptions for higher-density urban development has not been accepted universally by either architects or policy critics, many of whom argue that this strategy creates more problems than it solves. Randal O'Toole questions the basic assumption that more compact urban design leads to a cleaner and more healthy environment. He argues that those metropolitan areas with the highest housing densities also have the worst reported problems with air pollution. More crowded urban landscapes have more buses plying the streets, increases in traffic volume, reduced travel speeds, and ultimately the worst commuting bottlenecks. He also contends that greater housing densities characteristic of neotraditional neighborhoods lead to higher housing costs and a worse crime rate than that found in lower-density suburban communities (O'Toole 1996).

Rather than rejecting low-density suburban sprawl, free market advocate Wendell Cox suggests that this form of development is an important contributing factor in achieving the high standard of living enjoyed by Americans. Growing reliance on the automobile for transportation has enhanced the efficiency of labor markets, because the relatively free movement they engender permits workers to better connect with employers who desire their skills. Spacious urban areas have also encouraged increased retail competition provided by large shopping malls and large-scale retailers, while further helping to reduce consumer prices (Cox 1999). Even more, advocates see little in the future that will alter the tastes and preferences of Americans for the benefits that suburban living offers. The ongoing technological revolution is allowing people to work more and more out of their homes located in low-density suburban or rural locations where they do not have to worry about the many problems associated with urban life. Peter Gordon and Harry W. Richardson argue that "[n]o developer gets rich by building housing and projects people don't like . . . people throughout the country are choosing to live away from commercial areas, enjoying the private spaces afforded by single-family homes set back from streets and the mobility and accessibility offered by the private automobile" (Gordon and Richardson 2000).

III. Recent Trends in the Debate over Sprawl

The Smart Growth Movement

The preceding review demonstrates that the debate over urban sprawl has never represented a clean distinction between the forces of the free market and the regulatory state. Rather, they constitute rival notions of appropriate governmental intervention in the free market. Should the government continue to offer generous tax breaks, lending policies, and other inducements to developers that underwrite new development on the periphery of metropolitan areas? Or, should government require that landowners and business entrepreneurs adhere to a variety of development restrictions that shift this investment into other avenues of opportunity?

Concerns about sprawl and calls for growth management have been on the rise in American politics in recent decades. Environmental activists have long sought to protect wilderness areas and watersheds from the ravages of urban encroachment. More recently, growth management has become popular among farmland preservationists and urban activists who are pushing for greater public investment and inner-ring communities. Much less organized, but equally important, are growing numbers of suburban residents themselves who are distressed by the loss of open space, rising traffic congestion, overcrowded schools, and rising taxes in their communities.

Since the early 1990s "Smart Growth" coalitions have formed around the United States, based on the new consensus that seems to be emerging on sprawl. Journalist David Bollier contends that, unlike earlier movements, these groups are seeking to overcome the deadlock among antigrowth and progrowth interests that has long stymied progress. They espouse a philosophy that better regional planning and cooperation in metropolitan areas can bring positive outcomes for all concerned parties—environmentalists, advocates for affordable housing, farmland preservationists, banking interests, home builders, and real estate developers alike (Bollier 1998). Although a wide variety of initiatives are presently included under the Smart Growth label, a few common elements are readily apparent. All seem to call for restricting public subsidies to more compact, higher-density urban development on the metropolitan fringe. They also favor greater public investment in mass-transit systems, and more substantial public and private investments in older, central city neighborhoods. Underlying these proposals is a strong faith in the notion that regional cooperation is vital to achieving these goals. By working together older cities and the newer suburbs that surround them can achieve the twin goals of suburban growth and urban revitalization. This is certainly the base upon which several recent statewide antisprawl initiatives have been built. In turn a flurry of diverse urban coalitions have appeared in metropolitan areas promoting the Smart Growth agenda, along with regional conferences, state legislative committee hearings, and considerable media attention.

The Property Rights Challenge

Growth management has long faced a challenge from both citizens and business interests that perceive it as an attack on individual freedoms. The modern property rights movement, as it is known, dates back to the late 1970s. It coalesced largely in response to federal environmental laws, state planning statutes, and the popularity of restrictive growth measures at the local level. Alarmed by the ability of regulatory agencies to set restrictions on private land without compensation as guaranteed under the Fifth Amendment of the U.S. Constitution, groups at both the national and grassroots levels were launched to deter or block uncompensated "takings." These efforts were greatly aided by an increasingly sympathetic majority on the Supreme Court in the 1980s. In particular, the court affirmed the validity of uncompensated takings claims among plaintiffs in two key decisions handed down in *Lucas v. South Carolina Coastal Council* (505 U.S. 1003 [1992]), and *Dolan v. City of Tigard* (No. 93-518 Slip. Op., at 17 [U.S. June 24, [1994]).

Growing public resentment against regulation of land has also been expressed through state legislation designed to provide protection from such governmental action. By 1997 Hertha Lund identified a total of twenty-five states that had adopted laws of varying severity.

Although there is considerable variation among these policies, state property rights laws have generally come in two different forms. In so-called look-before-you-leap (LBYL) laws, a takings liability analysis modeled after the EPA environmental impact statement is required by law. Most laws require the state attorney general to develop guidelines for agencies to use in determining whether their actions have constitutional takings implications. This assessment includes an analysis of the likelihood that an action may result in a constitutional taking, alternatives that would reduce the impact on private property and reduce the risk of a taking, and an estimate of the financial cost for compensation if the action is determined to be a taking. The second most popular measure designed to safeguard property rights includes so-called takings quantification laws. These provide a "trigger point" after which inverse condemnation is presumed to have occurred—typically, this is set at 50 percent of the value of the property or more. Such laws automatically entitle a property owner to compensation when evidence is provided demonstrating that the value of a property has been reduced by environmental laws or land use zoning (Lund 1995).

The growing popularity of the property rights movement poses a significant challenge to the Smart Growth agenda and its advocates. Because local and state planning practices that limit sprawl through restrictive land use measures have a direct impact on adjacent property values, the enormous potential financial burden associated with fully compensating landowners in many cases would render the implementation of these laws almost null and void. At a deeper level the property rights movement challenges the fundamental assumptions of urban growth management that higher societywide values take precedence over individual freedoms.

The property rights movement has also stimulated a series of alternative policy prescriptions for dealing with sprawl that are believed to represent less of a threat to individual free choice. Popular among free market organizations like the Heritage Foundation are various types of pricing mechanisms. To reduce suburban traffic congestion, for example, free market advocates propose "smart roads" for which cars would be equipped with transponders that would enable highway managers to charge variable fees for using roads. These fees could be increased during rush hour to steer motorists off the roads and into public transit.

A full-cost pricing system for new infrastructure like that incorporated into a 1997 Maryland state law is also favored to preserve open space. Such mechanisms compel real estate developers to pay the entire bill for new sewers, water improvements, roads, and the like in rural areas where no such facilities are in place. The high costs associated with development in open areas encourages realtors and builders to build on properties located in developed areas where infrastructure already exists and would therefore be less costly in the consumer market. Another commonly cited policy is ending public transit systems and replacing them with a deregulated, highly flexible, private-sector system that would better serve the needs of consumers (Shaw and Utt 2000).

New Federal Initiatives

Policy questions dealing with urban sprawl have been traditionally relegated to elected officials at the state and local level. Is there a role for the federal government in addressing these important policy issues?

Direct federal involvement in land use planning has always invited a storm of controversy in the United States. Critics regard such initiatives as an unconstitutional breach of federal powers, claiming that local and state governments better serve the needs of the people. Consequently, few initiatives have been successful. For example, urban development grants established in the mid-1950s once mandated the creation of regional planning agencies, but these were stripped of funds and finally dismantled in the late 1960s after years of lobbying by local officials who resented this intrusion into their own jurisdictions. In 1970 a bill was introduced in Congress calling for the creation of state-level land use planning agencies that would prepare comprehensive inventories of natural resources, analyze economic trends, and prepare statewide land use plans. Even though the National Land Use Policy bill was pushed as an effective tool for accomplishing popular environmental policy goals, Sidney Plotkin maintains that it was soundly defeated by a coalition of private business interests and local governments that feared a loss of local control (Plotkin 1987).

Those in favor of federal involvement argue that the federal government has always been closely linked to sprawl-induced patterns of development. Jane Holtz Kay cites copious federal transportation funds made available to state and local governments that are used for the construction of new highways and roads, federally backed insurance for home mortgages, and tax policies that underwrite suburban home building as examples (Kay 1997). These advocates have sought to shift these programs toward a new emphasis on growth management. The Intermodal Surface Transportation Efficiency Act of 1991, for example, channeled a portion of federal highway funds toward supporting regional planning and mass transit alternatives in larger metropolitan areas. This provision was preserved in the 1998 Transportation Equity Act as well. By the mid-1990s, substantial federal EPA grant funds had also been established to assist state and local governments in the cleanup of heavily polluted brownfield sites situated in older industrial communities.

At the end of the decade the Clinton administration took an even more direct role with the launching of two initiatives timed to coincide with the release of its fiscal year 2000 federal budget. The Livability Agenda is designed to give state and local governments more resources for containing sprawl, rebuilding inner cities, and fostering greater commitment to civic and community values in suburban areas. A report titled "Building Livable Communities" released by the Clinton administration in June 1999 echoed these themes:

Our goal is to help build livable communities for the twenty-first century—places where young and old can walk, bike, and play together; where historic neighborhoods are preserved, as well as farms, forests, and other green spaces; where parents spend less time in traffic and more time with their children, spouses, and neighbors; where older neighborhoods thrive once again, and all can share in our new prosperity. Places with safe streets, good schools, and public and private places that help foster a spirit of community. (*Building Livable Communities* 1999)

The main instrument for the Livability Agenda is a new financing tool called Better America Bonds, which are to be administered by the Environmental Protection Agency. These commit $9.5 billion in bond authority to preserve open space, protect water quality, and clean up urban brownfields. Bond-holding entities would receive tax credits from the federal government equal to the amount of interest they would have received, providing a much better deal than a traditional tax-exempt bond. Under this arrangement local governments can work together in partnerships with other local governments, private land trusts, environmental organizations, and businesses to develop proposals that meet federal goals.

Another large investment of $1.6 billion in transportation funds was proposed to reduce congestion, encourage mass transit, and improve air quality through more carefully considered growth planning. Under a twin effort called the Lands Legacy initiative, an additional $588 million was allocated to the Interior and Agriculture Departments for the purpose of land acquisition, open space planning grants, and farmland protection.

The Clinton administration claims new federal initiatives have been launched without an attempt to overstep the traditional land use decision-making authority of state and local governments. The federal role is relegated to providing information and resources to help communities understand the future impact of different growth scenarios. The only significant change is that federal policy will now contain more incentives that encourage cooperation across local boundaries, through state and regional planning agencies. Opposition to this agenda has been rising, however. John Carlisle and other opponents see the administration's antisprawl agenda as just another attempt to create more costly federal programs and chip away at state and local powers (Carlisle 1999).

Whatever the outcome of these debates, the issue of sprawl has risen in significance across the nation. The November 1998 elections provided ample evidence of this heightened public concern. Ten states held referenda on constitutional amendments and legislative questions dealing with sprawl, while another 240 local governments considered similar questions as well. As urban growth pressures continue unabated in the context of continued economic growth around the country, there is little doubt that sprawl will figure prominently in the public debates that follow.

References

Abbott, Carl, Deborah Howe, and Sy Adler, eds. 1994. *Planning the Oregon Way: A Twenty-Year Evaluation.* Corvallis, OR: Oregon State University.

American Farmland Trust. 1994. *Farming on the Edge: A New Look at the Importance and Vulnerability of Agriculture Near American Cities.* Washington, DC: American Farmland Trust.

Barnett, Jonathan. 1995. *The Fractured Metropolis: Improving the New City, Restoring the Old City, Reshaping the Region.* New York: Harper-Collins.

Benfield, F. Kaid, Matthew D. Raimi, and Donald D. T. Chen. 1999. *Once There Were Greenfields: How Suburban Sprawl Is Undermining America's Environment, Economy and Social Fabric.* Washington, DC: Natural Resources Defense Council.

Bollier, David. 1998. *How Smart Growth Can Stop Sprawl.* Washington, DC: Essential Books.

Brown, Ann, et al. 1998. *The Dark Side of the American Dream: The Costs and Consequences of Suburban Sprawl.* San Francisco: Sierra Club.

Building Livable Communities: A Report from the Clinton-Gore Administration (June 1999). Available on-line at http://www.livablecommunities.gov/report2k.htm.

Burchell, Robert W. 1992. "Issues, Actors, and Analyses in Statewide Comprehensive Planning." In *State and Regional Comprehensive Planning: Implementing New Methods for Growth Management.* Edited by Peter A. Buchsbaum and Larry J. Smith. Chicago: American Bar Association.

Calthorpe, Peter. 1993. *The Next American Metropolis.* New York: Princeton Architectural Press.

Carlisle, John. 1999. **"The Campaign against Urban Sprawl: Declaring War on the American Dream."** *Report No. 239* (April). Washington, DC: National Center for Public Policy Research.

Cox, Wendell. 1999. **"The President's New Sprawl Initiative: A Program in Search of a Problem."** *Heritage Foundation Backgrounder* 1263 (March 18).

Cronon, William. 1983. *Changes in the Land: Indians, Colonists, and the Ecology of New England.* New York: Hill and Wang.

Daniels, Tom. 1999. *When City and Country Collide: Managing Growth in the Metropolitan Fringe.* Washington, DC: Island Press.

DeGrove, John M. 1992. *The New Frontier for Land Policy: Planning and Growth Management in the States.* Cambridge, MA: Lincoln Institute of Land Policy.

DeLong, James V. 1997. *Property Matters: How Property Rights Are under Assault and Why You Should Care.* New York: Free Press.

Downs, Anthony. 1994. *New Visions for Metropolitan America.* Washington, DC: Brookings Institution and the Lincoln Institute of Land Policy.

Garreau, Joel. 1991. *Edge City: Life on the New Frontier.* New York: Doubleday.

Gordon, Peter, and Harry W. Richardson. 2000. **"Critiquing Sprawl's Critics."** *Policy Analysis Paper No. 365.* Washington, DC: Heritage Foundation.

Hanson, Susan, ed. 1986. *The Geography of Urban Transportation.* New York: Guilford Press.

Jackson, Kenneth T. 1985. *Crabgrass Frontier: A History of Suburbanization in the United States.* New York: Columbia University Press.

Kay, Jane Holtz. 1997. *Asphalt Nation: How the Automobile Took Over America and How We Can Take It Back.* New York: Crown Publishers.

Kunstler, James H. 1996. *Home from Nowhere: Remaking Our Everyday World for the Twenty-First Century.* New York: Simon and Schuster.

Langdon, Philip. 1995. *A Better Place to Live: Reshaping the American Suburb.* Amherst, MA: University of Massachusetts Press.

Lewis, Eugene. 1973. *The Urban Political System.* Hinsdale, IL: Dryden Press.

Lund, Hertha. 1995. **"The Property Rights Movement and State Legislation."** In *Land Rights: The 1990s' Property Rights Rebellion.* Edited by Bruce Yandle. Lanham, MD: Rowman & Littlefield.

Moe, Richard, and Carter Wilkie. 1997. *Changing Places: Rebuilding Community in an Age of Sprawl.* New York: Henry Holt.

National Agricultural Statistics Service. 1998. *Statistical Highlights of Agriculture.* Washington, DC: U.S. Department of Agriculture.

Nature Conservancy. 1998. *The 1997 Species Report Card: The State of U.S. Plants and Animals.* The Nature Conservancy.

Orfield, Myron. 1997. *Metropolitics: A Regional Agenda for Community and Stability.* Washington, DC: Brookings Institution and the Lincoln Institute of Land Policy.

O'Toole, Randal. 1996. **"The Vanishing Automobile and Other Urban Myths."** *Different Drummer* 3 (Spring): 2–62.

Paton, J. John. 1995. *The Suburbs.* New York: McGraw-Hill.

Peirce, Neal. 1999. **"Suburbia's Dangerously Dull, Not Safe."** Nationally syndicated column, appearing on May 22 in the Springfield *Union News.*

Plotkin, Sidney. 1987. *Keep Out: The Struggle for Land Use Control.* Berkeley, CA: University of California Press.

Porter, Douglas R. 1997. *Managing Growth in America's Communities.* Washington, DC: Island Press.

Savas, E. S. 1987. *Privatization: The Key to Better Government.* Chatham, NJ: Chatham House Publishers.

Shaw, Jane S., and Ronald D. Utt, eds. 2000. *A Guide to Smart Growth: Shattering Myths, Providing Solutions.* Washington, DC: Heritage Foundation.

Staley, Samuel R. 1999. **"The Sprawling of America: In Defense of the Dynamic City."** *Policy Study No. 251.* Reason Public Policy Institute.

Staley, Samuel, and Lynn Scarlett. 1997. **"Market-Oriented Planning: Principles and Tools."** *Policy Study No. 236.* Reason Public Policy Institute.

U.S. Bureau of Economic Analysis. 1998. *Survey of Current Businesses, 1994–1997.* Washington, DC: U.S. Department of Commerce.

U.S. Conference of Mayors. 1999. *Recycling America's Land: A National Report on Brownfields Redevelopment.* Washington, DC: U.S. Conference of Mayors.

2

Chronology

1867 The city of San Francisco enacts the first land use zoning ordinance in the country to restrict the placement of slaughterhouses and meat-curing plants in the city.

1869 The first planned suburb in the United States is created outside of Chicago at Riverside, Illinois, under the direction of architects Frederick Law Olmstead and Calvert Vaux.

1877 The U.S. Supreme Court recognizes that the public has an interest in the use and development of privately owned land in *Munn v. Illinois.*

1880 The U.S. Census reveals that New York City is the first community in the country to reach the one million population mark.

1888 The first electric trolley is constructed in Richmond, Virginia. It soon becomes the dominant means of transportation in America and a major impetus for urban sprawl.

1891 The first private, nonprofit land trust is begun in Massachusetts under the name Trustees of Reservations.

1901 New York City creates a tenement house department to administer and strictly enforce its building construction code, becoming a model for similar programs throughout the United States.

1907 The Connecticut state legislature authorizes the creation of the first permanent, locally elected planning board for the city of Hartford.

1909 The first metropolitan regional plan is developed for the city of Chicago under the direction of Daniel H. Burnham and Edward H. Bennett.

Wisconsin becomes the first state to enable its local governments to adopt full planning powers.

The city of Los Angeles institutes the first major use of land use zoning to direct its future development.

1910 The number of registered automobiles in the country passes the 500,000 mark.

1913 New Jersey becomes the first state to institute mandatory referral of subdivision plats for local government approval, instituting the beginning of subdivision control as a function of city planning.

1916 New York City adopts the first comprehensive zoning code in the nation.

1922 Los Angeles County adopts the first county planning board in the country as a means for controlling sprawling suburban expansion.

The first suburban, auto-oriented shopping center is constructed at the Country Club Plaza in Kansas City, Missouri.

1925 The planning commission of Cincinnati is the first to adopt a long-range, comprehensive plan for a major American city.

1926 The U.S. Supreme Court validates the use of comprehensive zoning for the first time in *Village of Euclid v. Ambler Realty Company*, which becomes the constitutional building block for all future zoning ordinances.

New York is the first state to provide public funding for the construction of lower-middle-income housing.

1934 The first federally supported public housing project is begun in Cleveland, Ohio.

The Federal Housing Administration (FHA) is created, with authority to provide insurance for private home loans and establish minimum housing construction standards.

1940 The U.S. Census reveals that central cities are beginning to lose population to surrounding suburban areas.

1945 The Pennsylvania legislature passes the first state urban redevelopment act.

1947 The first large-scale suburban residential housing project is developed at Levittown, New York, subsidized by federal Veterans Administration (VA) and FHA loan insurance programs.

1949 The Housing Act authorizes the first federal funds to support slum clearance programs in older cities.

The first regional shopping center, known as the Town and Country Shopping Center, is built in Columbus, Ohio.

1950 The U.S. Census reports that suburban population has grown by 35 percent since 1940, while central-city populations have increased by only 13 percent.

1954 Section 701 of the Housing Act provides federal funding for the development of state, metropolitan, and other regional comprehensive plans.

1956 The Interstate Highway Act provides $60 billion in federal funds to assist states in the construction of over 40,000 miles of limited-access highways.

The nation's first enclosed suburban mall opens in Minneapolis, Minnesota.

1958 The term "urban sprawl" is first used in an essay written by William H. Whyte.

1960 The U.S. Census reports a suburban population growth

1960
cont.
rate of 47 percent since 1950, while central cities grew by only 5 percent.

1961 Hawaii enacts the first comprehensive statewide land use law, which puts all authority over development decisions in the hands of county and state officials.

1965 A massive riot rocks inner-city Los Angeles for five days, triggering other violent riots in central cities across the nation.

Congress creates the federal Department of Housing and Urban Development (HUD), elevating federal urban policy to cabinet-level status.

1966 The Model Cities program empowers local community groups to have authority over the expenditure of federal urban development funds.

1968 Congress authorizes HUD to subsidize the construction of six million housing units over the next ten years.

1969 The federal government mandates that areawide regional planning agencies review all proposals for local participation in federal urban development programs.

1970 The U.S. Census reports that for the first time more Americans are living in suburbs than in central cities.

Suburbs are supplying the majority of jobs in nine of the nation's fifteen largest metropolitan areas.

1971 The city of Petaluma, California, is the first local government to impose severe development controls on sprawl.

Reacting to popular alarm about the loss of rural lands to developments and rising property taxes, the Vermont legislature adopts Act 200, which mandates that all large development projects be subject to review by regional commissions.

1972 The California state legislature passes the Coastal Zone Conservation Act, which establishes six regional commissions to prepare coastal plans in cooperation with local governments and gives these commissions authority to approve all future large waterfront development projects.

In *Golden v. Planning Board of Ramapo,* the New York Court of Appeals upholds a zoning ordinance designed to manage growth.

1973 The state of Oregon adopts the Land Conservation and Development Act, the toughest statewide growth management law in the nation. It establishes nineteen state planning goals designed to limit sprawl and mandates that all counties and municipal governments adopt plans in conformity with state goals.

1974 The U.S. Supreme Court rules that school desegregation plans may not cross local government boundaries in *Milliken v. Bradley,* thus insulating suburbs from mandated racial integration and directly impacting the future development of metropolitan America.

1975 The American Law Institute releases a new Model Land Development Code. It calls for a complete revision of old 1920s-era planning and zoning acts so as to enhance the role of state and regional governments in reviewing and overriding local zoning decisions, especially with regard to large-scale development projects and locally unwanted land uses.

1977 Massachusetts and Maryland are the first states in the nation to set aside public funds for the purchase of development rights to safeguard productive farmland from urban encroachment.

1978 North Carolina is the first state to pass a right-to-farm law that protects its farmers from nuisance law suits. All other states quickly adopt similar laws over the next seven years.

1979 Congress cuts off the last federal funding supporting community and regional planning.

1980 The U.S. Census reveals that the nation's older central cities collectively lost 2.85 million residents over the previous decade—a decline of 6.1 percent.

1984 After forty years of experiencing the highest urban growth rates in the nation, the state of Florida adopts its State and Regional Planning Act. It mandates the preparation of a state comprehensive plan to develop a statewide strategy for dealing with urban growth pressures. In addition, eleven regional plans are to be prepared in conformity with the state plan.

1985 Florida amends its 1984 law by requiring each local government to prepare and adopt local growth management plans consistent with regional and state plans. The law forbids granting any more development permits unless adequate public facilities are concurrently made available.

New Jersey passes a State Planning Act. It establishes statewide growth management goals, calls for the creation of a state development and redevelopment plan, and classifies all land in the state into categories that are designed to assist local decision makers in locating future development. However, the state plan has only advisory status.

1988 Vermont adopts Act 250, which creates twelve statewide planning goals to function as guides for local government planning.

Maine adopts a Comprehensive Planning and Land Management Act, which mandates the preparation of local comprehensive plans that conform with ten statewide growth management goals.

The Rhode Island legislature passes the Comprehensive Planning and Land Use Regulation Act. It creates ten state growth management goals and mandates that all local governments henceforth draw up their own comprehensive plans. These must be reviewed and approved by a state agency, and be in conformity with statewide goals.

1989 The state of Georgia passes the Planning Act, which calls for the creation of state and regional growth plans. Local governments are offered incentives to adopt their own comprehensive plans that conform with regional and state goals.

1990 The U.S. Census reports that 102 million Americans—41 percent of the population—are residing in suburbs, while older central cities hold just 17 percent.

The state of Washington adopts the Growth Management Act. This requires all counties facing serious urban growth pressures to prepare comprehensive growth management plans that are in conformity with state guidelines.

Barnstable County, Massachusetts, adopts the Cape Cod Commission Act, which gives a countywide agency full authority to review and approve local growth management plans.

1991 In the midst of recession and facing severe political pressure, the Maine state budget eliminates funding for implementation of its statewide growth management law and dissolves its state planning office.

1992 The state of Maryland adopts the Economic Growth, Resource Protection and Planning Act. It requires all local governments to conform to a series of growth management goals in the preparation of their own local plans.

1995 Thirteen states pass "takings" bills designed to protect private property from the excesses of federal and state environmental regulations. This brings the total number of states with similar takings statutes to twenty-four across the United States.

1996 Colorado Governor Roy Romer hosts a much-publicized Smart Growth Summit, which results in seventy-four policy recommendations that include a variety of initiatives to fight urban sprawl.

1997 Maryland enacts its Smart Growth Act. It mandates all local governments to designate growth areas that are most suited for development or redevelopment and eliminates state funding for all infrastructure projects located outside of them.

1998 Vice President Al Gore announces the Livable Communities initiative, the first comprehensive federal plan to fight

1998
cont.

urban sprawl through enhanced support for urban planning, land acquisition, brownfields redevelopment, park
restoration, and a variety of other components.

The Tennessee state legislature enacts a law requiring each
county to develop a mandatory growth management plan
that identifies urban growth boundaries for each municipality within its borders.

In the 1998 elections, voters approve antisprawl ballot
measures to protect open space in eight of ten statewide
initiatives. An additional 124 ballot questions proposing
open space funding are passed by voters out of a total of
148 votes taken in county and municipal elections.

2000   Republican Senator Lincoln Chaffee introduces the Community Character Act, which proposes state grants of up to
$500,000 to develop or revise state land use plans and plan-
ning legislation aimed at addressing public transit, affordable housing, open space preservation, and other
anti-sprawl initiatives.

Pennsylvania's Republican Governor Tom Ridge signs
"smart growth" legislation into law that provides incentives for local government to create general plans that include preservation of open space, energy conservation,
and use of renewable energy sources. Additionally, it permits local governments to create "transfer of development
rights" programs so as to preserve open space.

3

Biographical Sketches

Ron Arnold

Ron Arnold is one of the most outspoken activists in the property rights movement whose extensive early involvement dating back to the 1970s has earned him the title "Father of the Wise Use Movement."

Arnold was raised in Houston and San Antonio, Texas. He studied fine arts at the University of Texas and later pursued business administration at the University of Washington, although he never received a formal degree. Even so, Arnold has been a prolific author and veteran journalist who has worked on many assignments dealing with government, environmental issues, business, and the economy in many different magazines. His projects have been covered by major media outlets including the *New York Times, Washington Post, Chicago Tribune, Los Angeles Times,* CBS News *60 Minutes,* ABC News *Nightline,* CNN's *Network Earth, Time* magazine, *Newsweek, U.S. News and World Report, People, Outside,* and magazines of major environmental organizations. He is a frequent contributor to *USA Today,* in which his 8-part series "The Environmental Battle" earned the American Business Press Editorial Achievement Award for best magazine series in 1981. From 1984 to 1987, he hosted a weekly radio show titled "Economics 101 on the Air," featuring interviews with notable figures in academia, business, and politics. For eight years, he served as an opinion columnist for the *Bellevue Journal-American.*

Arnold has written numerous books over the previous twenty years. His books cover a wide range of topics, but all articulate a libertarian philosophy on public policy issues. Among those books that deal with land use issues and property rights are a book he coauthored with Alan Gottlieb titled *Trashing the Economy: How Runaway Environmentalism Is Wrecking America* (1993), along with *Stealing the National Parks* (1987), *It Takes a Hero: The Grassroots Battle Against Environmental Oppression* (1994), and *Battered Communities* (1998). He founded the Free Enterprise Press in 1987 to create an outlet for those who share his views on economics. In this capacity, he has supervised the production of more than thirty books. He has also served as executive vice president of the Center for the Defense of Free Enterprise (formerly known as the Wise Use Action Center) since 1984. He has also worked as an adviser for National Lands Conference meetings held between 1988–1992.

Jonathan Barnett

Jonathan Barnett has been an urban design adviser to many U.S. cities and federal government agencies. He has participated in the design of large urban redevelopment projects, planned communities, and master plans for suburban areas. For over two decades, he has sought to promote urban planning and design initiatives that overcome the growing split between older central cities and fast-growing suburbs that result from sprawl patterns of development.

He is a magna cum laude graduate of Yale University and has a master's degree from the University of Cambridge and a master's of architecture from Yale. He is a fellow of the American Institute of Architects and a certified planner. He has held a teaching position as Professor of City and Regional Planning at the University of Pennsylvania and written numerous books. These include the introductory textbook *Introduction to Urban Design* (1982) as well as two critical commentaries on urban design and city planning: *The Elusive City: Five Centuries of Design Ambition and Miscalculation* (1987); and more recently, *The Fractured Metropolis: Improving the New City, Restoring the Old City, Reshaping the Region*. Published in 1996, this book has received much recognition both for its incisive commentary and abundant policy recommendations that seek to counteract the forces of sprawl. Barnett's position is that our nation's aging inner cities and traditional downtown neighborhoods can and should be revitalized. He argues that the only way this is attainable is to shift public and private financing and program resources away from the sprawling suburban developments and related infrastructure.

Peter Calthorpe

Peter Calthorpe is widely recognized in the architectural world as a leading proponent of the New Urbanist perspective. A practicing architect since 1972, Calthorpe attended Antioch College and studied architecture at Yale University. He founded Calthorpe Associates in 1983 and has lectured widely throughout the United States, Europe, Australia, and South America. He has taught at the University of California, Berkeley, the University of Washington, the University of Oregon, and the University of North Carolina. Since forming Calthorpe Associates in 1983, his work has ranged from large community planning projects to commercial complexes and public buildings. He has also worked as a consultant with the Department of Housing and Urban Development on transportation planning and community design for federal Empowerment Zones.

Calthorpe has been working to convince fellow architects that the United States must move away from sprawl and toward more compact, mixed-use, and economically diverse communities. The neotraditional design of many of his projects reflects an earlier era, both in scale and building style. Through these designs, he hopes to bring people closer together and foster a sense of community. He first achieved recognition for these views in a book that he coauthored with Sim Van Der Ryn titled *Sustainable Communities: A New Design Synthesis for Cities, Suburbs, and Towns* (1986). More recently, he compiled some twenty-four regional urban plans reflecting the New Urbanist philosophy in *The Next American Metropolis: Ecology, Community, and the American Dream* (1993). He is the recipient of numerous honors and awards that include three National Housing and Urban Development awards for energy-efficient designs, two Progressive Architecture Citations, a National AIA Design Award, and two National Endowment of the Arts grants. He was selected to represent the United States in an exchange with Russia on city and regional planning issues and was appointed by President Bill Clinton to serve on the President's Council for Sustainable Development. Recently, he was cited by *Newsweek* as one of twenty-five "innovators on the cutting edge." He currently serves on the Board of Directors of the Congress of New Urbanism, which he helped to found in 1993.

John M. DeGrove

John M. DeGrove is recognized as a leading scholar and policy advisor on the subject of statewide planning laws designed to combat sprawl. He is a founder of the Joint Center for Environmental and Urban Problems at Florida Atlantic University, at which he was director from 1972–1998. He also serves as a professor of political science and a leading figure in growth management in Florida as well as a nationally recognized authority in state-level planning initiatives. As secretary of Florida's Department of Community Affairs from 1983–1985, he was instrumental in the conception and passage of the 1985 Growth Management Act and the State Comprehensive Plan. He is a member of the Governor's Commission for a Sustainable South Florida and continues to work as an adviser to state, regional, and local planning and growth management agencies in fifteen states.

DeGrove received degrees from Rollins College and Emory University before going on to obtain a Ph.D. from the University of North Carolina in 1958. A frequent contributor to a variety of academic journals and law reviews, he has been published widely on the origins and development of growth management policy across the United States. Through his books, which include *Land, Growth, and Politics* (1984), *Balanced Growth: A Planning Guide for Local Government* (1991), and *The New Frontier for Land Policy: Planning and Growth Management in the States* (1992), DeGrove has chronicled the evolution of land use policy. His research has focused on identifying processes and patterns that have led some states to adopt comprehensive growth management legislation, while others have seen this kind of initiative blocked and defeated. As a leading advocate of growth management initiatives in state government, he has used this knowledge to assist state and local agencies with the implementation of land use policies.

Reid Ewing

Reid Ewing is among the leading authorities on urban design and transportation planning in the United States. He has devoted his career as a professional planner to developing policy recommendations that are designed to alleviate problems caused by urban sprawl, and has been the author of numerous publications and manuals that explain complex urban design principles in easily understandable language. He holds a master's degree in engineering and city planning from Harvard University and a Ph.D. in transportation systems and policy planning from the Massachusetts Institute of Technology.

Ewing is an associate professor in the College of Architecture at Florida International University in Miami, Florida, and also served as a faculty associate of the Lincoln Institute of Land Policy in Cambridge, Massachusetts. He works as Research Director of the Surface Transportation Policy Project in Washington, D.C., and holds a position as a Senior Associate with Fehr & Peers Transportation Consultants based in Lafayette, California.

A scholar as well as a policy practitioner, Ewing has authored several books and monographs that provide concrete recommendations for community officials and planners who are seeking to harmonize new urban development with competing goals of energy efficiency, environmental preservation, and related quality of life issues. His *Developing Successful New Communities* (1991) was among the first compilations to analyze development projects inspired by the New Urbanist school. *Best Development Practices: Doing the Right Thing and Making Money at the Same Time* (1996) and *Transportation and Land Use Innovations: When You Can't Pave Your Way Out of Congestion* (1997) are devoted to reducing the complexities of planning and design principles into easily understood language. Most recently, he has written a widely distributed manual for the Smart Growth Network titled *Pedestrian- and Transportation-Friendly Design: A Primer for Smart Growth* (2000) that is based on a manual he prepared for the Florida Department of Transportation. In each of his works, he makes extensive use of graphics and nontechnical language to convey his message that real estate development can be compatible with the goals of energy efficiency and environmental preservation.

Robert H. Freilich

Robert H. Freilich is a partner in the nationally recognized law and planning firm of Freilich, Leitner, and Carlisle based in Kansas City, Missouri, and Aspen, Colorado. He has represented more than 200 cities, counties, and state governments in a variety of cases dealing with planning, land use regulations, and litigation defense. Freilich holds an A.B. from the University of Chicago, a Juris Doctor from Yale Law School, and M.I.A., L.L.M., and J.S.D. degrees from Columbia University. In 1968, he became Hulen Professor of Law in Urban Affairs at the University of Missouri–Kansas City School of Law.

His most significant case was the Ramapo decision won in the New York Court of Appeals in 1972 (*Golden v. Planning Board of Ramapo*, 334 N.Y.S. 2d 138). This case established an important legal precedent by recognizing that local communities like Ramapo Township could use a comprehensive plan and associated permitting system as a means for managing growth. From this point on, local zoning and permit systems were established across the country as a means for fighting urban sprawl.

Freilich is currently the editor of *The Urban Lawyer*, a national quarterly journal on state and local government law published by the American Bar Association. He is author of numerous articles on land use planning and cowrote with David L. Callies and Thomas E. Roberts *Case and Materials on Land Use* and *Model Subdivision Regulations: Planning and Law* (1979). The latter book stands out as one of the essential compilations among legal professionals in this subfield and has been cited extensively in land use cases that deal with issues related to urban sprawl since its publication. Most recently, he has written *From Sprawl to Smart Growth: Successful Legal, Planning, and Environmental Systems*. Published in 2000, this book explores in detail the wide array of policy alternatives being pursued by the state and local governments in the effort to slow down sprawl development.

Parris N. Glendening

Parris Glendening grew up in poverty in Florida before receiving a scholarship to attend Broward Community College. He eventually received a bachelor's degree in political science at Florida State University in 1962 and then went on to pursue an M.A. and Ph.D. that was completed in 1967. For the next 27 years, he taught as a professor at the University of Maryland, College Park, authoring a book titled *Pragmatic Federalism: An Inter-Governmental View of American Government* (1984).

He entered Maryland politics in the early 1970s, first winning election to the Hyattsville City Council in 1973. He then held several positions in county government. In this capacity, he was honored by *City and State* magazine as the "Most Valuable County Official" in the nation. In 1994, he was elected on the Democratic Party ticket to his first term as governor of the state of Maryland. A major component of his election campaign centered on sponsoring a new initiative designed to stem the tide of urban sprawl and protect existing open space while also reinvigorating neglected urban communities. Over several months, Glendening reached out to interest groups and citizens through numerous meetings and forums held in all twenty-three counties to generate support for his new antisprawl agenda.

This was the basis for the landmark 1997 Smart Growth law, which built strongly on an earlier blueprint adopted by the state in 1992. The Smart Growth law enacted under Glendening's leadership seeks to develop a coordinated strategy to better prepare the state for the growth of over 1 million new residents projected by the year 2020. Among the features of this new set of laws is the Smart Growth Areas Act, which limits state infrastructure spending to designated growth zones rather than subsidizing sprawl in the countryside. Other affiliated programs assist land preservation through open space acquisition, brownfields clean-up in older urban areas, and a Live Near Your Work program that subsidizes the purchase of homes near workplaces. After four years in office, Glendening won his race for reelection to a second term in 1998.

Albert Gore Jr.

Inaugurated as the forty-fifth vice president of the United States in 1992, Albert Gore and his running mate President Bill Clinton were reelected to office on the Democratic Party ticket in 1996. Gore received an undergraduate degree in government from Harvard University in 1969 and worked as a journalist with the *Nashville Tennessean* newspaper from 1973–1976 after service in the U.S. military. He followed in the footsteps of his father in pursuing elective office in Congress, first serving as a member of the U.S. House of Representatives from 1976 to 1984, and then as a member of the U.S. Senate until 1992. In 1988, he ran unsuccessfully for the Democratic Party's presidential nomination.

Vice President Gore has been widely recognized as the key champion of environmental causes in the Clinton administration, even though he previously had developed a record as a centrist in Congress, suffering from the criticism of environmental groups in his native state of Tennessee. His prominence in environmental issues was achieved through the publication of his 1992 book *Earth in the Balance: Ecology and the Human Spirit*. Here, he spelled out serious threats associated with the rapid loss of rainforests, air pollution, the deterioration of the ozone layer, and global warming. The book calls for a spiritual renewal and comprehensive global action to address these threats to survival.

With a strong background of involvement in environmental

policy, no other public figure has contributed more to elevating the issue of urban sprawl to the national level. In his position as vice president, he has been the chief sponsor of the Clinton administration's "Lands Legacy Initiative," which proposes $1 billion to expand federal protection of land across the United States. Other funds made available in the "Better America Bonds" will be passed on to states and local governments seeking to preserve local green spaces and implement more effective land use planning. Gore has also been instrumental in championing the Clinton administration's "Livable Communities" directive, which has sought to involve federal agencies in the fight against sprawl. In promoting this agenda, Gore has also traveled extensively across the United States articulating his concerns for the negative impacts of sprawl patterns of development in America's urban areas. The White House established an extensive "Livable Communities" web site in 1998, and published a report in June 1999 titled *Building Livable Communities* that spells out the position of the Clinton administration on these issues.

As the nominee of the Democratic Party ticket for president in the 2000 election, Al Gore has continued to promote his antisprawl agenda. In his campaign, he maintains that the Livable Communities agenda remains a vital tool in fighting sprawl, and has proposed setting aside $9.5 billion in federal funds to facilitate state and local smart growth initiatives. He has also called for more federal funds to be made available for cleaning up and redeveloping abandoned industrial sites known as brownfields.

Alan M. Gottlieb

Alan Gottlieb has served as president of the Center for the Defense of Free Enterprise (formerly Wise Use Action Center) since its founding in 1976 and has been active in libertarian political and civil projects for more than two decades. A graduate in nuclear engineering at the University of Tennessee, he later attended the Institute on Comparative Political and Economic Systems at Georgetown.

Early in his career, he served on the staff of the Young Americans for Freedom. In the 92nd Congress, Gottlieb worked on the staff of Congressmember John J. Duncan of Tennessee, and served as the National Director for the Youth Against McGovern organization during the 1972 presidential election.

Gottlieb has assumed a very prominent position articulating libertarian views on a variety of public policy topics that include opposition to environmental regulation, federal lands management, and gun control. He espouses the "wise use" view that questions the use of government regulation as an answer to social and environmental problems. Contrary to advocates of government land use planning and regulation as a means for combating sprawl, he believes that decisions made by private property owners are protected by the U.S. Constitution and should override the heavy-handed use of government controls. He is an active writer and has had his articles appear in the *Seattle Times, Manchester Union Leader, San Francisco Examiner, Washington Post, Orlando Sentinel, Cincinnati Enquirer, Chicago Tribune, USA Today, Guns & Ammo* magazine, and *Gun Week*. His strong views in favor of property rights have been conveyed through a compilation of articles he edited in *The Wise Use Agenda: The Citizen's Guide to Environmental Resource Issues* (1979), and a book he coauthored with Ron Arnold titled *Trashing the Economy: How Runaway Environmentalism is Wrecking America* (1998). Gottlieb has also had numerous appearances on television talk shows such as ABC's *Good Morning America, McNeil-Lehrer News Hour, Larry King Live*, CNN's *Crossfire*, and other nationally syndicated programs. Most recently, he has become the president of two radio stations in Portland, Oregon, and Spokane, Washington, as well as the chairman of the Talk America Radio Network. He is also chairman of the Citizens Committee for the Right to Keep and Bear Arms.

Bruce Katz

Bruce Katz serves as the Director of the Center on Urban and Metropolitan Policy at the Brookings Institute in Washington, D.C. In this capacity, he has been a prominent voice in articulating concerns about sprawl as well as pushing for policy solutions. He received a bachelor of arts degree from Brown University in 1981 and subsequently studied for a law degree at Yale University Law School. He worked as an associate in a Washington-based law firm before taking on several prominent positions in the federal government. He began public service as a staff expert working as senior counsel to the U.S. Senate Subcommittee on Housing and Urban Affairs. From 1993 to 1996, he served as Chief of Staff at the U.S. Department of Housing and Urban Development.

In his position at the Brookings Institute, he has been at the center of sponsoring new research and policy development in the problems of sprawl in metropolitan America. He intends that the center will help cities and suburbs better understand demographic, environmental, and social trends, economic challenges, and policy strategies that can facilitate transitions that will benefit all citizens. As such, he is an ardent advocate of the "smart growth" agenda. He has authored numerous articles on the subject of sprawl and the metropolitan agenda that have appeared in publications such as the *Brookings Review* and *Atlantic Monthly*. A book containing his perspective on future policy directions in metropolitan governance was published in 1999 titled *Reflections on Regionalism: Metropolitan Case Studies*. His most recent work has been a comprehensive analysis of welfare reform policy in America's cities.

Peter Katz

Peter Katz is an author and consultant who once helped developers market urban sprawl in the San Francisco region. Now, he is one of its chief critics. A leading proponent of New Urbanism, Katz has advocated alternatives to standard real estate developments that emphasize environmental balance, social integration, and building a true sense of community. Katz received a degree from the Cooper Union for the Advancement of Science and Art in New York, where he studied architecture and graphic design. Before his involvement with New Urbanism, he was principal of Stratagem Consultants, a San Francisco–based real estate and marketing consultancy. His projects included working with governmental agencies and private home and commercial developers.

He has played a key role in shaping the New Urbanist movement as founding executive director of the Congress for New Urbanism, which was created in 1993. This organization was created for the purpose of bringing together leading advocates of this philosophy and disseminating its views to both the professional community and general public. He is also coauthor with Vincent Scully of *The New Urbanism: Toward an Architecture of Community* (1993), a book that offers an overview of the general design principles associated with New Urbanism as well as its practical applications. In 1997, Katz founded a company called Urban Advantage that provides a range of educational and promotional materials reflecting the New Urbanism philosophy for clients that include developers, investors, city agencies, and community groups. He presently works as a consultant with the Citistates organization, in which capacity he offers assistance on such topics as marketplace applications of New Urbanist principles, public transit, and new technologies for citizen-based planning.

Charles E. Little

Charles E. Little is a Washington-based author and journalist who has made many contributions to the national policy debate on urban growth pressures and conservation-related issues. A former New York City advertising executive and conservation activist, Little came to Washington, D.C., in the early 1970s as senior associate at the Conservation Foundation. Here, he worked on promoting a comprehensive land use policy initiative then being championed by former Washington Senator Henry Jackson. He later accepted a position as head of natural resources policy research at the Congressional Research Service and in that capacity was responsible for drafting legislation to preserve the New Jersey pinelands as well as farmland protection measures and new approaches to cooperative planning for nationally recognized landscape areas.

In recent years, he has served as executive director of the Open Space Action Institute and was the founder and past president of the American Land Forum. He has published many magazine and journal articles and conducts a book review column for *Wilderness* magazine. Little is the author or coauthor of ten books. Among his many influential works dealing with environmental preservation and land use reform are *Challenge of the Land: Green Fields Forever* (1987), *Greenways for America* (1990), and *Hope for the Land* (1992). In these works, he offers the view that the only way for the United States to overcome its record of environmental despoliation is to understand that land is the basis of community. When the natural landscape is irrevocably altered and lost, individual and community life are forever diminished.

Thomas L. McCall

Oregon governor Thomas McCall led the fight for the adoption of the most comprehensive state-level initiative to combat the forces of urban sprawl. McCall graduated with a bachelor of arts degree in 1936 from the University of Oregon. He became a news correspondent before serving in the United States Naval Reserve from 1944–1946. He worked as a journalist and political analyst in Portland, Oregon, until 1964, when he took a job as administrative assistant to Governor Douglas McKay. In 1952, he was elected secretary of state on the Republican ticket, serving in that capacity from 1965–1966. An early champion of environmental issues, he ran for governor in 1966, in spite of opposition to his nomination from more conservative elements in his own party. He won the general election against Democrat Robert W. Straub, serving until 1974 when he chose to step down rather than seek reelection.

Throughout his term of office, McCall was an outspoken critic of urban sprawl and the unrestricted forces of commercial development. Concerned about the rapid loss of both farmland and wilderness areas of the state, he used his colorful and effective gift for speechmaking to press for a solution that would unite regulatory agencies operating at local, county, and state levels against sprawl. His first major victory came soon after his election with legislation known as the "Beach Bill," which granted the state government the power to zone Oregon's beaches and protect them from private development. Campaigning in support of greater timber production and an expansion of the state's industrial base during his race for reelection, he also insisted that the state's natural resources were in desperate need of protection. Once reelected to office, he introduced a comprehensive land use bill that would mandate planning and the establishment of urban growth boundaries. Although he faced severe opposition by political and economic interests that represented land developers, loggers, mining companies, and local home-rule advocates, McCall was still able to craft a law that allowed considerable freedom at the city and county level to adapt state-wide planning guidelines to local considerations. Almost thirty years later, this law remains the most thorough growth management policy in the country. McCall died in 1982 after a political career that spanned nearly four decades.

Richard Moe

A native of Duluth, Minnesota, Moe graduated from Williams College in 1959. He later earned a law degree from the University of Minnesota. After returning to Minnesota, Moe began a career in public service as an elected official in city and state government that eventually propelled him to the chairmanship of the Democratic Farm Labor Party. In 1972, he moved to Washington to serve as a staff assistant to then-Senator Walter Mondale. After the election of Jimmy Carter to the presidency, Moe was retained by the vice president as his chief of staff. He practiced law from

1981 until he assumed the presidency of the National Trust for Historic Preservation in 1993. Moe has also served on the Committee for the Preservation of the White House and the executive boards of the Ford Foundation and Civil War Trust. He was awarded an honorary doctorate from the University of Maryland in 1998 in recognition for his contributions in the field of historic preservation.

Moe coauthored *Changing Places: Rebuilding Community in the Age of Sprawl* with Carter Wilkie in 1997. This work chronicles the decline of large urban industrial centers and the phenomenon of urban sprawl and argues in favor of historic preservation as a tool for urban revitalization. Under his direction, the National Trust has become an outspoken advocate for controlling sprawl and has launched numerous efforts to demonstrate and document the effectiveness of preservation as a tool for strengthening American urban communities.

Myron Orfield

Myron Orfield was born in Minneapolis. He studied political science and history at the University of Minnesota and then completed a law degree at the University of Chicago. Working as an attorney in Minneapolis, he became interested in environmental issues while developing a growing concern for the plight of older industrial communities. In pursuit of this joint agenda, he won a seat in the state House of Representatives in 1990. Now serving his fifth term of office, Orfield has gained considerable notoriety in Minnesota state politics for his role in helping to forge a political alliance between declining central city communities and older threatened blue-collar suburbs on a platform promoting regional cooperation and governance for the Minneapolis–St. Paul region.

His research and analysis of the Minneapolis–St. Paul metropolitan region was published in 1997 as *Metropolitics: A Regional Agenda for Community and Stability.* This book provides a thorough analysis of metropolitan development patterns in the Twin City region, which highlight how public subsidies have promoted rapid sprawl development on the periphery while neglecting to address the needs of older, minority-dominated, inner-ring communities. Given the mutual dependence of all of the communities in the region, Orfield's position has been that inner- and outer-ring suburbs need to work together through regional governance, housing, land use, and transportation policies. The Metropolitan

Council of the Twin Cities represents the culmination of these efforts aimed at achieving regional cooperation among local governments. Although the book is devoted entirely to this case study, it has been widely recognized for its potential application elsewhere in the country.

A former special assistant attorney general of Minnesota, Orfield is running in 2000 for a seat in the Minnesota Senate. He has held a position as adjunct professor at the University of Minnesota Law School since 1995, and directs the Metropolitan Area Program of the National Growth Management Leadership Project.

Neal Peirce

A journalist and writer, Neal Peirce ranks among the leading commentators on the political and economic development of metropolitan America. A graduate of Princeton University in 1954, Peirce was one of the founders and a contributing editor of the *National Journal*, a leading political journal. He also worked as editor of *Congressional Quarterly* from 1960 to 1969 and later served on the National Civic League's executive committee from 1972 to 1995. His interest in governmental reform is evident in the role he has played in helping to found the National Academy of Public Administration's Alliance for Redesigning Government. Recognized widely for his expertise on urban issues, he has appeared on television programs that include *Meet the Press, The Today Show, McNeil/Lehrer News Hour, CNN,* and many local radio and television shows. He has been a fellow at the Woodrow Wilson International Center for Scholars and the Smithsonian Institution and served as the John L. Weinburg Distinguished Visiting Professor at the Woodrow Wilson School of International Affairs, Princeton University. In recent years, he has toured the lecture circuit, speaking at conferences across the United States.

In 1975, Peirce began writing the first nationally syndicated column focused on federal, state, and local political issues. Many of these opinions were incorporated into his ten-book series on America's states and regions, which culminated in the publication of *The Book of America: Inside 50 States Today* (1983).

His books *Corrective Capitalism* (1987) and *Enterprising Communities* (1990) cover the rise of community development corporations and other locally based initiatives aimed at revitalizing America's urban centers. Since then, his commentaries have covered a wide variety of topics related to state and local politics.

Among the most innovative and widely recognized are those views and proposals that focus on the political and economic dynamics of cities and their emerging national and global roles. He brought these views together in a book he authored in 1993 titled *Citistates: How Urban America Can Prosper in a Competitive World* (1993). More recently, he coauthored with Curtis Johnson *Breakthroughs: Recreating the American City* (1997), which describes numerous case studies around the United States that illustrate the potential and possibilities associated with regional cooperation and governance in America's large metropolitan areas.

He is presently working on this agenda through his chairmanship of the Citistates group. This organization was formed in 1996 to pull together a network of professionals who provide consulting services for cities that are facing serious challenges in transportation, economic renewal, regional cooperation, and growth management. The *Peirce Reports* represent detailed analyses and recommendations of urban case studies done by the Citistates team across the country.

Elizabeth Plater-Zyberk

An architect and town planner who cofounded Duany Plater-Zyberk & Company with architect husband Andres Duany in 1980, Elizabeth Plater-Zyberk has established herself as one of the leading advocates of the New Urbanist school of design and architecture. Her family immigrated to the United States from Poland in 1950 and she grew up near Philadelphia, Pennsylvania. She later received an undergraduate degree in architecture from Princeton University and a master's degree from Yale University School of Architecture. After moving to Miami, Florida, in 1974, she and her husband became increasingly disenchanted with standard architectural designs and urban development that underlay sprawl patterns of urbanization. In 1980, she and her husband founded their own architectural firm with the intention of designing more community-centered developments that reflected pre–World War II design patterns.

Since then, Plater-Zyberk has distinguished herself by popularizing innovative designs that articulate the "neotraditional" model promoted by New Urbanists. Among the exemplars of this style is the community of Seaside, Florida, a new town built with the intention of promoting closely knit community institutions, energy efficiency, and environmental conservation. She has also worked to retrofit existing downtowns and suburban locales to reflect these principles. In 1991, Plater-Zyberk helped write a Traditional Neighborhood Development Ordinance based on New Urbanist design principles for Miami-Dade County, Florida, which has been a model for other similar endeavors across the country. She helped to found a master of architecture program in suburb and town design at the University of Miami and has served as director for the Center for Urban and Community Design there as well. More recently, she has served as dean of the school of architecture.

She coauthored with Andres Duany and Jeff Speck a book titled *Suburban Nation: The Rise of Sprawl and Decline of the American Dream* (2000). The book investigates the causes of urban sprawl and shares the fruits of the coauthors' extensive experiences in designing new neighborhoods and community revitalization projects. She intends the book both to inform the general public about the issue of sprawl and to present a clear program of steps that can be taken to enhance the quality of life in America's suburbs and rekindle development in declining urban communities.

Her contributions have been recognized far beyond the confines of her adopted city of Miami. Over the past decade, she has been a visiting professor at many major North American schools of architecture, a resident at the American Academy in Rome, and a trustee of Princeton University. She currently sits on the board of directors of the Congress of New Urbanism, based in San Francisco, California, and continues to do architectural work on new towns for urban municipalities. Recent projects include designs in Trenton, New Jersey; St. Louis, Missouri; Cleveland, Ohio; Ft. Lauderdale, Florida; and Ottawa, Ontario.

David Rusk

David Rusk, the former mayor of Albuquerque, New Mexico, has emerged as one of the leading commentators on trends facing America's large metropolitan areas, including the issue of sprawl. Rusk graduated from the University of California at Berkeley in 1962, at which point he took on a job as a full-time civil rights and antipoverty activist with the Washington Urban League. In 1968, he entered government service as the legislative and program development director for the Manpower Administration in the U.S. Department of Labor.

In 1971, he and his wife moved to Albuquerque, New Mexico, where he continued working on labor issues for the city government. Four years later, he entered the world of local politics by winning a seat in the New Mexico House of Representatives. In this capacity, he oversaw the passage of a massive reorganization of state government agencies. This involvement in local issues ultimately led him to run for mayor of Albuquerque, which he won on the Democratic ticket in 1977. He served in this capacity in pursuit of a major downtown renewal project that also included new investments in open space acquisition and public transit. Since stepping down from politics, Rusk has directed the executive committee that runs New Mexico's largest energy utility while assuming increased visibility nationwide as a consultant and author. He has become a speaker and consultant to business groups, foundations, local governments, interfaith organizations, and civic coalitions in over ninety metropolitan areas in thirty-five states and several foreign countries.

Rusk's research has focused primarily on the social, economic, and fiscal impacts of sprawl-based urban development patterns in America. In this capacity, he has become one of the nation's leading advocates for regionalism. This is the idea that serious economic and political problems facing metropolitan areas can best be solved through cooperative solutions that transcend local government boundaries in favor of regionally based institutions. His 1993 book, *Cities Without Suburbs* (now in its second edition), provides an analysis of urban development in America, providing an explanation for why some cities have succumbed to serious decline while others have largely avoided such problems. Subsequent books titled *Baltimore Unbound* (1995) and *Inside Game/Outside Game* have provided considerable insight into urban issues through analyses of case studies from around the United States.

Samuel Staley

Samuel Staley is a leading advocate for incorporating more free market principles and less reliance on government in urban development, with experience as an economic development consultant, urban policy analyst, citizen planner, and economist. He has attained national prominence while serving as the director of the Urban Futures Program at the conservative Reason Foundation in Los Angeles, California, for over 10 years. He also serves as the vice president of research at the Buckeye Institute for Public Policy Solutions in Dayton, Ohio.

He has authored or coauthored more than three dozen professional articles and reports, including two books, *Drug Policy and the Decline of American Cities* (1992) and *Planning Rules and Urban Economic Performance: The Case of Hong Kong* (1994). His book on drug policy won first place in the 1993 Sir Antony Fisher International Memorial Awards sponsored by the Atlas Economic Research Foundation for its contribution to an understanding of a free economy. His work has also appeared in a variety of academic, professional, and popular publications that include the *Journal of the American Planning Association*, the *Economics of Education Review*, the *Wall Street Journal, Chicago Tribune*, and other leading newspapers.

He received his B.A. in economics and public policy from Colby College in 1984, an M.S. in social and applied economics from Wright State University in 1987, and his Ph.D. in public policy and management from the Ohio State University in 1997. He has served on the planning commission and board of zoning appeals in Bellbrook, Ohio, worked as an active economic development consultant for local governments, and taught economics at Wright State University.

4

Facts and Opinion

The Facts: What Trends Are Shaping Sprawl?

M uch of the current debate about urban sprawl centers around rival assumptions about trends in the use of land in the United States. The following tables contain facts and data that should help to provide some solid background for those seeking to learn what trends are shaping land use in America.

Table 4.1

How Land Is Used in the United States in the Contiguous Forty-Eight States
(data in millions of acres)

	1945	1954	1964	1974	1982	1992
Total cropland*	451	465	444	465	469	460
Cropland used for crops	363	381	335	361	383	337
Grassland pasture and range	659	632	636	595	594	589
Forest land	602	615	612	598	567	559
Urban land	15	19	29	35	50	58
Recreation/Wildlife areas	23	28	50	57	71	88
Misc. farmland areas**	15	12	10	8	8	6

* Includes cropland used for crops, cropland idled, and cropland used for pasture
** Includes farmsteads, farm roads, etc.
Source: U.S. Department of Agriculture, Economic Research Service (1999)

Table 4.2
Participation in Public Open Space Preservation Programs, 1995
(in acres)

Region*	Farmland Protection Programs**	Conservation Reserve Program	Wetlands Reserve Program***
Appalachia	1,255	1,158,124	18,514
Corn Belt	0	5,603,333	115,621
Delta States	0	1,248,403	148,667
Lake States	0	3,008,337	18,664
Mountain States	1,904	6,687,264	3,210
Northeast	337,092	226,411	6,383
Northern Plains	0	9,664,110	25,254
Pacific	56,435	1,791,182	27,910
Southeast	0	1,692,580	5,257
Southern Plains	0	5,342,989	21,798

*Regions divided as follows: Appalachia (KY, NC, TN, VA, WV), Corn Belt (IL, IN, IA, MO, OH), Delta States (AR, LA, MS), Lake States (MI, MN, WI), Mountain States (AZ, CO, ID, MT, NM, NV, UT, WY), Northeast (CT, DE, MA, ME, MD, NH, NJ, NY, PA, RI, VT), Northern Plains (KS, NE, ND, SD), Pacific (CA, OR, WA), Southeast (AL, FL, GA, SC), Southern Plains (OK, TX). Alaska and Hawaii were excluded.

**Currently, eleven states (CT, DE, KY, MD, MA, ME, NH, NJ, PA, RI, VT) have agricultural conservation easement programs.

***Includes emergency sign-ups.

Source: U.S. Department of Agriculture, Economic Research Service (1996)

Table 4.3
Large Metropolitan Areas of the United States with Projected Population Growth Rates of 10 Percent or Higher, 2000–2010, Ranked by Projected Increase in Growth Between 2000–2010

	2000 population	2000–2010 increase	2010 population	percentage change
Las Vegas, NV	1,262,000	306,000	1,568,000	24.2
Orlando, FL	1,605,000	358,000	1,963,000	22.3
Riverside-San Bernardino, CA	3,429,000	701,000	4,130,000	20.4
Sarasota-Bradenton, FL	602,000	121,000	723,000	20.1
Sacramento, CA	1,667,000	311,000	1,978,000	18.7
Boca Raton, FL	1,074,000	186,000	1,260,000	17.3
Phoenix-Mesa, AZ	2,773,000	459,000	3,232,000	16.6
Salt Lake City-Ogden, UT	1,327,000	220,000	1,547,000	16.6
Austin-St. Marcos, TX	1,077,000	174,000	1,251,000	16.2
Raleigh-Durham-Chapel Hill, NC	1,092,000	176,000	1,268,000	16.1
San Diego, CA	2,964,000	471,000	3,435,000	15.9
Seattle-Bellevue-Everett, WA	2,416,000	384,000	2,800,000	15.9
Fort Lauderdale, FL	1,527,000	237,000	1,764,000	15.5
Atlanta, GA	3,682,000	550,000	4,232,000	14.9
Tampa-St. Petersburg-Clearwater, FL	2,403,000	349,000	2,752,000	14.5

Table 4.3, continued

	2000 population	2000–2010 increase	2010 population	percentage change
Ventura, CA	785,000	114,000	899,000	14.5
Jacksonville, FL	1,075,000	154,000	1,229,000	14.3
Albuquerque, NM	711,000	100,000	811,000	14.1
Denver, CO	1,970,000	265,000	2,235,000	13.5
Orange County, CA	2,849,000	377,000	3,226,000	13.2
Fresno, CA	920,000	118,000	1,038,000	12.8
Portland-Vancouver, OR-WA	1,829,000	233,000	2,062,000	12.7
Monmouth-Ocean, NJ	1,142,000	145,000	1,287,000	12.7
Ft. Worth-Arlington, TX	1,599,000	201,000	1,800,000	12.6
Washington, DC-MD-VA-WV	4,860,000	594,000	5,454,000	12.2
Tucson, AZ	793,000	96,000	889,000	12.1
Dallas, TX	3,161,000	377,000	3,538,000	11.9
Houston, TX	4,020,000	471,000	4,491,000	11.7
Charlotte-Gastonia-Rock Hill, NC	1,361,000	158,000	1,519,000	11.6
Nashville, TN	1,155,000	133,000	1,288,000	11.5
San Antonio, TX	1,548,000	175,000	1,723,000	11.3
Middlesex-Somerset-Hunterdon, NJ	1,156,000	121,000	1,277,000	10.5
San Jose, CA	1,676,000	172,000	1,848,000	10.3
Oakland, CA	2,346,000	242,000	2,588,000	10.3
Greensboro-Winston-Salem-High Pt., NC	1,185,000	119,000	1,304,000	10.0

Table 4.4
Measures of Urban Sprawl in Fifty-Three Urbanized Areas, 1950–1990

	Growth in urbanized population (percent)	Growth in urbanized land (percent)	Land-to-population growth ratio	Density of new growth in 1980s (persons per square mile)	Density of central cities in 1950 (persons per square mile)
Akron, OH	44	162	4 to 1	747	4,778
Albuquerque, NM[a]	106	189	2 to 1	1,440[b]	3,580
Allentown-Bethlehem-Easton, PA-NJ	82	188	2 to 1	1,879	5,017
Atlanta, GA	325	977	3 to 1	2,577	7,822
Baltimore, MD	63	290	5 to 1	2,695	12,067
Buffalo, NY	7	133	20 to 1	-429	12,879
Charlotte, NC	223	601	3 to 1	2,029[b]	4,468
Chattanooga, TN	77	410	5 to 1	871	4,480
Chicago, IL	38	124	3 to 1	4,328	12,919
Cincinnati, OH-KY-IN	49	250	5 to 1	1,198	6,711
Cleveland, OH	21	112	5 to 1	-756	12,197
Columbus, OH	116	435	4 to 1	2,797[b]	9,541
Dayton, OH	77	337	4 to 1	2,160	9,755
Springfield, OH[c]	8	170	22 to 1	561	6,488
Detroit, MI	34	165	5 to 1	-144	12,066
Erie, PA	17	94	6 to 1	1,453	6,958
Fort Wayne, IN	77	365	5 to 1	1,496	7,107
Fort Worth, TX[d]	274	451	2 to 1	4,587[b]	3,467

(continues)

Table 4.4, continued

	Growth in urbanized population (percent)	Growth in urbanized land (percent)	Land-to-population growth ratio	Density of new growth in 1980s (persons per square mile)	Density of central cities in 1950 (persons per square mile)
Gainesville, FL[a]	82	111	1 to 1	2,440[b]	2,472
Grand Rapids, MI	92	378	4 to 1	920	7,543
Hartford, CT	82	356	4 to 1	784	10,195
Indianapolis, IN	82	418	5 to 1	1,823	7,739
Kalamazoo, MI	97	300	3 to 1	1,251	6,557
Kansas City, MO-KS	83	411	5 to 1	2,287	5,647
Lancaster, PA	154	965	6 to 1	1,769	14,831
Lorain-Elyria, OH[a]	50	78	2 to 1	1,488	3,490
Louisville, KY-IN	60	324	5 to 1	1,400	9,251
Memphis, TN-AR-MS	103	211	2 to 1	2,423	3,676
Minneapolis-St.Paul, MN-WI	111	360	3 to 1	3,514	7,859
Mobile, AL	64	458	7 to 1	260	5,079
Muskegon, MI[a]	11	138	12 to 1	1,516	5,369
Nashville, TN	121	800	7 to 1	673	7,923
New Haven-Meridan, CT	84	301	4 to 1	2,152	9,187
New Orleans, LA	58	148	3 to 1	535	6,633
Norfolk-Virginia Beach-Newport News, VA[a]	85	162	2 to 1	4,648	3,217
Oklahoma City, OK	185	865	5 to 1	557	4,927
Peoria, IL	57	289	5 to 1	−1,522	6,857
Pittsburgh, PA	10	207	22 to 1	−1,095	12,622
Portland, OR-WA	129	242	2 to 1	3,744[b]	5,720
Reading, PA	20	127	6 to 1	1,875	12,423
Richmond, VA	129	525	4 to 1	2,219	6,208
Rochester, NY	51	241	5 to 1	1,369	9,236
Saginaw, MI	32	168	5 to 1	100	5,597
San Antonio, TX	151	388	3 to 1	2,194[b]	5,877
Springfield, MA	49	80	2 to 1	1,165	5,123
St. Louis, MO-IL	39	220	6 to 1	1,351	10,968
Tallahassee, FL[a]	31	29	1 to 1	1,827	2,755
Toledo, OH	34	177	5 to 1	1,221	7,927
Utica-Rome, NY	-14	51	-5 to 1	1,050	6,426
Washington, DC	161	429	3 to 1	4,465	10,979
Worcester, MA	44	218	5 to 1	1,495	5,500
York, PA	81	529	7 to 1	1,752	14,275
Youngstown-Warren, OH	-6	12	-2 to 1	214	5,132
Unweighted mean	80	305	4 to 1	1,573	7,504

[a]Data from 1960 to 1990, except for Gainesville and Tallahassee (1970–1990).
[b]Both suburban and elastic central city growth.
[c]Springfield, OH (Clark County), is separated from the Dayton metropolitan area.
[d]Fort Worth and Dallas urbanized areas combined.
Source: David Rusk, *Inside Game/Outside Game* (1999)

Table 4.5
Sierra Club's Ranking of the Most Sprawl-Threatened Cities in the United States

Large Cities	
1. Atlanta, GA	11. Detroit, MI
2. St. Louis, MO	12. Baltimore, MD
3. Washington, DC	13. Cleveland, OH
4. Cincinnati, OH	14. Tampa, FL
5. Kansas City, MO	15. Dallas, TX
6. Denver, CO	16. Hampton Roads, VA
7. Seattle, WA	17. Pittsburgh, PA
8. Minneapolis-St. Paul, MN	18. Miami, FL
9. Ft. Lauderdale, FL	19. San Antonio, TX
10. Chicago, IL	20. Riverside/San Bernardino, CA
Medium Cities	Small Cities
1. Orlando, FL	1. McAllen, TX
2. Austin, TX	2. Raleigh, NC
3. Las Vegas, NV	3. Pensacola, FL
4. West Palm Beach, FL	4. Daytona Beach, FL
5. Akron, OH	5. Little Rock, AR

Source: Sierra Club (2000)

Public Opinion Polls on Urban Sprawl

What opinions do Americans have about sprawl? Do they consider it to be an important issue for government to address? And what policy prescriptions do they support? These questions were raised in opinion polls taken at the end of the 1990s by two organizations. The results are no doubt important in influencing the direction of the public debate about sprawl in the coming years.

"Straight Talk from Americans: 2000" National Survey

The Pew Center for Civic Journalism conducted a telephone survey of a representative sample of 1,006 adults age eighteen and older living in the forty-eight contiguous states between 6 and 31 October 1999. This survey provides evidence that the complex of issues known as sprawl, growth, traffic, roads, and infrastructure are a top concern, with 18 percent mentioning the issue. The survey confirmed the contention that traffic congestion, poorly maintained roads, inadequate sewer and water utilities, and crowded schools were being linked strongly to perceptions of urban growth and development.

Q: *"What do you think is the most important problem facing the community where you live?"*

Development/Sprawl/Traffic/Roads—18 percent
Crime/Violence—18 percent
Economic issues/The economy—13 percent
Education—10 percent
Child and teen issues—6 percent
Problems with politics/Politicians—3 percent
Racism/Discrimination/Intolerance—2 percent
Problems with immigrants—2 percent
The environment—2 percent
Law enforcement/Justice/Court system—2 percent
Moral decline/Decline of family values—3 percent
Health/Medicine—1 percent
Poverty/Hunger/Homelessness—1 percent
Natural disasters/Hurricanes/Floods—1 percent
Senior citizen issues/Care of the elderly—1 percent
Other—4 percent
Things are good here—3 percent
New to the area/Just moved here—1 percent
Nothing/No problems/None—6 percent
Don't know/Can't think of anything—5 percent
Refused/No comment—1 percent

The study also concluded that:

Sprawl is more of an issue for those in the suburbs than anywhere else, more of an issue for college-educated citizens and more of an issue among white Americans than African-Americans. And it is a huge issue in Denver and San Francisco.

Twenty-six percent of those who live in the suburbs mention sprawl-related issues as the most important local matters, more than the 14 percent who do so in more rural areas.

Twenty-four percent of those who have at least attended college mention it is an issue, compared with 13 percent of those who have not.

And 20 percent of the white Americans say it is a top local issue, compared with 8 percent of African-Americans.

There are enormous variations by city. In Denver, an astonishing 60 percent of residents name sprawl as the biggest problem facing the area. A strong 47 percent do so in San Francisco. Thirty-three percent mention it in Tampa and only 18 percent in Philadelphia. (Again, each of the local surveys was conducted in a multicounty area including the major city named. All local survey findings refer to those multicounty areas.)

Source: Pew Center for Civic Journalism, "Straight Talk from Americans: 2000" National Survey (1999)

1999 Consumer Survey on Growth Issues

A written survey was administered to 2,000 randomly selected households nationwide and 3,000 households in ten metropolitan areas by the National Association of Homebuilders during December 1998 and January 1999. This organization believes that these survey results confirm their contention that Americans are generally satisfied with life in their communities, support local government control of land use, and prefer current growth patterns over higher-density development that has been proposed by antisprawl advocates.

Q: *"In general, are you satisfied with the quality of life in your neighborhood?"*

Very satisfied—36 percent
Somewhat satisfied—53 percent
Not satisfied—10 percent
Not sure—1 percent

Q: *"Do you think addressing growth issues is mainly the responsibility of federal, state or local government?"*

Federal government—3 percent
State government—14 percent
Local government—72 percent
None of these—2 percent
Unsure—9 percent

Q: "Which of the following approaches should local government take to influence growth and development?"

Pass laws to stop growth—2 percent
Pass laws to restrict growth—12 percent
Plan and manage growth—75 percent
Let people use property as they see fit—11 percent

Q: "Would you support or oppose building single-family homes at a higher density (smaller lots or more homes per acre) in your neighborhood?"

Strongly oppose—40 percent
Oppose—37 percent
Does not matter—8 percent
Support—12 percent
Strongly support—3 percent

Q: "Would you support or oppose building townhouses in your neighborhood?"

Oppose—54 percent
Support—32 percent
Not sure—14 percent

Q: "Would you support or oppose building multifamily apartment buildings in your neighborhood?"

Oppose—78 percent
Support—12 percent
Not sure—10 percent

Source: National Association of Home Builders, *Smart Growth Report* (1999)

Quotations: Debating Urban Sprawl

As the debate over sprawl heats up across the country, rival positions are being staked out. The following section provides quotes from authorities on both sides of the debate in response to several key questions associated with the issue of urban sprawl.

Is Urban Sprawl a Problem?

"According to recent market research, most ordinary Americans, though still favoring detached, single-family homes, are increasingly fed up with the congestion and sprawling commercial development that too often come as part of the package. Today's consumers say they are particularly annoyed by commercial strips and that in principle they would prefer neighborhoods clustered around a downtown or village center."

Phillip J. Longman
U.S. News & World Report (27 April 1998), p. 22

"The prospect of everyone owning their own home evokes a nightmare image of endless single-family houses, apartment buildings, and condos sprawling over hill and dale, destroying farmland and forests, leading to increased car dependency, further fragmentation, excessive energy and resource consumption, and continued ecological damage. Neither the market nor the environment can support everyone in fulfilling this 'American Dream.'"

Ken Norwood and Kathleen Smith
Rebuilding Community in America (1995), p. 29

"Communities in every corner of the country . . . accept a developer's idea of how their community should be shaped, because they have few ideas of their own. How much better off they would be if they would step back from immediate development pressures, allow the community to decide what it wants to be, and then proceed to make it happen. Some communities, however, can't seem to find the wisdom to restrain themselves from making short-term decisions with long-term implications. The fact is, places everywhere subsidize sprawl because of imagined gains. Few of them ever pause to measure the true costs of such development proposals."

Richard Moe and Carter Wilkie
Changing Places (1997), p. 255

"The total amount of urbanized or built-up land is less than 5 percent of the total land area in the continental U.S., and the rate of land being developed, based on U.S. Geological Survey estimates, is about seven one-hundredths of one percent (0.07 percent). Some evidence suggests that the rate of 'sprawl' is actually lower today than it was in the 1950s and 1960s. The 'sprawl index,' a simple comparison of population growth and the rate of urbanization, has actually declined since 1980. Moreover, since the end of World War II, the amount of land set aside for parks, wilderness, and wildlife has grown twice as fast as urban areas. In 1969, there were 2.6 acres of conservation land for every acre of urbanized land; today there are about 4 acres of conservation land for every acre of urbanized land. (These figures exclude national parks and agricultural conservation land programs.) And private land conservation efforts are booming."

Steven Hayward, Pacific Research Institute for Public Policy
Testimony before the Public Works Committee, U.S. Senate, 17 March 1999

"What is disturbing about the crusade against urban sprawl is that anti-sprawl activists portray their agenda of 'smart-growth' initiatives as 'pro-suburban' to receptive voters concerned about improving the quality of life in their communities. In reality, anti-sprawl policies are profoundly anti-suburban. In cities such as Portland, Oregon, where aggressive anti-sprawl policies have been implemented, government planners have deliberately tried to increase traffic congestion, not diminish it, and have tried to force people to live in smaller houses in more crowded urban-like neighborhoods. To these activists, suburbs are the cause of sprawl, and the only way to stop sprawl is to dissuade people from moving to the suburbs. The campaign against urban sprawl is perilously close to a campaign against the American Dream."

John Carlisle, National Center for Public Policy Research (April 1999)

"Residential construction stimulates the economy directly by generating jobs, wages and tax revenues and indirectly as the demand for goods and services created by the construction of new homes ripples through the economy. The construction of 1,000 single-family homes generates 2,448 full-time jobs in construction and construction-related industries; $79.4 million in wages; and $42.5 million in combined federal, state and local revenues and fees. The construction of 1,000 multifamily units generates 1,030 full-time jobs in construction and construction-related industries; $33.5 million in wages; and $17.8 million in combined federal, state and local tax revenues and fees."

National Association of Home Builders, NAHB website, June 1999

Is Life in Suburbia Really That Bad?

"For all its apparent success, suburban sprawl sorely lacks many things that make life worth living, particularly civic amenities, which main street (once) offered in spades. Deep down, many Americans are dissatisfied with suburbia—though they have trouble understanding what's missing—which explains their nostalgia for the earlier model. Their dissatisfaction is literally a *dis-ease*. They feel vaguely and generally unwell where they are. Nostalgia in its original sense means homesickness."

   James H. Kunstler, *Home from Nowhere* (1996), p. 37

"Our dependence upon the car and its cohort, the single-family house in the suburbs, has seriously contributed to the fragmentation of the extended family and a lower quality of living for more and more people. We can get up in the morning, get in our car, and drive to work without encountering any other person face to face. Is this the American Dream? The way our neighborhoods are laid out and our housing is financed ensures that residential areas are segregated by economic class, age, and race. Is this the American Dream? It is obvious that the housing industry has not been a social/family/community-oriented process, but merely a way of doing business and making a profit, as if a house were like any other product sold over the counter."

   Ken Norwood and Kathleen Smith, *Rebuilding Community in America* (1995), p. 18

"The United States has become a predominately suburban nation, but not a very happy one. Today more than three-quarters of the American people live in metropolitan areas, and more than two-thirds of those live in suburbs. Each year development pushes out across more than a million acres, yet the expansion of highways, housing tracts, and other suburban construction rouses fewer cheers than at any time in the past. The problem is not simply that a sensible person can no longer believe in the rightness of turning huge expanses of farmland, forest, desert, and other rural landscapes into additional suburbs. The problem is that the suburbs we build are fostering an unhealthy way of life. . . . There is a strong connection between the ills we exhibit as a people and the suburban 'communities' (to use a much abused word) that we inhabit."

   Philip Langdon, *A Better Place to Live* (1994), p. 1

"An alien observer looking down at us from another planet

might easily conclude that the automobile was the dominant life form in America. What the alien would see is a network of pavement linking shopping malls, commercial strips, interstate highways, and suburban housing tracts to the parking lots where the beasts come to rest. For people, modern highways and the clutter that developed along them divided communities as effectively as the Berlin Wall, and parking lots wasted nearly every open space in sight. In the age of auto madness, we paved paradise and put in a parking lot."

Terry Pindell, *A Good Place to Live* (1995), p. 375

"Sprawl will be unabated in the future despite the howls of critics and government planners; housing developments will continue eating up rural land on the suburban fringe, moving ever farther from the already distant central city. This decentralization will be driven not only by technology, but also prevailing attitudes. Surveys indicate that suburban residents enjoy the moderate concentration of services provided by shopping malls, strip plazas, and office parks, but dislike the heavier densities of the typical downtown. And they will oppose strongly any efforts to transform their uncrowded neighborhoods into copies of the congested urban model."

G. Scott Thomas, *The United States of Suburbia* (1998), p. 108

"Americans value their freedom to choose where they live and work and how they travel. People continue to live and work in the suburbs because they enjoy the quality of life in those communities. So-called 'smart-growth' plans aimed at increasing housing densities and limiting highway capacity will restrict home and travel choices. While some growth management is necessary to help alleviate the challenges associated with growth, such policies should follow, and not dictate, public sentiment. Growth-management policies must work with, not against, the overwhelming preference in this country: the detached, single-family home."

Quality Growth Coalition, *Building Better Communities* (2000), p. 19

Is More Compact Urban Development a Better Way to Organize Our Cities?

"Houses of the past have lessons from which today's suburbs can profit. In recent decades Americans have been focusing too much on the house itself and too little on the neighborhood, too much on interior luxury and too little on public amenity. By reconsidering the design of our houses, we might begin again to create walkable, stimulating, more affordable neighborhoods where sociable pleasures are always within reach. The country can learn much from the neighborly kinds of housing we used to build. They made—and continue to make—good places for living."

Philip Langdon, *A Better Place to Live* (1994), p. 171

"The taming of sprawl and the creation of more sustainable places require a concerted effort at promoting compact communities—human settlement patterns that consume considerably less natural and open land and that achieve higher average densities than current development patterns. In fact, the compact form of cities and towns has historically manifested itself in ways that facilitate human interaction and commerce. The enduring success of a number of European cities and older American communities illustrates that this is neither a new nor an outmoded concept. From Boston's Beacon Hill to Washington, D.C.'s Georgetown to the older districts of Charleston, South Carolina, and Savannah, Georgia, compact, dense cities and neighborhoods continue to thrive."

Timothy Beatley and Kristy Manning, *The Ecology of Place* (1997), p. 42

"Study after study has shown that increasing the distance over which service and infrastructure must travel increases costs. The greatest cost savings come from reducing the total amount of linear infrastructure, especially roads and water and sewer lines, required to serve a given number of households or businesses. One synthesis of several studies concluded that directing growth to areas with existing infrastructure and modestly increasing the density of development could reduce the total capital costs for roads by 25 percent and water and sewer infrastructure by 15 percent. Other research has put the savings even higher—up to 60 percent for roads and 40 percent for water and sewer lines."

F. Kaid Benfield, Matthew D. Raimi, and Donald D. T. Chen, *Once There Were Greenfields* (1999), p. 115

"What would American society be like if over the past hundred years the peripheral growth of urban areas had been tightly constricted? Scores of millions would be living in crowded buildings. Housing for the urban poor in particular would be more cramped, more substandard, and much more expensive. The nation's extraordinarily diverse ethnicities might collide more frequently, much as they did when packed into the cities of the nineteenth century. The number of persons exposed to crime, congestion, and environmental hazards such as carcinogenic particulates in the air would be greater than it is today. Restraints on the locus of capital investment would have pinched the national economy, making a majority of Americans less prosperous. Clearly, liberal access to space beyond the boundaries of our central cities has helped the United States thrive and avoid some of the afflictions that especially in recent years have sapped the economies of several European countries and Japan."

Pietro S. Nivola, *Laws of the Landscape* (1999), pp. 88–89

"Smart Growth's assumptions and 'solutions' are wrong because they are based on an antiquated economic model that is wrong. Maryland's Smart Growth, which offers increased density as a cure for density-related problems, is based on the state's 2020 Plan for growth management, issued in 1989. The 2020 Plan, and most others like it around the country, is based on a 1974 economic study, *The Costs of Sprawl*, commissioned by the U.S. Council on Environmental Quality (CEQ). . . . It found that high-density, planned communities are less costly to build and live in than low-density 'sprawl.' It also suggested that sprawl produces more pollution than planned high-density developments. *The Costs of Sprawl* was powerful, persuasive, and—according to the evidence—egregiously defective. At least in terms of real-world applications. In the real world, as population densities increase, so do traffic congestion, air pollution, taxes, infrastructure, and other costs. More importantly, so does crime—especially violent crime."

Frieda Campbell, Cato Institute *Regulation* (Spring 1998), p. 11

Does Urban Sprawl Contribute to Inner-City Decline?

"Even with flourishing downtowns, inner cities decline. Inner-city neighborhoods deteriorate as places to raise families. With shrinking tax bases, city budgets are unable to meet rising social needs. Enterprise zones, community development banks, non-

profit inner-city housing developments—all the tools of 'empowerment'—are not futile efforts. They will produce some new businesses, some new jobs, some new homes, and some revitalized neighborhoods. They will be more effective, however, if carried out within a framework of actions to bring down the walls between city and suburb. Absent efforts at reunification, such programs will be unable to reverse the downward slide of the inner cities."
    David Rusk, *Cities Without Suburbs* (1993), p. 121

    "The new metropolitan geography, with its fragmentation of traditional communities and the migration of jobs away from older urban centers, is a major cause not only of environmental stress and traffic gridlock, but of unemployment, alienation, and the breakdown of law and order. The evolution of the metropolitan region has left most low-income people concentrated in older deteriorating neighborhoods of cities and towns, while jobs and the tax base to support education and social services have migrated elsewhere. Separating the poor from access to jobs and leaving them in places where both public and private investment is being withdrawn is a recipe for social tragedy."
    Jonathan Barnett, *The Fractured Metropolis* (1995), p. 114

    "Urban areas and older, declining suburbs don't escape the harmful effects of sprawl. As families flee to the countryside, a city's tax base disappears, forcing mayors to raise taxes on remaining taxpayers to pay for city services. And the so-called 'brownfields' don't get cleaned up, because businesses are given incentives to relocate to outer 'greenbelts.' Sprawl destroys downtown commerce by pulling shoppers from once-thriving locally owned stores and restaurants to large regional malls. Unemployment, lowered property values, and fewer investment opportunities all result when cities lose their vitality and livability."
    Kathryn Hohmann, Director, Environmental Quality Program of the Sierra Club (17 March 1999)

    "Rejuvenating America's urban cores and inner-ring suburbs with new housing requires a joint effort on the part of local governments and home builders. If people don't want to buy close-in because of concerns about security, property values, or public schools, no amount of innovative housing will convince them otherwise. . . . Cities can encourage infill housing and amplify its impact on existing development patterns by providing/rebuilding infrastructure, cleaning environmentally tainted sites, revising liability laws for brownfields sites, increasing crime prevention, improving inner-city schools, promoting community support for projects, increasing predictability and efficiency in the permitting process, streamlining and expediting development approvals, (and) offering builder and buyer incentives, tax credits, financing, partnerships and contributing land."

National Association of Home Builders, *NAHB's Smart Growth Report* (2000), p. 13

"Many cities suffer from poorly functioning school systems, high tax rates, anticompetitive regulations, and a deteriorating housing stock. These obstacles become formidable barriers to development. . . . City governments, then, need to carefully assess and restructure their own policies to provide a more investor-, family-, and entrepreneur-friendly business climate. Deregulating central cities and lowering overall taxes mitigate the 'push' factor in suburbanization."

Samuel Staley, *The Sprawling of America* (1999), pp. 37–38

Is Mass Transit an Effective Way to Fight Sprawl?

"Home buyers have few choices in transportation. They are only guaranteed long car trips, ozone depletion, and a house they may never be able to sell because of the oversupply of remote location tracts that are too far from services. In many of this country's urban regions, commutes of 60 miles or more each way are not uncommon. Americans drove one trillion more miles in 1990 than they did in 1973, and since 1982, gas consumption has gone up 10 percent. Improved fuel consumption and cleaner fuels will not be enough, because increased emissions from car trips generated by faulty land use policy will soon exceed the emission levels previously set."

Ken Norwood and Kathleen Smith, *Rebuilding Community in America* (1995), p. 26

"Traffic congestion is an annoyance faced by urban residents on a daily basis. Almost 70 percent of peak-hour travel on the urban interstate system occurs under near stop-and-go conditions. Congestion is consistently identified by metropolitan area residents as one of the most serious urban problems, even when compared with crime, education, and human services. The economic impact of congestion is significant. Most people consider time spent stalled in traffic as wasted. How that time would be divided between productive work and leisure activities is hard to determine, but both alternatives are valuable. Congestion also inhibits the movement of goods, which raises prices. The U.S. Government Accounting Office estimates that the annual cost of congestion (excluding environmental impacts) in the United States is $130 billion. Perhaps most insidiously, the automobile destroys the cohesion of our communities. The construction of roads results in physical divisions, and the reliance on automobiles has been partially responsible for breaking down identification with community. Urban dwellers have become less likely to know their neighbors and shop at local stores."

Daniel Carlson, *At Road's End* (1995), pp. 6–7

"In the annals of history, many recognize that we have moved as far as we can go on untamed wheels. A nation in gridlock from its auto-bred lifestyle, an environment choking from its auto exhausts, a landscape sacked by its highways has distressed Americans so much that even this go-for-it nation is posting 'No Growth' signs on development from shore to shore. All of these dead ends make this a time for larger considerations. The future of our motorized culture needs change."

Jane Holtz Kay, *Asphalt Nation* (1997), p. 9

"U.S. rail transit investments have been costly failures that have paradoxically resulted in less transit use as bus funds were cannibalized for rail. Los Angeles, as a typical example, has lost more than a fifth of its transit riders since it started spending billions of dollars on rail. As for the much-touted Portland light rail (MAX), every Portland freeway carries four to five times more riders per day . . . transit accounts for only 2.8 percent of trips, with a mere 0.3 percent using MAX, and only about one percent of the Tri-Met's service area population is within walking distance of MAX stations."

Peter Gordon and Harry Richardson, Cascade Policy Institute, *"Why Sprawl Is Good"* (1997), p. 1

"Few communities have the kinds of mass-transit systems in place to accommodate a significant share of current commuting trips. Indeed, most urban mass-transit systems are neither

efficient nor cost effective under current policies. Light-rail systems are too inflexible and costly to be effective mass-transit alternatives. Until cities deregulate their transit industry or institute 'curb rights'—reducing burdensome licensing and inspection systems for taxi, van and bus services—cost-effective mass transit is unlikely to emerge."
Samuel Staley, *The Sprawling of America* (1999), p. 39

"If the public road system represents a subsidy of any kind, it is, at least in the United States, a subsidy of virtually every man, woman, and child in the country. If something benefits all citizens and if it is a 'good' that has been supplied by civil organizations since the beginning of history, can it be a subsidy? Even the very few citizens who may enter a car only rarely still depend on the roads for the transport of their food and everything else they use. Nonmotorists who use rail mass transit are the truly subsidized. No such rail system comes close to paying for its operating costs, much less paying off the investment in its construction and maintenance."
James D. Johnson, *Driving America* (1997), p. 195

"Census Bureau surveys show that average commuting times have remained remarkably constant for decades at about 22 minutes each direction. About one out of six commuters takes over 35 minutes, but another one of six takes under 10 minutes. Moreover, commuting times are roughly the same across all cities and across different types of commutes: suburbs to suburbs, suburbs to central city, and central city to suburbs. . . . Auto commuters take about 20 minutes, while bus and light rail commuters average closer to 35. This isn't because mass transit commuters go further; on average they don't go as far. Instead, it is because mass transit is slower: an average of 13 miles per hour compared with more than 30 miles per hour by car."
Randal O'Toole, *The Vanishing Automobile* (1996), p. 27

Does Urban Sprawl Threaten American Farming?
"According to a 1997 American Farmland Trust study, every state in the nation is sacrificing irreplaceable agricultural resources to urban sprawl. We are converting a total of 1 million acres a year, and while the quantity of top-quality agricultural land being lost varies from state to state, the process of conver-

sion increases the pressures on agriculture even beyond the acres that are actually taken out of production."
American Farmland Trust, *Why Save Farmland* (2000)

"(T)he amount of land in urban use is projected to double in fifty years. But the impact of urban development on farmland and open space cannot be measured just in terms of acres converted or higher land prices. Often the knowledge that development is likely will cause farmers to reduce investment in buildings and equipment, as they foresee the eventual sale of the farm. Another important factor is the compatibility, or lack of it, between new houses, offices, stores, and factories and nearby farms. Once farmland becomes interspersed with houses and other development, farm operations change to small vegetable farms, horticulture greenhouses, and horse farms or the land is sold to grow more buildings."
Tom Daniels and Deborah Bowers, *Holding Our Ground* (1997), pp. 10–11

"Farmland that is the basis of a healthy local economy, provides critical environmental benefits, or is of exceptional value for food production should be protected from conversion to nonagricultural uses. The governors recommend that the Farmland Protection Program continue to authorize one-to-one federal matching grants to states and state-approved local jurisdictions. Organizations such as nonprofit land trusts and conservancies should be allowed to hold easements purchased with the grants."
National Governors' Association, Policy Position adopted at Annual Meeting (1999)

"Cities are not crowding out agricultural production. Expanding urban areas do not threaten agricultural production. Since 1950, U.S. agricultural acreage has fallen by 15 percent, while production has risen by more than 105 percent. The area required for agricultural production has declined, quite independently of urban expansion. Between 1960 and 1990, the area taken out of agricultural production was greater than that of Texas and more than eight times the area consumed by expanding urban areas."
Wendell Cox, *The President's New Sprawl Initiative: A Program in Search of a Problem* (1999), p. 4

"This must be the silliest of pet causes. Why should farms near cities be preserved? If you want parks, forests, recreation facilities or anything else, okay, but why farms? So they will be within easy wagon distance in case we forget how to use our trucks and airplanes? In the whole United States, only 92.4 million acres are developed—less than 5 percent of our total surface area of 1.9 billion acres. Cropland takes up 382 million acres. Even in the crowded Middle Atlantic states, only 10 percent of the land is developed. There is no crisis. Nonetheless, planning efforts solemnly worry about this terrible threat, preserving farmland while residential development is forced further out and commutes lengthen."

James V. DeLong, *Property Matters* (1997), p. 241

"What is often overlooked in the farmland debate is that major technological advances in food production require less and less farmland to produce record crop yields. The United States Department of Agriculture's (USDA) index of national farm output shows that the United States increased its food production by nearly 48% since 1970, despite a reduction in agricultural acreage. The U.S. Bureau of Economic Analysis shows that total farm income increased by 63% between 1980 and 1994. The value of farm production is expected to grow nearly 26% even though the number of farms continues to decline and the number of farm workers is expected to fall by 4.9%. . . . In a 1997 report, the USDA's Economic Research Service concluded that 'losing farmland to urban uses does not threaten total cropland or the level of agricultural production which should be sufficient to meet food and fiber demand into the next century.'"

John Carlisle, National Center for Public Policy Research, Report No. 239, *The Campaign Against Urban Sprawl* (April 1999)

5

Documents

What Is the Best Way to Deal with Urban Sprawl?

The following documents offer a sampling of initiatives that are already in place at the state and metropolitan level, and what is being proposed at the federal level of government.

The first document presented is the 1993 charter for the metropolitan government that was created to govern the three-county urban region that surrounds Portland, Oregon. With the adoption of this innovative regional government, the people of this area placed primary responsibility for land use planning in the hands of an elected regional council that is overseen by an elected executive. It offers a model for other communities faced with similar growth pressures.

The next two documents represent policy initiatives to contain urban sprawl at the state level. First presented is the statewide planning law that was adopted by Oregon in 1973. It seeks to better manage growth statewide by coordinating land use planning by the many local, county, and state agencies that all have an impact on development. Almost a dozen states have followed suit with growth management laws patterned after Oregon. The third document is the "smart growth" law passed by the Maryland state legislature in 1997. The significance of this law is that it provides both incentives and disincentives to promote less wasteful use of land resources, with the intention of pushing new development into previously developed corridors, while preserving relatively pristine rural areas.

The final series of documents revolve around federal initiatives of the Clinton-Gore administration to foster growth management through coordinated action by federal agencies. It provides grant programs to states and localities to encourage in-fill development and more comprehensive planning. This section also contains a rebuttal from the National Association of Home Builders, which has embraced the "smart growth" agenda with some important reservations.

Charter of the Metropolitan Government of Portland, Oregon, 1993

Preamble

We, the people of the Portland area metropolitan service district, in order to establish an elected, visible and accountable regional government that is responsive to the citizens of the region and works cooperatively with our local governments; that undertakes, as its most important service, planning and policy making to preserve and enhance the quality of life and the environment for ourselves and future generations; and that provides regional services needed and desired by the citizens in an efficient and effective manner, do ordain this charter for the Portland area metropolitan service district, to be known as Metro.

Names and Boundaries

Section 1. Title of Charter.   The title of this charter is the 1992 Metro Charter.

Section 2. Name of Regional Government.   The Portland area metropolitan service district, referred to in this charter as the "Metropolitan Service District," continues under this charter as a metropolitan service district with the name "Metro."

Section 3. Boundaries.   The Metro area of governance includes all territory within the boundaries of the Metropolitan Service District on the effective date of this charter and any territory later annexed or subjected to Metro governance under state law. This charter refers to that area as the "Metro area." Changes of Metro boundaries are not effective unless approved by ordinance. No change of Metro boundaries requires approval by a local government boundary commission or any other state agency unless required by law. The custodian of Metro records shall keep an accurate description of Metro boundaries and make it available for public inspection.

Functions and Powers

Section 4. Jurisdiction of Metro.   Metro has jurisdiction over matters of metropolitan concern. Matters of metropolitan concern include the powers granted to and duties imposed on Metro by current and future state law and those matters the council by ordinance determines to be of metropolitan concern. The council shall specify by ordinance the extent to which Metro exercises jurisdiction over matters of metropolitan concern.

Section 5. Regional Planning Functions. (1) Future Vision.

(a) Adoption. The council shall adopt a Future Vision for the region between January 15, 1995, and July 1, 1995. The Future Vision is a conceptual statement that indicates population levels and settlement patterns that the region can accommodate within the carrying capacity of the land, water and air resources of the region, and its educational and economic resources, and that achieves a desired quality of life. The Future Vision is a long-term, visionary outlook for at least a 50-year period. As used in this section, "region" means the Metro area and adjacent areas.

(b) Matters addressed. The matters addressed by the Future Vision include but are not limited to: (1) use, restoration and preservation of regional land and natural resources for the benefit of present and future generations, (2) how and where to accommodate the population growth for the region while maintaining a desired quality of life for its residents, and (3) how to develop new communities and additions to the existing urban areas in well-planned ways.

(c) Development. The council shall appoint a commission to develop and recommend a proposed Future Vision by a date the council sets. The commission shall be broadly representative of both public and private sectors, including the academic community, in the region. At least one member must reside outside the Metro area. The commission has authority to seek any necessary information and shall consider all relevant information and public comment in developing the proposed Future Vision. The commission serves without compensation.

(d) Review and amendment. The Future Vision may be reviewed and amended as provided by ordinance. The Future Vision shall be completely reviewed and revised at least every fifteen years in the manner specified in subsection (1)(c) of this section.

(e) Effect. The Future Vision is not a regulatory document. It is the intent of this charter that the Future Vision have no effect that would allow court or agency review of it.

(2) Regional framework plan.

(a) Adoption. The council shall adopt a regional framework plan by December 31, 1997 with the consultation and advice of the Metro Policy Advisory Committee (MPAC) created under Section 27 of this charter. The council may adopt the regional framework plan in components.

(b) Matters addressed. The regional framework plan shall address: (1) regional transportation and mass transit systems, (2) management and amendment of the urban growth boundary, (3) protection of lands outside the urban growth boundary for natural resource, future urban or other uses, (4) housing densities, (5) urban design and settlement patterns, (6) parks, open spaces and recreational facilities, (7) water sources and storage, (8) coordination, to the extent feasible, of Metro growth management and land use planning policies with those of Clark County, Washington, and (9) planning responsibilities mandated by state law. The regional framework plan shall also address other growth management and land use planning matters which the council, with the consultation and advice of the MPAC, determines are of metropolitan concern and will benefit from regional planning. To encourage regional uniformity, the regional framework plan shall also contain model terminology, standards and procedures for local land use decision making that may be adopted by local governments. As used in this section, "local" refers only to the cities and counties within the jurisdiction of Metro.

(c) Effect. The regional framework plan shall: (1) describe its relationship to the Future Vision, (2) comply with applicable statewide planning goals, (3) be subject to compliance acknowledgment by the Land Conservation and Development Commission or its successor, and (4) be the basis for coordination of framework plan after seeking the consultation and advice of the MPAC.

(d) Implementation. To the maximum extent allowed by law, the council shall adopt ordinances: (1) requiring local comprehensive plans and implementing regulations to comply with the regional framework plan within three years after adoption of the entire regional framework plan. If the regional framework plan is subject to compliance acknowledgment, local plans and implementing regulations shall be required to comply with the regional framework plan within two years of compliance acknowledgment; (2) requiring the council to adjudicate and determine the consistency of local comprehensive plans with the regional framework plan; (3) requiring each city and county within the jurisdiction of Metro to make local land use decisions consistent with the regional framework plan until its comprehensive plan has been determined to be consistent with the regional framework plan. The obligation to apply the regional framework plan to local land use decisions shall not begin until one year after adoption and compliance acknowledgment of the regional framework plan; and (4) allowing the council to require changes in local land use standards and procedures if the council determines changes are necessary to remedy a pattern or practice of decision making inconsistent with the regional framework plan.

(3) Priority and funding of regional planning activities.

The regional planning functions under this section are the primary functions of Metro. The council shall appropriate funds sufficient to assure timely completion of those functions.

Section 6. Other Assigned Functions. Metro is also authorized to exercise the following functions: (1) Acquisition, development, maintenance and operation of: (a) a metropolitan zoo, (b) public cultural, trade, convention, exhibition, sports, entertainment, and spectator facilities, (c) facilities for the disposal of solid and liquid wastes, and (d) a system of parks, open spaces and recreational facilities of metropolitan concern; (2) Disposal of solid and liquid wastes; (3) Metropolitan aspects of natural disaster planning and response coordination; (4) Development and marketing of data; and (5) Any other function required by state law or assigned to the Metropolitan Service District or Metro by the voters.

Section 7. Assumption of Additional Functions. (1) Assumption ordinance.

The council shall approve by ordinance the undertaking by Metro of any function not authorized by sections 5 and 6 of this charter. The ordinance shall contain a finding that the function is of metropolitan concern and the reasons it is appropriate for Metro to undertake it.

(2) Assumption of local government service function.

(a) An ordinance authorizing provision or regulation by Metro of a local government service is not effective unless the ordinance is approved by the voters of Metro or a majority of the members of the MPAC. Voter approval may occur by approval of a referred measure (1) authorizing the function or (2) relating to finances and authorizing financing or identifying funds to be used for exercise of the function. As used in this section, "local government service" is a service provided to constituents by one or more cities, counties or special districts within the jurisdiction of Metro at the time a Metro ordinance on assumption of the service is first introduced.

(b) An ordinance submitted to the MPAC for approval is deemed approved unless disapproved within 60 days after submission.

(c) No approval under this subsection is required for the compensated provision of services by Metro to or on behalf of a local government under an agreement with that government.

(3) Assumption of other service functions.

The council shall seek the advice of the MPAC before adopting an ordinance authorizing provision or regulation by Metro of a service which is not a local government service.

(4) Assumption of functions and operations of mass transit district.

Notwithstanding subsection (2) of this section, Metro may at any time assume the duties, functions, powers and operations of a mass transit district by ordinance. Before adoption of this ordinance the council shall seek the advice of the Joint Policy Advisory Committee on Transportation or its successor. After assuming the functions and operations of a mass transit district, the council shall establish a mass transit commission of not fewer than seven members and determine its duties in administering mass transit functions for Metro. The members of the governing body of the mass transit district at the time of its assumption by Metro are members of the initial Metro mass transit commission for the remainder of their respective terms of office.

(5) Boundary commission functions.

The council shall undertake and complete a study of the Portland Metropolitan Area Local Government Boundary Commission, with advice of the MPAC, by September 1, 1995. The council shall implement the results of the study and shall seek any legislative action needed for implementation.

Section 8. Preservation of Authority to Contract.   All Metro officers shall preserve, to the greatest extent possible, the ability of Metro to contract for all services with persons or entities who are not Metro employees.

Section 9. General Grant of Powers to Carry Out Functions; Construction of Specified Powers.   When carrying out the functions authorized or assumed under this charter: (1) Metro has all powers that the laws of the United States and this state now or in the future could allow Metro just as if this charter specifically set out each of those powers, (2) the powers specified in this charter are not exclusive, (3) any specification of power in this charter is not intended to limit authority, and (4) the powers specified in this charter shall be construed liberally.

Finance

Section 10. General Authority. Except as prohibited by law or restricted by this charter, Metro may impose, levy and collect taxes and may issue revenue bonds, general and special obligation bonds, certificates of participation and other obligations. The authority provided under this section supplements any authority otherwise granted by law.

Section 11. Voter Approval of Certain Taxes. Any ordinance of the council imposing broadly based taxes of general applicability on the personal income, business income, payroll, property, or sales of goods or services of all, or a number of classes of, persons or entities in the region requires approval of the voters of Metro before taking effect. This approval is not required (1) to continue property taxes imposed by the Metropolitan Service District, (2) for the rate or amount of any payroll tax imposed by a mass transit district as of June 1, 1992, if the functions of that district are assumed by Metro, or (3) for additional payroll tax revenues for mass transit imposed to replace revenues lost by withdrawal of any locality from the service area of the mass transit district after June 1, 1992. For purposes of sections 11, 13 and 14 of this charter, "taxes" do not include any user charge, service fee, franchise fee, charge for the issuance of any franchise, license, permit or approval, or any benefit assessment against property.

Section 12. Voter Approval of General Obligation Bonds. Issuance of general obligation bonds payable from ad valorem property taxes requires the approval of the voters of Metro.

Section 13. Prior Consultation for Tax Imposition. Before imposing any new tax for which voter approval is not required, the council shall establish and seek the advice of a tax study committee that includes members appointed from the general population, and from among businesses and the governments of cities, counties, special districts and school districts, of the Metro area.

Section 14. Limitations on Expenditures of Certain Tax Revenues. (1) General. Except as provided in this section, for the first fiscal year after this charter takes effect Metro may make no more than $12,500,000 in expenditures on a cash basis from taxes imposed and received by Metro and interest and other earnings on those

taxes. This expenditure limitation increases in each subsequent
fiscal year by a percentage equal to (a) the rate of increase in the
Consumer Price Index, All Items, for Portland-Vancouver (All
Urban Consumers) as determined by the appropriate federal
agency or (b) the most nearly equivalent index as determined
by the council if the index described in (a) is discontinued.

(2) Exclusions from limitation. This section does not apply
to (a) taxes approved by the voters of Metro or the Metropolitan
Service District and interest and other earnings on those taxes,
(b) payroll taxes specified in section 11 of this charter, and (c)
tax increment financing charges on property.

Section 15. Limitations on Amount of User Charges. Except to the extent
receipts in excess of costs from food and beverage sales, parking
and other concessions are dedicated to reducing charges for the
provision of goods or services to which the concession directly
relates, charges for the provision of goods or services by Metro
may not exceed the costs of providing the goods or services.
These costs include, but are not limited to, costs of personal services, materials, capital outlay, debt service, operating expenses,
overhead expenses, and capital and operational reserves attributable to the good or service.

Form of Government
Section 16. Metro Council. (1) Creation and Powers.

The Metro council is created as the governing body of
Metro. Except as this charter provides otherwise, and except for
initiative and referendum powers reserved to the voters of
Metro, all Metro powers are vested in the council.

(2) Composition.

Beginning January 2, 1995, the council consists of seven
councilors, each nominated and elected from a single district
within the Metro area. Until that date the council consists of the
13 members of the governing body of the Metropolitan Service
District whose terms begin or continue in January 1993 and
whose districts continue until replaced as provided in this section. The terms of those members expire January 2, 1995.

(3) Apportionment of council districts.

(a) Creation and appointment of apportionment commission. A Metro apportionment commission of seven commissioners is created. To appoint the commission the council shall
divide itself into five pairs of councilors and one group of three
councilors. Each pair and group of councilors shall be from contiguous districts and appoints one commissioner. The presiding

officer appoints one commissioner and the commission chair. At least two commissioners must be appointed from each of the three counties within the Metro area, and each commissioner appointed by a pair or group of councilors shall reside in one of the districts from which the councilors making the appointment are elected or appointed. All appointments to the commission shall be made by February 1, 1993.

(b) Appointment by executive officer. If all appointments to the commission are not made by February 1, 1993, the executive officer shall appoint all commissioners and designate its chair by March 1, 1993. The executive officer shall appoint at least two commissioners from each of the three counties within the Metro area and may not appoint more than one commissioner from a single council district.

(c) Disqualifications from commission membership. No commissioner, or his or her spouse, children, or stepchildren may (1) be a Metro councilor, executive officer or employee, (2) be an elected officer or employee of any city, county or special district, (3) have an economic interest which is distinct from that of the general public in any policy or legislation adopted by Metro or the Metropolitan Service District within the previous two years or which is being considered for adoption, or (4) be engaged, directly or indirectly, in any business with Metro which is inconsistent with the conscientious performance of the duties of commissioner. No commissioner may be a candidate for the office of councilor or executive officer in the first primary and general elections after adoption of this charter. Any challenge of the qualifications of a commissioner shall be made by May 1, 1993.

(d) Commission vacancies. A vacancy on the commission is filled by action of the authority that appointed the commissioner whose position is vacant.

(e) Filing of apportionment plan. Not later than July 1, 1993, the commission shall adopt and file with the council an apportionment plan dividing the Metro area into seven council districts. Councilors from those districts are first elected in the first statewide primary and general elections after adoption of this charter for a term of office beginning January 2, 1995. The affirmative vote of four commissioners is required to adopt the apportionment plan.

(f) Appointment of apportionment referee. If the commission fails to file an apportionment plan by July 1, 1993, the council shall appoint an apportionment referee by July 15, 1993. The provisions of subsection (3)(c) of this section apply to appointment of the referee. The referee shall prepare and file with the council an apportionment plan within 60 days after his or her appointment.

(g) Effective date of apportionment plan. An apportionment plan filed under this subsection becomes effective on the 30th day after filing unless a voter of Metro petitions for judicial review of the plan as provided by law.

(h) Criteria for districts. As nearly as practicable, all council districts shall be of equal population and each shall be contiguous and geographically compact. The council may by ordinance prescribe additional criteria for districts that are consistent with the requirements of this subsection.

(i) Appropriation of funds. The council shall appropriate sufficient funds to enable the commission and referee to perform their duties under this section.

(j) Abolition of commission. The commission is abolished upon filing the apportionment plan required by this section or on July 2, 1993, whichever is earlier.

(k) Repeal of subsection. Subsection (3) of this section is repealed January 1, 1994. Upon repeal its provisions shall be stricken from this charter and the other subsections of this section renumbered.

(4) Initial terms of office.

The terms of office of the four councilors receiving the highest number of votes among the seven councilors elected in 1994 end January 4, 1999. The terms of office of the other three councilors end January 6, 1997. Thereafter the term of office of councilor is four years.

(5) Council presiding officer.

At its first meeting each year the council shall elect a presiding officer from its councilors.

(6) Council meetings.

The council shall meet regularly in the Metro area at times and places it designates. The council shall prescribe by ordinance the rules to govern conduct of its meetings. Except as this charter provides otherwise, the agreement of a majority of councilors present and constituting a quorum is necessary to decide affirmatively a question before the council.

(7) Quorum.

A majority of councilors in office is a quorum for council business, but fewer councilors may compel absent councilors to attend.

(8) Record of proceedings.

The council shall keep and authenticate a record of council proceedings.

Section 17. Metro Executive Officer.   (1) Creation.

The office of Metro executive officer is created. The executive officer is elected from the Metro area at large for a term of four years. The executive officer serves full time and may not be employed by any other person or entity while serving as executive officer.

(2) Duties.

The primary duty of the executive officer is to enforce Metro ordinances and otherwise to execute the policies of the council. The executive officer shall also: (a) administer Metro except for the council and the auditor, (b) make appointments to Metro offices, boards, commissions and committees when required to do so by this charter or by ordinance, (c) propose for council adoption measures deemed necessary to enforce or carry out powers and duties of Metro, (d) prepare and submit a recommended annual Metro budget to the council for approval, and (e) keep the council fully advised about Metro operations.

(3) Transition from Metropolitan Service District.

The Metropolitan Service District executive officer in office when this charter takes effect is the Metro executive officer until January 2, 1995 when his or her term expires. The Metro executive officer is elected in the first statewide primary or general election after adoption of this charter for a term beginning January 2, 1995.

(4) Veto.

(a) Except as provided in this subsection, the executive officer may veto the following legislative acts of the council within five business days after enactment: (1) any annual or supplemental Metro budget, (2) any ordinance imposing, or providing an exception from, a tax, and (3) any ordinance imposing a charge for provision of goods, services or property by Metro, franchise fees or any assessment.

(b) The council, not later than 30 days after a veto, may override a veto by the affirmative vote of (1) nine councilors while the council consists of 13 positions and (2) five councilors after the council consists of seven positions as provided by section 16(2) of this charter. (c) A legislative act referred to the voters of Metro by the council is not subject to veto.

Section 18. Metro Auditor.   (1) Creation.

The office of Metro auditor is created. The auditor is elected from the Metro area at large for a term of four years. The auditor serves full time and may not be employed by any other person or entity while serving as auditor.

(2) First election; disqualification for other Metro elected offices.

The auditor is first elected in the first statewide primary or general election after adoption of this charter for a term beginning January 2, 1995. During the term for which elected, and for four years thereafter, the auditor is ineligible to hold the offices of Metro executive officer or Metro councilor.

(3) Duties.

The auditor shall: (a) make continuous investigations of the operations of Metro including financial and performance auditing and review of financial transactions, personnel, equipment, facilities, and all other aspects of those operations, and (b) make reports to the Metro council and executive officer of the results of any investigation with any recommendations for remedial action. Except as provided in this section, the auditor may not be given responsibility to perform any executive function.

Section 19. Term of Office.   The term of office of an officer elected at a primary or general election begins the first Monday of the year following election and continues until a successor assumes the office.

Officers, Commissions, and Employees
Section 20. Qualifications of Elected Officers.   (1) Councilor.

A councilor shall be a qualified elector under the constitution of this state when his or her term of office begins and shall have resided during the preceding 12 months in the district from which elected or appointed. When the boundaries of that district have been apportioned or reapportioned during that period, residency in that district for purposes of this subsection includes residency in any former district with area in the district from which the councilor is elected or appointed if residency is established in the apportioned or reapportioned district within 60 days after the apportionment or reapportionment is effective.

(2) Executive officer and auditor.

The executive officer and auditor shall each be a qualified elector under the constitution of this state when his or her term of office begins and shall have resided during the preceding 12 months within the boundaries of Metro as they exist when the term of office begins. At the time of election or appointment the auditor shall also hold the designation of certified public accountant or certified internal auditor.

(3) Multiple elected offices.

A Metro elected officer may not be an elected officer of the state, or a city, county or special district during his or her term of office. As used in this charter, special district does not include school districts.

(4) Judging elections and qualifications.

The council is the judge of the election and qualification of its members.

Section 21. Compensation of Elected Officers. (1) Council.

The salary of the council presiding officer is two-thirds the salary of a district court judge of this state.

The salary of every other councilor is one-third the salary of a district court judge of this state. A councilor may waive a salary.

(2) Executive officer.

The salary of the executive officer is the salary of a district court judge of this state.

(3) Auditor.

The salary of the auditor is eighty percent of the salary of a district court judge of this state.

(4) Reimbursements.

The council may authorize reimbursement of Metro elected and other officers for necessary meals, travel and other expenses incurred in serving Metro.

Section 22. Oath. Before assuming office a Metro elected officer shall take an oath or affirm that he or she will faithfully perform the duties of the office and support the constitutions and laws of the United States and this state and the charter and laws of Metro.

Section 23. Vacancies in Office. (1) Councilor.

The office of councilor becomes vacant upon the incumbent's: (a) death, (b) adjudicated incompetence, (c) recall from office, (d) failure following election or appointment to qualify for the office within 10 days after the time for his or her term of office to begin, (e) absence from all meetings of the council within a 60-day period without the council's consent, (f) ceasing to reside in the district from which elected or appointed, except when district boundaries are reapportioned and a councilor is assigned to a district where the councilor does not reside and the councilor becomes a resident of the reapportioned district within 60 days after the reapportionment is effective, (g) ceasing to be a qualified elector under state law, (h) conviction of a felony or conviction of a federal or state offense punishable by loss of liberty and pertaining to his or her office, (i) resignation from office, or (j) becoming an elected officer of the state or a city, county or special district.

(2) Executive officer and auditor.

The offices of executive officer or auditor become vacant in the circumstances described in subsection (1)(a)-(d) and (g)-(j) of this section, or if the executive officer or auditor ceases to reside in the Metro area. The office of auditor also becomes vacant if the incumbent ceases to hold the designation of certified public accountant or certified internal auditor.

(3) Vacancy after reapportionment.

If a councilor vacancy occurs after the councilor has been assigned to a reapportioned district under section 32 of this charter, the vacancy is in the district to which that councilor was assigned.

(4) Determination of vacancy.

The council is the final judge of the existence of a vacancy.

Section 24. Filling Vacancies. A majority of councilors holding office shall fill a vacancy by appointment within 90 days after it occurs. The term of office of the appointee runs from the time he or she qualifies for the office after appointment until a successor is duly elected and qualifies for the office. If the vacancy occurs more than 20 days before the first general election after the beginning of the term for that office, the term of office of the appointee runs only until the first council meeting in the year immediately after that election. A person shall be elected for the remainder of the term at the first primary or general election after the beginning of the term.

Section 25. Limitations of Terms of Office. No person may be elected councilor for more than three consecutive full terms. No person may be elected executive officer for more than two consecutive full terms. The limitations of this section apply only to terms of office beginning on or after January 2, 1995.

Section 26. Appointive Offices and Commissions. (1) Appointments and confirmation.

The executive officer appoints all employees in the office of the executive officer, all department directors, and all other positions this charter or ordinance requires the executive officer to appoint. Appointments of department directors are subject to council confirmation. The council by ordinance may require confirmation of other positions.

(2) Removal.

Employees in the office of the executive officer and department directors serve at the pleasure of the executive officer. Staff employed by the council serve at the pleasure of the council. The executive officer may remove his or her other appointees as provided by ordinance.

Section 27. Metro Policy Advisory Committee. (1) Creation and composition.

The Metro Policy Advisory Committee (MPAC) is created. The initial members of the MPAC are:

(a) One member of each of the governing bodies of Washington, Clackamas and Multnomah Counties appointed by the body from which the member is chosen;

(b) Two members of the governing body of the City of Portland appointed by that governing body;

(c) One member of the governing body of the second largest city in population in Multnomah County appointed by that governing body;

(d) One member of the governing body of the largest city in population in Washington County appointed by that governing body;

(e) One member of the governing body of the largest city in population in Clackamas County appointed by that governing body;

(f) One member of a governing body of a city with territory in the Metro area in Multnomah County other than either the City of Portland or the second largest city in population in Multnomah County, appointed jointly by the governing bodies of cities with territory in the Metro area in Multnomah County other than the City of Portland or the second largest city in population in Multnomah County;

(g) One member of a governing body of a city with territory in the Metro area in Washington County other than the city in Washington County with the largest population, appointed jointly by the governing bodies of cities with territory in the Metro area in Washington County other than the city in Washington County with the largest population;

(h) One member of a governing body of a city with territory in the Metro area in Clackamas County other than the city in Clackamas County with the largest population, appointed jointly by the governing bodies of cities with territory in the Metro area in Clackamas County other than the city in Clackamas County with the largest population;

(i) One member from the governing body of a special district with territory in the Metro area in Multnomah County appointed jointly by the governing bodies of special districts with territory in the Metro area in Multnomah County;

(j) One member from the governing body of a special district with territory in the Metro area in Washington County appointed jointly by the governing bodies of special districts with territory in the Metro area in Washington County;

(k) One member from the governing body of a special district with territory in the Metro area in Clackamas County appointed jointly by the governing bodies of special districts with territory in the Metro area in Clackamas County;

(l) One member of the governing body of Tri-County Metropolitan Transportation District of Oregon appointed by the governing body of that district; and,

(m) Three persons appointed by the executive officer and confirmed by the council. No person appointed under this part of subsection (1) may be an elected officer of or employed by Metro, the state, or a city, county or special district. Each person appointed under this part of subsection (1) shall reside in the Metro area during the person's tenure on the MPAC.

(2) Change of composition.

A vote of both a majority of the MPAC members and a majority of all councilors may change the composition of the MPAC at any time.

(3) Duties.

The MPAC shall perform the duties assigned to it by this charter and any other duties the council prescribes.

(4) Bylaws.

The MPAC shall adopt bylaws governing the conduct and record of its meetings and the terms of its members.

Section 28. Metro Office of Citizen Involvement.   (1) Creation and purpose.

The Metro office of citizen involvement is created to develop and maintain programs and procedures to aid communication between citizens and the council and executive officer.

(2) Citizens' committee in office of citizen involvement.

The council shall establish by ordinance (a) a citizens' committee in the office of citizen involvement and (b) a citizen involvement process. The council shall appropriate sufficient funds to operate the office and committee.

Elections and Reapportionment

Section 29. State Law.   Except as this charter or a Metro ordinance provides otherwise, a Metro election shall conform to state law applicable to the election.

Section 30. Elections of Metro Officers. (1) Generally.
Except for certain elections to fill a vacancy in office, the first vote for councilor, executive officer or auditor occurs at an election held at the same time and places in the Metro area as the statewide primary election that year. If one candidate for a Metro office receives a majority of the votes cast at the primary election for all candidates for that office, that candidate is elected. If no candidate receives a majority of the votes cast at the primary election, the candidates receiving the two largest numbers of votes cast for the office are the only names to appear on the general election ballot that year as candidates for that office. The candidate who receives the largest number of votes cast at the general election for that office is elected.

(2) Nonpartisan offices.
All elections of Metro officers are nonpartisan. Election ballots shall list the names of candidates for Metro offices without political party designations.

Section 31. Multiple Candidacies. No person may be a candidate at a single election for more than one Metro elected office.

Section 32. Reapportionment of Council Districts after Census. (1) General requirements.
Within three months after an official census indicates that the boundaries of council districts deny equal protection of the law, the council shall change the boundaries to accord equal protection of the law and shall assign councilors to the reapportioned districts. As nearly as practicable, all council districts shall be of equal population and each shall be contiguous and geographically compact. The council may by ordinance specify additional criteria for districts that are consistent with this section.

(2) Failure to reapportion.
If the council fails to establish council district boundaries as provided by this section, the executive officer shall establish the boundaries within 60 days.

Section 33. Recall. (1) Generally.
An elected officer of Metro may be recalled in the manner and with the effect described by the constitution and laws of this state.

(2) Effect of reapportionment.
Upon the effective date of a council reapportionment under section 32 of this charter, a councilor is subject to recall by the voters of the district to which the councilor is assigned and not by the voters of the district of that councilor existing before the reapportionment.

Section 34. Initiative and Referendum. The voters of Metro reserve to themselves the powers of initiative and referendum. The council may provide for the exercise of those powers in a manner consistent with law.

Section 35. Amendment and Revision of Charter. The council may refer, and voters of Metro may initiate, amendments to this charter. A proposed charter amendment may embrace only one subject and matters properly connected with it. The council shall provide by ordinance for a procedure to revise this charter.

Ordinances

Section 36. Ordaining Clause. The ordaining clause of an ordinance adopted by the council is: "The Metro Council ordains as follows:." The ordaining clause of an initiated or referred ordinance is: "The People of Metro ordain as follows:."

Section 37. Adoption by Council. (1) General requirements.

The council shall adopt all legislation of Metro by ordinance. Except as this charter otherwise provides, the council may not adopt any ordinance at a meeting unless: (a) the ordinance is introduced at a previous meeting of the council, (b) the title of the ordinance is included in a written agenda of the meeting at which the ordinance is adopted, (c) the agenda of that meeting is publicized not less than three business days nor more than ten days before the meeting, and (d) copies of the ordinance are available for public inspection at least three business days before that meeting. The text of an ordinance may be amended, but not substantially revised, at the meeting at which it is adopted.

(2) Immediate adoption.

The provisions of this section do not apply to an ordinance adopted by unanimous consent of the council and containing findings on the need for immediate adoption.

(3) Vote required.

Adoption of an ordinance requires the affirmative votes of (a) seven councilors while the council consists of 13 positions, and (b) four councilors after the council consists of seven positions as provided by section 16(2) of this charter.

Section 38. Endorsement. The person presiding over the council when an ordinance is adopted shall endorse the ordinance unless the council prescribes a different procedure by general ordinance.

Section 39. Effective Date of Ordinances. (1) Generally.

An ordinance takes effect 90 days after its adoption unless

the ordinance states a different effective date. An ordinance may state an earlier effective date if (a) an earlier date is necessary for the health, safety or welfare of the Metro area, (b) the reasons why this is so are stated in an emergency clause of the ordinance, and (c) the ordinance is approved by the affirmative vote of two-thirds of all councilors. An ordinance imposing or changing a tax or charge, changing the boundaries of Metro, or assuming a function may not contain an emergency clause.

(2) Vetoed and referred ordinances.

If the executive officer vetoes an ordinance and the council overrides the veto, the date of adoption is the date on which the veto is overridden. If the council refers an ordinance to the voters of Metro, the ordinance effective date is the 30th day after its approval by a majority of the voters voting on the measure unless the ordinance specifies a later date. If a referendum petition is filed with the filing officer not later than the 90th day after adoption of an ordinance, the ordinance effective date is suspended. An ordinance is not subject to the referendum after it is effective. An ordinance referred by a referendum petition (a) does not take effect if a majority of the voters voting on the measure reject it and (b) takes effect, unless the ordinance specifies a later date, on the date the results of the election are certified by a majority of the council.

Section 40. Content of Ordinances. Each ordinance may embrace only one subject and all matters properly connected with it. The council shall plainly word each ordinance and avoid technical terms as far as practicable.

Section 41. Public Improvements and Special Assessments. General ordinances govern the procedures for making, altering, vacating or abandoning a public improvement and for fixing, levying and collecting special assessments against real property for public improvements or services. State law governs these procedures to the extent not governed by general ordinances.

Miscellaneous Provisions
Section 42. Transition Provisions. All legislation, orders, rules, and regulations of the Metropolitan Service District in force when this charter takes effect remain in force after that time to the extent consistent with this charter and until amended or repealed by the council. All rights, claims, causes of action, duties, contracts, and legal and administrative proceedings of the Metropolitan Service District that exist when this charter takes effect continue and are unimpaired by the charter. Each is in the

charge of the officer or agency designated by this charter or by its authority to have charge of it. The unexpired terms of elected officers of the Metropolitan Service District continue as provided by this charter. Upon the effective date of this charter, the assets and liabilities of the Metropolitan Service District are the assets and liabilities of Metro.

Section 43. Effective Date.   This charter takes effect January 1, 1993.

Section 44. Severability.   The terms of this charter are severable. If a part of this charter is held invalid, that invalidity does not affect any other part of this charter unless required by the logical relation between the parts.

Section 45. State Legislation.   By adopting this charter the voters of Metro direct the council to seek, and request the Legislative Assembly of this state to enact, any legislation needed to make all parts of this charter operative.

Statewide Planning Program, State of Oregon, 1973

The Statewide Planning Goals
Since 1973 Oregon has maintained a strong statewide program for land use planning. The foundation of that program is a set of nineteen statewide planning goals. The goals express the state's policies on land use and on related topics, such as citizen involvement, housing, and natural resources.

Most of the goals are accompanied by "guidelines," which are suggestions about how a goal may be applied. As noted in Goal 2, guidelines are not mandatory. The goals have been adopted as administrative rules (Oregon Administrative Rules, Chapter 660, Division 15).

Goal 1: Citizen Involvement   To develop a citizen involvement program that insures the opportunity for citizens to be involved in all phases of the planning process. The governing body charged with preparing and adopting a comprehensive plan shall adopt and publicize a program for citizen involvement that clearly defines the procedures by which the general public will be involved in the on-going land-use planning process. The citizen involvement program shall be appropriate to the scale of the planning effort. The program shall provide for continuity of citizen participation and of information that enables citizens to identify and comprehend the issues. Federal, state and regional agencies, and special-purpose districts shall coordinate their planning efforts with the affected governing bodies and make use of existing local citizen involvement programs established by counties and cities.

Goal 2: Land Use Planning   To establish a land use planning process and policy framework as a basis for all decisions and actions related to use of land and to assure an adequate factual base for such decisions and actions. City, county, state and federal agency and special district plans and actions related to land use shall be consistent with the comprehensive plans of cities and counties and regional plans adopted under ORS Chapter 268.

All land use plans shall include identification of issues and problems, inventories and other factual information for each applicable statewide planning goal, evaluation of alternative courses of action and ultimate policy choices, taking into consideration social, economic, energy and environmental needs. The required information shall be contained in the plan document or in supporting documents. The plans, supporting documents and implementation ordinances shall be filed in a public office or other place easily accessible to the public. The plans shall be the basis for specific implementation measures. These measures shall be consistent with and adequate to carry out the plans. Each plan and related implementation measure shall be coordinated with the plans of affected governmental units.

All land-use plans and implementation ordinances shall be adopted by the governing body after public hearing and shall be reviewed and, as needed, revised on a periodic cycle to take into account changing public policies and circumstances, in accord with a schedule set forth in the plan. Opportunities shall be provided for review and comment by citizens and affected governmental units during preparation, review and revision of plans and implementation ordinances.

Goal 3: Agricultural Lands   To preserve and maintain agricultural lands. Agricultural lands shall be preserved and maintained for farm use, consistent with existing and future needs for agricultural products, forest and open space and with the state's agricultural land use policy expressed in ORS 215.243 and 215.700.

Goal 4: Forest Lands   To conserve forest lands by maintaining the forest land base and to protect the state's forest economy by making possible economically efficient forest practices that assure the continuous growing and harvesting of forest tree species as the leading use on forest land consistent with sound management of soil, air, water, and fish and wildlife resources and to provide for recreational opportunities and agriculture.

Forest lands are those lands acknowledged as forest lands

as of the date of adoption of this goal amendment. Where a plan is not acknowledged or a plan amendment involving forest lands is proposed, forest land shall include lands which are suitable for commercial forest uses including adjacent or nearby lands which are necessary to permit forest operations or practices and other forested lands that maintain soil, air, water and fish and wildlife resources.

Goal 5: Open Spaces, Scenic and Historic Areas, and Natural Resources   To protect natural resources and conserve scenic and historic areas and open spaces. Local governments shall adopt programs that will protect natural resources and conserve scenic, historic, and open space resources for present and future generations. These resources promote a healthy environment and natural landscape that contributes to Oregon's livability.

Goal 6: Air, Water and Land Resources Quality   To maintain and improve the quality of the air, water and land resources of the state. All waste and process discharges from future development, when combined with such discharges from existing developments shall not threaten to violate, or violate applicable state or federal environmental quality statutes, rules and standards. With respect to the air, water and land resources of the applicable air sheds and river basins described or included in state environmental quality statutes, rules, standards and implementation plans, such discharges shall not exceed the carrying capacity of such resources, considering long-range needs; degrade such resources; or threaten the availability of such resources.

Goal 7: Areas Subject to Natural Disasters and Hazards   To protect life and property from natural disasters and hazards. Developments subject to damage or that could result in loss of life shall not be planned nor located in known areas of natural disasters and hazards without appropriate safeguards. Plans shall be based on an inventory of known areas of natural disaster and hazards.

Goal 8: Recreational Needs   To satisfy the recreational needs of the citizens of the state and visitors and, where appropriate, to provide for the siting of necessary recreational facilities including destination resorts.

Goal 9: Economic Development   To provide adequate opportunities throughout the state for a variety of economic activities vital to the health, welfare, and prosperity of Oregon's citizens. Comprehensive plans and policies shall contribute to a stable and healthy economy in all regions of the state. Such plans shall be based on inventories of areas suitable for increased economic growth and activity after taking into consideration the health of the current economic base; materials and energy availability and cost; labor market factors; educational and technical training programs; availability of key public facilities; necessary support facilities; current market forces; location relative to markets; availability of renewable and nonrenewable resources; availability of land; and pollution control requirements. Comprehensive plans for urban areas shall:

1. Include an analysis of the community's economic patterns, potentialities, strengths, and deficiencies as they relate to state and national trends;

2. Contain policies concerning the economic development opportunities in the community;

3. Provide for at least an adequate supply of sites of suitable sizes, types, locations, and service levels for a variety of industrial and commercial uses consistent with plan policies;

4. Limit uses on or near sites zoned for specific industrial and commercial uses to those which are compatible with proposed uses.

In accordance with ORS 197.180 and Goal 2, state agencies that issue permits affecting land use shall identify in their coordination programs how they will coordinate permit issuance with other state agencies, cities and counties.

Goal 10: Housing   To provide for the housing needs of citizens of the state. Buildable lands for residential use shall be inventoried and plans shall encourage the availability of adequate numbers of needed housing units at price ranges and rent levels which are commensurate with the financial capabilities of Oregon households and allow for flexibility of housing location, type and density.

Goal 11: Public Facilities and Services   To plan and develop a timely, orderly and efficient arrangement of public facilities and services to serve as a framework for urban and rural development. Urban and rural development shall be guided and supported by types and levels of urban and rural public facilities and services appropriate for, but limited to, the needs and requirements of the urban, urbanizable, and rural areas to be served. A provision for key facilities shall be included in each plan. Cities or counties shall develop and adopt a public facility plan for areas within an urban growth boundary containing a population greater than 2,500 persons. To meet current and long-range needs, a provision for solid waste disposal sites, including sites for inert waste, shall be included in each plan.

Counties shall develop and adopt community public facility plans regulating facilities and services for certain unincorporated communities outside urban growth boundaries as specified by Commission rules.

Local governments shall not allow the establishment or extension of sewer systems outside urban growth boundaries or unincorporated community boundaries, or allow extensions of sewer lines from within urban growth boundaries or unincorporated community boundaries to serve land outside those boundaries, except where the new or extended system is the only practicable alternative to mitigate a public health hazard and will not adversely affect farm or forest land. Local governments shall not rely upon the presence, establishment, or extension of a water or sewer system to allow residential development of land outside urban growth boundaries or unincorporated community boundaries at a density higher than authorized without service from such a system.

In accordance with ORS 197.180 and Goal 2, state agencies that provide funding for transportation, water supply, sewage, and solid waste facilities shall identify in their coordination programs how they will coordinate that funding with other state agencies and with the public facility plans of cities and counties.

Goal 12: Transportation To provide and encourage a safe, convenient and economic transportation system. A transportation plan shall:

1. Consider all modes of transportation including mass transit, air, water, pipeline, rail, highway, bicycle and pedestrian;

2. Be based upon an inventory of local, regional and state transportation needs;

3. Consider the differences in social consequences that would result from utilizing differing combinations of transportation modes;

4. Avoid principal reliance upon any one mode of transportation;

5. Minimize adverse social, economic and environmental impacts and costs;

6. Conserve energy;

7. Meet the needs of the transportation disadvantaged by improving transportation services;

8. Facilitate the flow of goods and services so as to strengthen the local and regional economy; and

9. Conform with local and regional comprehensive land use

plans. Each plan shall include a provision for transportation as a key facility.

Goal 13: Energy Conservation To conserve energy. Land and uses developed on the land shall be managed and controlled so as to maximize the conservation of all forms of energy, based upon sound economic principles.

Goal 14: Urbanization To provide for an orderly and efficient transition from rural to urban land use. Urban growth boundaries shall be established to identify and separate urbanizable land from rural land. Establishment and change of the boundaries shall be based upon considerations of the following factors:

1. Demonstrated need to accommodate long-range urban population growth requirements consistent with LCDC goals;

2. Need for housing, employment opportunities, and livability;

3. Orderly and economic provision for public facilities and services;

4. Maximum efficiency of land uses within and on the fringe of the existing urban area;

5. Environmental, energy, economic and social consequences;

6. Retention of agricultural land as defined, with Class I being the highest priority for retention and Class VI the lowest priority; and,

7. Compatibility of the proposed urban uses with nearby agricultural activities.

The results of the above considerations shall be included in the comprehensive plan. In the case of a change of a boundary, a governing body proposing such change in the boundary separating urbanizable lands from rural land shall follow the procedures and requirements as set forth in the Land Use Planning goal (Goal 2) for goal exceptions. Any urban growth boundary established prior to January 1, 1975, which includes rural lands that have not been built upon shall be reviewed by the governing body, utilizing the same factors applicable to the establishment or change of urban growth boundaries.

Establishment and change of the boundaries shall be a cooperative process between a city and the county or counties that surround it. Land within the boundaries separating urbanizable land from rural land shall be considered available over time for urban uses. Conversion of urbanizable land to urban uses shall be based on consideration of:

1. Orderly, economic provision for public facilities and services;

2. Availability of sufficient land for the various uses to insure choices in the market place;

3. LCDC goals or the acknowledged comprehensive plan; and,

4. Encouragement of development within urban areas before conversion of urbanizable areas.

In unincorporated communities outside urban growth boundaries counties may approve uses, public facilities and services more intensive than allowed on rural lands by Goal 11 and 14, either by exception to those goals, or as provided by Commission rules which ensure such uses do not:

1. adversely affect agricultural and forest operations, and

2. interfere with the efficient functioning of urban growth boundaries.

Goal 15: Willamette River Greenway   To protect, conserve, enhance and maintain the natural, scenic, historical, agricultural, economic and recreational qualities of lands along the Willamette River as the Willamette River Greenway.

Goal 16: Estuarine Resources   To recognize and protect the unique environmental, economic, and social values of each estuary and associated wetlands; and to protect, maintain, where appropriate develop, and where appropriate restore the long-term environmental, economic, and social values, diversity and benefits of Oregon's estuaries.

Comprehensive management programs to achieve these objectives shall be developed by appropriate local, state, and federal agencies for all estuaries. To assure diversity among the estuaries of the State, by June 15, 1977, LCDC with the cooperation and participation of local governments, special districts, and state and federal agencies shall classify the Oregon estuaries to specify the most intensive level of development or alteration which may be allowed to occur within each estuary. After completion for all estuaries of the inventories and initial planning efforts, including identification of needs and potential conflicts among needs and goals and upon request of any coastal jurisdiction, the Commission will review the overall Oregon Estuary Classification.

Comprehensive plans and activities for each estuary shall provide for appropriate uses (including preservation) with as much diversity as is consistent with the overall Oregon Estuary Classification, as well as with the biological, economic, recreational, and aesthetic benefits of the estuary. Estuary plans and activities shall protect the estuarine ecosystem, including its natural biological productivity, habitat, diversity, unique features and water quality. The general priorities (from highest to lowest) for management and use of estuarine resources as implemented through the management unit designation and permissible use requirements listed below shall be:

1. Uses which maintain the integrity of the estuarine ecosystem;

2. Water-dependent uses requiring estuarine location, as consistent with the overall Oregon Estuary Classification;

3. Water-related uses which do not degrade or reduce the natural estuarine resources and values;

4. Nondependent, nonrelated uses which do not alter, reduce or degrade estuarine resources and values.

Goal 17: Coastal Shorelands   To conserve, protect, where appropriate, develop and where appropriate restore the resources and benefits of all coastal shorelands, recognizing their value for protection and maintenance of water quality, fish and wildlife habitat, water-dependent uses, economic resources and recreation and aesthetics. The management of these shoreland areas shall be compatible with the characteristics of the adjacent coastal waters; and to reduce the hazard to human life and property, and the adverse effects upon water quality and fish and wildlife habitat, resulting from the use and enjoyment of Oregon's coastal shorelands.

Programs to achieve these objectives shall be developed by local, state, and federal agencies having jurisdiction over coastal shorelands. Land use plans, implementing actions and permit reviews shall include consideration of the critical relationships between coastal shorelands and resources of coastal waters, and of the geologic and hydrologic hazards associated with coastal shorelands. Local, state and federal agencies shall within the limit of their authorities maintain the diverse environmental, economic, and social values of coastal shorelands and water quality in coastal waters. Within those limits, they shall also minimize man-induced sedimentation in estuaries, nearshore ocean waters, and coastal lakes. General priorities for the overall use of coastal shorelands (from highest to lowest) shall be to:

1. Promote uses which maintain the integrity of estuaries and coastal waters;

2. Provide for water-dependent uses;

3. Provide for water-related uses;

4. Provide for nondependent, nonrelated uses which retain flexibility of future use and do not prematurely or inalterably commit shorelands to more intensive uses;

5. Provide for development, including nondependent, non-related uses, in urban areas compatible with existing or committed uses;

6. Permit nondependent, nonrelated uses which cause a permanent or long-term change in the features of coastal shore-lands only upon a demonstration of public need.

Goal 18: Beaches and Dunes   To conserve, protect, where appropriate develop, and where appropriate restore the resources and benefits of coastal beach and dune areas; and to reduce the hazard to human life and property from natural or man-induced actions associated with these areas.

Coastal comprehensive plans and implementing actions shall provide for diverse and appropriate use of beach and dune areas consistent with their ecological, recreational, aesthetic, water resource, and economic values, and consistent with the natural limitations of beaches, dunes, and dune vegetation for development.

Goal 19: Ocean Resources   To conserve the long-term values, benefits, and natural resources of the near shore ocean and the continental shelf. All local, state, and federal plans, policies, projects, and activities which affect the territorial sea shall be developed, managed and conducted to maintain, and where appropriate, enhance and restore, the long-term benefits derived from the near shore oceanic resources of Oregon. Since renewable ocean resources and uses, such as food production, water quality, navigation, recreation, and aesthetic enjoyment, will provide greater long-term benefits than will nonrenewable resources, such plans and activities shall give clear priority to the proper management and protection of renewable resources.

City and County Planning

Oregon's statewide goals are achieved through local comprehensive planning. State law requires each city and county to have a comprehensive plan and the zoning and land-division ordinances needed to put the plan into effect.

The local comprehensive plans must be consistent with the statewide planning goals. Plans are reviewed for such consistency by the state's Land Conservation and Development Commission (LCDC). When LCDC officially approves a local government's plan, the plan is said to be "acknowledged." It then becomes the controlling document for land use in the area covered by that plan.

Oregon's planning laws apply not only to local governments, but also to special districts and state agencies. The laws strongly emphasize coordination—keeping plans and programs consistent with each other, with the goals, and with acknowledged local plans.

A Partnership

Oregon's planning program is a partnership between state and local governments. The state requires cities and counties to plan, and it sets the standards for such planning. Local governments do the planning and administer most of the land use regulations. The resulting mosaic of state-approved local comprehensive plans covers the entire state.

The state does not write comprehensive plans. It doesn't zone land or administer permits for local planning actions like variances and conditional uses. And unlike some other states, Oregon does not require environmental impact statements.

The Land Conservation and Development Commission

Oregon's statewide planning program is directed by the Land Conservation and Development Commission (LCDC). The commission's seven members are unsalaried volunteers, appointed by the governor and confirmed by the state senate. The term of appointment is four years.

The Department of Land Conservation and Development

The LCDC's administrative arm is the Department of Land Conservation and Development (DLCD). The DLCD is a small state agency with its main office in Salem. The department has field representatives in Portland, Newport, and Bend.

The Land Use Board of Appeals

The state has a special "court," the Land Use Board of Appeals, that reviews appeals of land use decisions. The LUBA has three members, known as "referees." It is based in Salem.

Citizen Involvement

It's no coincidence that Citizen Involvement is the first among Oregon's nineteen planning goals. Extensive citizen participation has been the hallmark of the state's planning program from its outset. Every city and county has a Committee for Citizen Involvement (CCI) to monitor and encourage active citizen participation. The state's Citizen Involvement Advisory Committee (CIAC) also encourages such participation in all aspects of planning.

The Local Comprehensive Plan

The local comprehensive plan guides a community's land use, conservation of natural resources, economic development, and public services. Each plan has two main parts. One is a body of data and information called the inventory, background report, or factual base. It describes a community's resources and features. It must address all of the topics specified in the applicable statewide goals. The other part is the policy element. That part of the plan sets forth the community's long-range objectives and the policies by which it intends to achieve them. The policy element of each community's plan is adopted by ordinance and has the force of law.

Local plans may be changed through plan amendments or periodic review. Plan amendments are smaller, unscheduled adjustments to a plan. Periodic reviews are broad evaluations of an entire plan that occur every four to ten years. A plan may be modified extensively after such a review.

Each plan is accompanied by a set of implementing measures. There are many different kinds. The two most common measures are zoning and land division ordinances. Every city and county in Oregon has adopted such land use controls.

Source: Oregon Department of Land Conservation and Development, 1996

Smart Growth and Neighborhood Conservation Initiatives, State of Maryland, 1997

An Overview

In 1996, Governor Parris N. Glendening announced his priority commitment to develop and secure passage of a wide-ranging package of legislation to strengthen the state's ability to direct growth and to enhance our older developed areas. The goal was to develop a coordinated strategy to better prepare for the growth of over one million people in the next twenty years and to preserve Maryland's desired quality of life for tomorrow's generations.

Over several months, the Governor and key staff reached out to hundreds of interested groups and citizens. Meetings and forums were held in all 23 counties and Baltimore City; letters and phone calls seeking input and ideas were generated. By the end of the year, over 100 legislative and administrative suggestions were submitted. This effort resulted in a package of five bills and one budget item submitted to the General Assembly for its consideration. Within four months, the General Assembly approved the following:

Smart Growth Areas Act: A law limiting most State infrastructure funding related to development to existing communities or to those places designated by State or local governments for growth.

Rural Legacy: A grant program to create greenbelts to protect geographically large rural areas from sprawl through purchase of easements and development rights.

Brownfields—Voluntary Cleanup and Revitalization Incentive Program: Three programs to facilitate clean-up of contaminated areas and commercial/industrial development on those sites.

Job Creation Tax Credit: Income tax credits to businesses which create new jobs within designated areas to promote development.

Live Near Your Work Demonstration Program: State, employer and local government matching cash grants to home buyers who purchase homes near their workplace.

Collectively, these initiatives employ the power of planning and the purse to improve older urban areas, encourage infill and compact new development and preserve rural areas. Other incentives, especially administrative initiatives, are under consideration. An overview of the 1997 Smart Growth Initiatives follows:

Smart Growth Areas

Smart Growth Areas or "Priority Funding Areas" reflect Maryland's policy to support, and where necessary, revitalize existing communities. These are areas where there already is significant financial investment in existing infrastructure. This policy fosters economic vitality and improves the quality of life by maintaining and improving infrastructure and services in existing communities.

The 1997 Smart Growth Areas Act builds on the foundation created by the set of Visions for Maryland's Future adopted as State policy in the 1992 Growth Act. That Act requires local governments to revise and periodically update their Comprehensive Plans to reflect these Visions.

The 1997 Smart Growth Areas Act capitalizes on the influence of State expenditures on economic growth and development. This legislation directs State spending to "Priority Funding Areas." Priority Funding Areas are existing communities and other logically designated areas, consistent with the

1992 Visions, where State and local governments want to encourage and support economic development and new growth. Focusing State spending in these areas will provide the most efficient and effective use of taxpayer dollars, avoid higher taxes which would be necessary to fund infrastructure for sprawl development, and reduce the pressure for sprawl into agricultural and other natural resource areas.

The Smart Growth legislation automatically designates several areas which form the traditional core of the State's urban development locations targeted for economic development, as Priority Funding Areas: municipalities, Baltimore City, areas inside the Baltimore and Washington beltways, neighborhoods which have been designated by the Maryland Department of Housing and Community Development for revitalization, Enterprise Zones, and Heritage Areas within county designated growth areas.

This legislation authorizes counties to designate additional Priority Funding Areas which meet established minimum criteria. Priority Funding Areas designated by counties must be based on an analysis which determines the capacity of land area available for development, and the land area which would be necessary to satisfy demand for development. With this analysis in hand, counties may designate areas as Priority Funding Areas if they meet specified use, water and sewer service, and residential density requirements. Counties may designate existing communities and areas where industrial or other economic development are desired. In addition, counties may designate areas planned for new residential development. Areas eligible for county designation are:

Areas with industrial zoning (Areas with new industrial zoning after January 1, 1997, must be in a county-designated growth area and be served by a sewer system.);

Areas with employment as the principal use which are served by, or planned for, a sewer system (Areas zoned after January 1, 1997, must be in a county-designated growth area.);

Existing communities (as of January 1, 1997) within county-designated growth areas which are served by a sewer or water system and which have an average density of 2 units per acre;

Rural villages designated in local Comprehensive Plans before July 1, 1998; and

Other areas within county-designated growth areas that:

—reflect a long-term policy for promoting an orderly expansion of growth and an efficient use of land and public services,

—are planned to be served by water and sewer systems, and

—have a permitted density of 3.5 or more units per acre for new residential development.

Counties are not required to designate Priority Funding Areas or to designate all of the eligible areas. In addition, county designation of Priority Funding Areas does not restrict the location of private sector or county employment. County-designated Priority Funding Areas simply are areas the county wants to be eligible for State funded growth projects. One goal of directing State projects to Priority Funding Areas is to make these areas more attractive for residents, potential residents and private sector development and redevelopment.

Beginning October 1, 1998, the State must direct funding for "growth-related" projects to Priority Funding Areas. "Growth-related" projects defined in the legislation include most State programs which encourage or support growth and development such as highways, sewer and water construction, economic development assistance, and State leases or construction of new office facilities. State funding in communities with only water service (without a sewer system) and in rural villages is restricted to projects which maintain the character of the community. The projects must not increase the growth capacity of the village or community.

The Smart Growth bill does recognize that there are times when the State will need to fund projects that are outside Priority Funding Areas and makes provision for determining and approving those exceptions on a case-specific basis.

Rural Legacy

The 1997 Rural Legacy initiative establishes a grant program to protect targeted rural greenbelts from sprawl through the purchase of easements and development rights in "Rural Legacy Areas." The mission of the program is to protect "Rural Legacy Areas"—regions rich in a multiple of agriculture, forestry, natural and cultural resources that, if conserved, will promote resource-based economies, protect green belts and greenways and maintain the fabric of rural life. The Rural Legacy Program provides the focus and funding necessary to protect large contiguous tracts of land and other strategic areas from sprawl development, and enhance natural resource, agricultural, forestry and environmental protection through cooperative efforts among State and local governments and land trusts. Protection is provided through the acquisition of easements and fee estates from willing landowners and the supporting activities of Rural Legacy sponsors and local governments.

Local governments and private land trusts are being encouraged to identify Rural Legacy Areas and to competitively apply for funds to complement existing land conservation efforts or create new ones. This Program is in addition to—not in place of—existing programs such as the Agricultural Land Preservation Program and Program Open Space.

For fiscal year 1998 through 2002, $71.3 million has been authorized. If funding is continued at this level after five years, the State could protect up to 200,000 acres of resource lands by the year 2011.

The program is administered by the Rural Legacy Board. Board members are the Secretary of Natural Resources, the Secretary of Agriculture and the Director of the Maryland Office of Planning. An eleven-member advisory committee is comprised of government officials, agricultural and forestry and mineral industry representatives, environmental and conservation organization representatives, developers and a private land owner.

The Voluntary Cleanup and Brownfields Programs

Many unused or abandoned properties that are contaminated, or even perceived to be contaminated, are not attractive to commercial and industrial developers because of the uncertainty about future liability. Because of these liability concerns, developers and businesses often choose to locate on "greenfields"—pristine farms and open spaces—without needed infrastructure, such as roads and utilities. This contributes to the loss of farms and open spaces, increases the amount of taxpayer dollars spent on funding new infrastructure and impedes neighborhood revitalization efforts.

This package of three bills aims to make development on these former industrial sites more feasible and desirable—and a reality.

Voluntary Cleanup

The Voluntary Cleanup Program, administered by the Department of the Environment, reforms the process used to clean up eligible properties that are or are perceived to be contaminated by hazardous waste. In addition to providing a streamlined cleanup process, the legislation changes the liability scheme for certain prospective owners of eligible properties in the Program to encourage the transfer of properties. These changes provide more "certainty" regarding environmental requirements to both responsible persons and future owners of a property, thereby allowing parties to more accurately predict costs and time lines associated with a cleanup and increasing the likelihood of cleanup and redevelopment.

Brownfields Programs

The Department of Business and Economic Development's Brownfields Revitalization Incentive Program provides economic incentives to certain properties proposed to be purchased by someone who has not previously owned the site and who has not been responsible for the contamination of the site. The property must be a former industrial or commercial site located in a densely populated urban area and substantially underutilized. Furthermore, an existing site which poses a threat to the public health and the environment qualifies for economic incentives, provided that in all of the above cases the jurisdiction where it is located has adopted local ordinances granting a Brownfield Property Tax Credit.

Brownfield Site Assessment

The Maryland Department of the Environment is continuing its Brownfield Assessment Initiative, using federal funding to conduct site assessments at no cost to property owners on certain brownfield sites. To be eligible for the program, sites must be vacant or underutilized. Remediation must be feasible. Finally, sites must allow for redevelopment which will create jobs and improve the local tax base. The assessments conducted by MDE include complete Phase I and Partial Phase II assessments. To date, assessments have been conducted at 24 sites; 29 new assessments are planned.

Job Creation Tax Credit

The Job Creation Tax Credit Act, passed in 1996, was expanded to encourage midsized and smaller businesses to invest in Smart Growth Areas around the State. Small businesses comprise almost 80 percent of Maryland business and generate the majority of new job growth in the State.

This new initiative will encourage small business development and job growth in areas accessible to available labor pools and will encourage more efficient use of the State's existing infrastructure. It promotes job creation by providing income tax credits to "targeted growth sector" businesses which create at least 25 jobs in Priority Funding Areas or 60 jobs outside those areas.

The jobs must be full-time, permanent and pay at least 150 percent of the minimum wage. Positions filled after December, 1996, must be newly created in a single Maryland location. As of July 1, 1997, the State had issued 43 certifications (associated with 10,300 new jobs, paying an average of $36,000) and received 39 additional letters of intent (associated with 4,600 jobs) statewide.

Live Near Your Work

The Live Near Your Work initiative provides a package of incentives, support services and partnerships with local governments, financial institutions and private market employers to encourage employees to buy homes near their work. The Maryland Department of Housing and Community Development is administering this pilot program. This initiative will stabilize the neighborhoods surrounding the State's major employers by stimulating home ownership in targeted communities. In addition to providing resources for programs sponsored by public and private institutions, the State is participating as a major employer.

Three hundred thousand dollars have been appropriated for fiscal year 1998 for this program. The State hopes to continue to expand this pilot program in future years to other employers and jurisdictions. Through the program, a participating employer contributes $1,000 for every employee. The $1,000 is matched by $1,000 from the state and $1,000 from the local government. The employee also contributes $1,000 as part of the down-payment or closing costs of the house. Currently, 24 employer partners have opted to take part in the program. They include small and large businesses and institutions in Baltimore City, Baltimore County, College Park, Denton, Hagerstown, Salisbury, and Silver Spring. More businesses have expressed interest and undoubtedly will participate.

Source: Maryland Office of Planning, 1998 Annual Report

Vice President Al Gore's Livable Communities Speech, Delivered at the Brookings Institution, Washington, D.C., 2 September 1998

Since it was first seen by human eyes, the new world has been a revelation to the old. The American countryside used to make travelers stand still in astonishment. That's how beautiful it was. From the Lakota storytellers who described the vast clearness of the Western sky as a metaphor for inner courage; to the Hudson River painters whose canvases and brush strokes grew ever larger and wider in an effort to show old Europe just how majestic were the cliffs of the Storm King; from Thoreau, who saw an entire pilgrimage in a still body of water in a Massachusetts meadow; to Mark Twain, who wrote back to his Eastern readers that the Tahoe depths were so lucid, you could see straight down a mile to the stones on the lake's bed; to Spanish settlers who named the high places in California after the views they commanded—Buena Vista and Alta Vista; all these Americans knew that their home was a place of natural grace.

This nation's cities and villages used to be a model of civil life. We were the experts at creating the gathering places, the very architecture, that set the stage for democracy: the Puritans built their villages around common greens; the livestock grazed there, but, more importantly, the village green was where news was proclaimed, and where neighbors chatted or argued over the issues of the day. As our cities grew, their life took the vibrant shape of America: the mixed-use building of dwellings over small shops allowed people to work long hours, raise families close by, and start the climb up the economic ladder; as the nineteenth century drew to an end and America looked around at its new wealth and diversity, the City Beautiful movement was inaugurated: proud civic buildings—libraries and post offices, town halls and colleges, parks and recreation areas for working men and women's days off, ornate commercial buildings and statuary—proclaimed to the world that though Cleveland or Milwaukee or Corvallis or Tuscaloosa were new, they had plenty to be proud of. The great civic buildings and recreation areas drew the people together in the heart of the cities: at best, the working people mingled with the affluent, Latin families picnicked alongside Anglos, and students of Chinese parentage sat in reading rooms alongside those whose folks were Irish. The civic spaces, by drawing people together in pride and enjoyment, also helped create the diversity and self-respect that characterized our bold new country.

In the hearts of our cities, those who are willing to seek them still find the precious gifts of culture and history. Our communities are a reflection of who we are as a people, and where we have been. From 18th Street and Vine District in Kansas City; to the Bronzeville area in Chicago, one of the homes of jazz; to historic Beale Street in Memphis—our cherished landscape tells the story of how we came to be just who we are. We can still see the greatness of what those Americans saw in our natural and civic landscape—but all too often, in too many places, what we see is only the traces. Because over the last thirty years, bad planning has too often distorted our towns and landscapes out of all recognition. We drive the same majestic scenery, but in too many places, the land we pass through is often burdened by an ugliness that leaves us with a quiet sense of sadness. The burden is national. No state has escaped it.

From the desert Southwest to the forested Northeast, from the most pristine snowfields in Alaska, to the loveliest hollows of the Carolinas—thickets of strip development distort the landscape our grandparents remember. We walk through the hearts of the cities, but too often the downtown is a wasteland of boarded-up storefronts that goes silent at night, as commuters start their grueling commute to further and further periphery suburbs. Many of our walkable main streets have emptied out, and their small shops closed, one by one, leaving a nighttime vacuum for crime and disorder. Acre upon acre of asphalt have transformed what were once mountain clearings and congenial villages into little more than massive parking lots. The ill-thought-out sprawl hastily developed around our nation's cities has turned what used to be friendly, easy suburbs into lonely cul-de-sacs, so distant from the city center that if a family wants to buy an affordable house they have to drive so far that a parent gets home too late to read a bedtime story. In many such developments, an absence of sidewalks, amenities, and green spaces discourages walking, biking, and playing—and kids learn more about Nintendo and isolation than about fresh air and taking turns.

Houses in such places were built fast and heedlessly by bulldozing flat an ecosystem, and ripping out the century-old trees that had sustained the neighborhood's birds and wildlife. People move in and make their lives, but as the bulldozers leapfrog their dreams, they begin to long for something they remember—the meadow that used to be the children's paradise at the end of the suburban street, the local shops where neighbors passed the local news from one to another, the park where families shared picnics.

The problem which we suffer in too many of our cities, suburbs, and rural areas is made up of so many different pieces that until recently it has been a problem that lacked a name. "Sprawl" hardly does justice to it. But Americans are resourceful people. While the blight of poor development and its social consequences have many names, the solutions, pioneered by local citizens, are starting to coalesce into an American movement. Some call it "sustainability;" some call it "smart growth;" others refer to "metropolitan strategies;" still others prefer to talk about "regionalism." In New York and Portland, in towns like Celebration, Florida, and in many other areas nationwide, it's been called the movement for "livability." And that's as good a name as any to describe the many solutions that local citizens are crafting.

This movement across the country is showing us how we can build more livable communities—places where families work, learn, and worship together—where they can walk and bike and shop and play together—or choose to drive—and actually find a parking place!—and get out and have fun. A livable suburb or city is one that lets us get home after work fast—so we can spend more time with friends and family, and less time stuck in traffic. "Road rage" is only one of the newest manifestations of this commuting-induced stress. It is one that restores and sustains our historic neighborhoods, so they are not abandoned and bulldozed under, but are alive with shops and cultural events. It is one that preserves among the new development some family farms and green spaces—so that even in the age of cyberspace, kids can still grow up knowing what it's like to eat locally grown produce, or toss a ball in an open field on a summer evening. Most of us can't afford to travel to Yellowstone or the Grand Canyon every time we want to enjoy the rich American landscape; a livable neighborhood lets you and your spouse walk through a natural ecosystem as you simply take an evening stroll down your street. That's spiritually renewing.

A livable community cares about parks as well as parking lots, and develops in a way that draws on local strength and uniqueness—resisting the "cookie-cutter monster" that has made so much of our country look all the same. And increasingly, in the 21st Century, a livable community will be an economically powerful community: a place where a high quality of life attracts the best-educated and trained workers and entrepreneurs. A place where good schools and strong families fuel creativity and productivity. A place where the best minds and the best companies share ideas and shape our common future. So many towns and suburbs are building more livable communities, and showing that you can embrace community development while growing stronger economically in the process. Indeed, first and foremost, our cities, suburbs, and neighborhoods need continued economic growth and strength to thrive. That is why our efforts to make communities more livable today must emphasize the right kind of growth—sustainable growth. Promoting a better quality of life for our families need never come at the expense of economic growth. Indeed, in the 21st Century, it can and must be an engine for economic growth.

In the last fifty years, we've built flat, not tall: because land is cheaper the further out it lies, new office buildings, roads, and malls go up farther and farther out, lengthening commutes and adding to pollution. This outward stretch leaves a vacuum in the cities and suburbs which sucks away jobs, businesses, homes, and hope; as people stop walking in downtown areas, the vacuum is filled up fast with crime, drugs, and danger. Drive times and congestion increase; Americans waste about half a billion hours a year stuck in traffic congestion. And the number is growing rapidly. An hour-and-a-half commute each day is ten full workdays a year spent just stuck in traffic. The problem isn't the cars themselves; for so much of this century, cars have given us the chance to pursue our dreams. We just never expected to hit a traffic jam along the way. So the exhausted commuter seeks affordable housing further out—and can't help pushing local farmers out of business, since family farms can't pay the rising property taxes. Orchards and dairy farms go under; the commute gets even longer; and nobody wins, least of all our children. America, which is now losing 50 acres of farmland to development every single hour, could become the largest net importer of food by the next century, instead of the world's largest exporter.

This kind of uncoordinated growth means more than a long drive to work; it means a half hour to buy a loaf of bread; it means that working families have to spend thousands of dollars a year more on transportation costs when they might want the option of spending that money instead toward a year of a good college for a son or daughter. It means that people coming off welfare and eager to work, especially if they have children, find that they don't have a way to reach an available job and still pick a child up from day care. It means mothers isolated with small children far from playmates, and older Americans stuck in their homes alone. Air and water quality go down; taxes go up; there are no sidewalks, and even if there were, nowhere to walk to. We gather at the mall, but there is nowhere to sit outside with family on a fine day. And suddenly we see: this is not the community that we were really looking for.

I've often referred to the well-known theory called "broken windows." When a criminal sees a community with broken windows, garbage strewn on the street, and graffiti on the walls, there is a powerful message, if often an unverbalized message: if you're looking for a place to commit a crime, it's here, because this community has a high tolerance for disorder. If a young family is looking for a place to live, or an entrepreneur is looking for a place to start an exciting new business, what kind of message is sent by a community that has no parks and green spaces; nowhere to shop and walk and play with your children; no running paths to help people stay well and productive; no nearby countrysides or family farms?

The message is clear: you'd better not raise your family here, because we don't value the quality of life that you want. But a livable, walkable, playable community—like a safe community or a good, modern classroom, sends a very different message: we care about this place, we place a high value on it, and you should, too. So many generations moved out to the suburbs to find the good life—more space, more safety, more privacy, and a better quality of life. Today, it is where the vast majority of new jobs are created. We should be able to reclaim that dream. We're starting to see that the lives of suburbs and cities are not at odds with one another, but closely intertwined. No one in a suburb wants to live on the margins of a dying city. No one in the city wants to be trapped by surrounding rings of parking lots instead of thriving, livable suburban communities. And no one wants to do away with the open spaces and farmland that give food, beauty, and balance to our postindustrial, speeded-up lives.

Fortunately, all across America, communities are coming together to meet these new challenges of growth—to restore historic neighborhoods, to protect centuries-old farmland, to turn shopping malls into village squares, to preserve both our natural and our cultural heritage. These communities are proving that America can grow according to its *values*—which include goodness, and also include beauty. By working together, they show us we can build an America that is not just better off, but *better*. What is being gained is not just livability, but also new life for our democracy. As citizens come together to plan their common future—as they realize that they can make a difference right in their own neighborhoods—we open the door to more vibrant civic life and self-government on a much broader scale. That is why smart, sustainable growth must happen at the local and community level.

The American Heritage Rivers initiative rewards communities that restore their rivers and waterfronts. Empowerment zones unite communities to revitalize central cities. These initiatives reveal that rediscovering the pride of *place*, the delight of home, has an unparalleled power to reinvigorate democracy. In the words of Daniel Kemmis, who was one of several thinkers who joined Tipper and me at our home eighteen months ago for a series of lengthy discussions on this subject, "what holds people together long enough to discover their power as citizens is their common inhabiting of a single place." In other words, to paraphrase the TV show: "everyone needs a place where everybody knows your name." When I was a child, I spent a lot of time living in a community just like that—Carthage, Tennessee. I've often described it as a place where people know about it when you're born, and care about it when you die. There are a lot of Americans who want to live with their families in a community that has that feeling.

Let me share a few examples of what America is doing about it, and they're causing to happen across the country: Consider Chattanooga, a city of black and white families, both affluent and working class, in my home state of Tennessee. Like the Spanish settlers who made their home on the Buena Vista, Chattanooga's founders were entranced by the beauty of the land that lies between two majestic mountains and a sweeping bend of the Tennessee River. Each feature of the landscape speaking to the soul, in Wordsworth's memorable phrase, "like a mighty voice." But by the time I was growing up, that voice had grown hoarse. The smog was so thick people couldn't even see the mountains. The air was so polluted that on some occasions, when women wore nylon stockings outside, their legwear actually disintegrated from the pollution. The riverfront was littered with dilapidated warehouses and a vacant high school, and you couldn't even see the river. The town's oldest bridge was considered so unsafe the state wanted to tear it down. According to one council member, in Chattanooga, "the prosperity of one generation became the burden of the next one." Then the people of Chattanooga decided to reclaim the natural beauty of the place. More than 2,500 people turned out for public meetings and listening sessions. They looked at pictures of different neighborhoods and communities, and they were consulted for their ideas and preferences. Students proposed turning the old warehouses into an aquarium that families could visit. Soon after, the vacant high school reopened as a nationally recognized magnet school. The old bridge was reinforced and reopened as the country's longest pedestrian walkway over a beautiful river. As Tennessee's senator, I was proud to help Chattanooga develop an electric bus system to give people an alternative to all those hours in traffic. And best of all—just as those students had dreamed—those old warehouse properties were turned into the largest freshwater aquarium in the world—attracting 1.3 million visitors every year since it has opened, making kids, retailers, and fish very happy. Today, Chattanooga is not only cleaner than it has been in decades—it led the entire state in job growth for the first half of last year.

I joined the President's Council on Sustainable Development at a two-day meeting in Chattanooga where we talked about these new development patterns. In St. Paul, people like Mary Gruber are showing us the power of citizen action. She is a nurse living with her husband—a pipe fitter—in the working class north end of St. Paul. She is also active in the St. Paul Ecumenical Alliance of Congregations. In the early 1990s, she met a social worker who told her that she spent the first six weeks of every school year looking for shoes for the children. She saw that poverty was undermining their community's efforts to provide a good education. But when she wondered where all the jobs would come from, all she saw in her neighborhood were abandoned old factories. Doing a little research, she found that there were more 4,000 acres of abandoned factories in inner cities, barring job growth.

Together with the members of her religious coalition, she helped bring together 45 inner-city and suburban churches, environmental groups, synagogues, developers, and government officials to clean up those old sites and bring jobs back. They came up with their own slogan: "Turn Polluted Dirt Into Pay Dirt." They held rallies, they sent letters, they met with state legislators. And they persuaded the legislature to pass a seven-year plan to reclaim 175 acres of polluted sites, create more than 2,000 new jobs there, and leverage up to $70 million in private investment in the once-neglected community. One of them summed it up this way: "I hate to sound like a civic cheerleader, but . . . you come away thinking that this is worth your time." In St. Paul, changing the physical landscape meant a change for the better in people's lives.

In Routt County, Colorado, in the Rocky Mountains, residents and businesses became concerned that an explosion of year-round resorts and tourism was degrading the character of their small ranching and mining community. On summer weekdays, in a town with a population of just 15,000, it wasn't unusual for 28,000 cars to come through the town. One bank president said: "It's not a question of whether we are going to grow. It's a question of how we're going to manage that growth to maintain the things we all came here for." They also realized that destroying their rural way of life would also hurt tourism. So more than 1,000 residents worked on a plan called "Controlling Our Own Destiny," which led to plans for affordable housing, more open space, and better transportation and schools. Now, more than 10,000 acres have been set aside as permanent land-ranches that the town can grow around. And former adversaries, from ranchers to business people to conservationists, are now working closely together for strong, sustainable, and beautiful growth.

And then there is the City of Detroit. Lots of folks remember how, just a few years ago, Detroit seemed to be in a free-fall— losing jobs, losing businesses, gaining crime and poverty. Distrust between the city and the surrounding suburbs was the norm. Today, Detroit is experiencing an economic renaissance— and much of that progress is due to Mayor Dennis Archer's efforts to work with the surrounding counties. Our Empowerment Zone in Detroit not only helped them attract $4 billion in private investment and thousands of jobs to the once-ravaged city core, it also linked the zone's residents with available jobs out in the suburbs. The natural surroundings benefit, too. Communities have come together to protect and preserve the Detroit River as one of our new American Heritage Rivers. Thirteen communities, three counties, and the state have banded together to fight urban blight along Detroit's northern border. And last year, city residents even approved $38 million in improvements for recreational facilities located out in the suburbs. The partnership is really working. Diverse religions are seeing a common interest. They all realize that the only way to achieve growth and prosperity for everyone is to work together.

In the 1970's, Portland, Oregon was consuming 30,000 acres of its rich agricultural land every year, and threatening the pristine forests leading to Mount Hood. To protect the land, Portland passed a smart growth plan—creating a more walkable, livable community while preserving historic areas rather than builder farther and farther out. They were told that it would be impossible—that the new emphasis on quality of life would force out businesses and force down property values. Instead, the opposite has come to pass: high-tech campuses sprung up, home values have increased, Portland's population has swelled with families fleeing sprawl and congestion elsewhere—and a new light rail system has attracted 40 percent of all commuters in the city. Today, the environment is better protected; developers advertise "not sprawl but community villages;" new developments, crafted with care, boast community spaces, light rail stations, and on-the-block day care; and Portland's community spirit has become one of joy. As one newspaper described: "many of the newer companies in Oregon—like Hewlett-Packard, Intel, and Hyundai—say they moved here *because* there are forests, fruit orchards and meandering creeks just across the street from the contained urban areas. The employers said they wanted to locate in an area that could attract educated workers who were as interested in quality of life as a paycheck." Or as one employee of Intel put it: "companies that can locate anywhere they want will go where they can attract good people in good places." Coming together as a community made good common sense, and made good economic sense. And we see this kind of success across the nation—from Chicago to Fresno to South Florida to Indianapolis to San Antonio. I could mention many other examples.

How, then, can the federal government encourage and strengthen smarter, more livable, sustainable growth? Again, smart growth is about local and community decisions, and we don't want to tell anyone where to live, or where to locate a business. But I believe there is nevertheless an important role for federal support for local energies. We in the federal government can start by getting our own house in order, and making it look good. We should start paying closer attention to livability in the building and planning we provide to taxpayers—such as where we locate new post offices, new libraries, new federal buildings and so on, and whether we should fix up beautiful old buildings in historic areas before rushing to build bland new ones farther out.

Secondly, we can get our own house in order by reexamining federal policies that may have been well intentioned, but have encouraged and subsidized the wrong kind of growth and runaway sprawl. For example, in some cases, federal subsidies actually gave handsome financial rewards to communities to extend sewage lines far out into undeveloped areas, rather than spending those funds for needed improvements and expansions in places where families already relied on them. And until we changed the policy, the federal government gave employers big subsidies to offer parking spaces to their employees, but much less help if they wanted to help cover their employees' mass transit costs. We need a national dialogue on the kinds of policies that actually subsidize and encourage the wrong kind of development.

Third, we can provide carefully targeted incentives to encourage smarter growth—such as support for mass transit and light rail systems—not to restrict growth in any way, but to reward growth that strengthens family-friendly communities.

Fourth, we can play an enormously positive role as a partner with cities, suburbs, and rural areas, as we have already started to do through our empowerment initiative and through our work with the U.S. Conference of Mayors and the National Association of County Organizations on their brand-new Joint Center for Sustainable Communities. That way, whole regions can create a vision and build together for their common future.

President Clinton and I have already worked hard to make the federal government a better partner—part of the solution. We are cleaning up old brownfield sites and toxic waste dumps, and replacing them with parks, new businesses, and new homes. The President's Council on Sustainable Development has worked very hard to encourage better, more livable communities. Our community empowerment strategy is bringing billions of dollars in new private investment to central cities, and breathing new life into America's central cities. We passed targeted tax cuts for families, small businesses, and communities. We are rebuilding and modernizing crumbling schools. With our new transportation bill, we are giving local communities an unprecedented local control over the kind of infrastructure they choose, and we will make sure that control is preserved. We are putting 100,000 community police on the sidewalks—police who walk a neighborhood beat and know the kids on the sidewalk by name. We have taken new action to help local communities protect their farmland, wetlands, and private forests.

And today, on behalf of President Clinton, I am pleased to announce three additional steps that we will take to help encourage smarter growth and more livable communities all across America. First, today I am announcing that FANNIE MAE will launch a new $100 million pilot program that will recognize an economic reality that has long been ignored by our mortgage system: families that live near mass transit save as much as hundreds of dollars a month, and therefore should qualify for larger mortgages than they presently do according to formulas that don't take these savings into account. These new location-efficient mortgages, which come with a 30-year transit pass, will give families more choices, by enabling them to live in more desirable neighborhoods, with higher property values. They will also illuminate whether this financial innovation will encourage smarter growth nationwide. We hope and believe that it will.

Second, I am announcing two new initiatives to give more information to communities that want to pursue livability options. We will offer grants that enable communities to obtain and display federal information on easy-to-understand computerized maps, to see all the parks and buildings and farmlands in the region, and to chart predictions of future growth. This will make it dramatically easier to envision and plan smarter, more livable growth for the future.

Third, we are taking new action to protect our farmland. If you lose an acre of fertile farmland, you lose it forever. That's why, two years ago, we reached out to states, tribes, and local governments and asked them to help us protect our farmland through the purchase of easements. Today, I am proud to announce today that we are awarding more than $17 million to 19 states to ensure that thousands of acres of our very best farmland are preserved for generations to come. This investment will protect more than 53,000 acres of precious farmland on 217 farms across America. It is a good beginning. Our kids *will* see horses, cows, and farms outside books and movies.

This is just the beginning of a renewed federal commitment to smarter, more livable growth—and I will be announcing additional actions in the coming months. But in every case, our goal will be to put more control, more information, more decision-making power into the hands of families, communities, and regions—to give them all the freedom and flexibility they need to reclaim their own unique place in the world. That is why I will begin this fall by holding several listening sessions on livability and smart growth, to hear firsthand what is working, and what the federal government can do to become a better partner. In the coming months, members of the President's Cabinet will hold several additional sessions around the country as well.

What is clear to the local and federal governments, more and more, is something any parent has known when struggling to afford and then protect a home, and that is: places matter to people; they shape people, for good or ill. Our communities must be more than mere plots of bulldozed land, more than mere networks of roads and soulless buildings. They must allow us to come together, to walk and bike and play with our children, to know that we can shape the communities we want for *their* children. They are a reflection of who we are as a people.

We must preserve and protect what is special about our natural landscape, and about our built landscape as well. That is why America must always seek strong and aggressive growth—but growth that is consistent with local values. Wallace Stegner once reminded us that, as deeply as we treasure the mythic cowboys and pioneer men and women and lone rangers who tamed America's great frontier, we treasure our traditions of homesteading and community building just as much. As Stegner wrote: "This is the native home of hope. When [America] fully learns that cooperation . . . is the pattern that most characterizes and preserves it, then it will have achieved itself and outlived its origins. Then, [we have] a chance to create a society to match [our] scenery." All across America, you and your neighbors have started to do just that. And it's high time. Because this land is your land. From California to the New York island—from the Redwood Forests to the Gulf Stream waters—this land was made for you and me.

Source: Office of the Vice President

Clinton-Gore Livability Agenda: Building Livable Communities for the Twenty-First Century

Vice President Gore is today launching a comprehensive Livability Agenda to help communities across America grow in ways that ensure a high quality of life and strong, sustainable economic growth. This billion dollar initiative will strengthen the federal government's role as a partner with the growing number of state and local efforts to build "livable communities" for the 21st century.

Key elements of the interagency initiative—to be included in President Clinton's proposed FY 2000 budget—will provide communities with new tools and resources to preserve green space, ease traffic congestion, and pursue regional "smart growth" strategies. As part of the Livability Agenda, the Administration will continue to work with and learn from states, communities, and other stakeholders, and to develop new strategies to provide them with additional tools and resources.

Livability Goals
The Clinton-Gore Livability Agenda aims to help citizens and communities:

Preserve green spaces that promote clean air and clean water, sustain wildlife, and provide families with places to walk, play and relax.

Ease traffic congestion by improving road planning, strengthening existing transportation systems, and expanding use of alternative transportation.

Restore a sense of community by fostering citizen and private sector involvement in local planning, including the placement of schools and other public facilities.

Promote collaboration among neighboring communities—cities, suburbs or rural areas—to develop regional growth strategies and address common issues like crime.

Enhance economic competitiveness by nurturing a high quality of life that attracts well-trained workers and cutting-edge industries.

FY 2000 Livability Initiatives
The President's FY 2000 budget request to Congress will propose significant new investments to support major Livability programs:

Better America Bonds
To help communities reconnect with their land and water, preserve green space for future generations, and provide attractive settings for economic development, the Administration is proposing a new financing tool generating $9.5 billion in bond authority for investments by state, local and tribal governments. The President's budget will propose tax credits totaling more than $700 million over five years—to support Better America Bonds, which can be used to preserve green space, create or restore urban parks, protect water quality, and clean up brownfields (abandoned industrial sites). The program will be coordinated through an interagency process.

Community Transportation Choices
To help ease traffic congestion, the proposed Department of Transportation budget for FY 2000 will include a record $6.1 bil-

lion for public transit and $2.2 billion—a total 16 percent increase over FY 1999—to aggressively implement innovative community-based programs in the Transportation Equity Act for the 21st Century. Such programs provide flexible support to help communities create regional transportation strategies, improve existing roads and transit, and encourage broader use of alternative transportation. This includes $1.6 billion for the Congestion Mitigation and Air Quality Improvement Program, which supports state and local projects that reduce congestion and improve air quality.

Regional Connections Initiative
To promote regional "smart growth" strategies and to complement the Administration's other regional efforts, the Department of Housing and Urban Development will provide $50 million as matching funds for local partnerships to design and pursue smarter growth strategies across jurisdictional lines. Strategies will include (a) compact development incentives, (b) coordinated reinvestment in existing infrastructure, and (c) ways to manage and better reinforce the region's overall development strategy.

Other Livability Initiatives
The President's proposed FY 2000 budget will include funding for several other initiatives supporting local livability efforts:
Community-Centered Schools A new $10 million grant program administered by the Department of Education to encourage school districts to involve the community in planning and designing new schools.
Community-Federal Information Partnership A new $40 million program funded by several agencies to provide communities with grants for easy-to-use information tools to help develop strategies for future growth.
Regional Crime-Data Sharing $50 million will be provided to expand programs to help communities share information to improve public safety. These programs will: (1) improve and continue to computerize national, state, and local criminal history records; and (2) develop or upgrade local communications technologies and criminal justice identification systems to help local law enforcement share information in a timely manner.

The Livability Agenda integrates the commitments of more than a dozen federal agencies. The Agenda also supplements the various programs that make up the Administration's Community Empowerment Agenda, which is designed to encourage reinvestment in existing communities and provide greater opportunity for their residents.

Source: Remarks by Vice President Al Gore at American Institute of Architects on 2 September 1998

Testimony for the Senate Environment and Public Works Committee, Hearing on Open Space, by Gary Garczynski, President, National Association of Home Builders, 17 March 1999

Where We Live, Work and Play

The concept of "Smart Growth" has exploded onto the national consciousness as one of the most critical issues confronting America today. It touches on choices we Americans hold close to our hearts—where we live, work and play, the education of our children, commute times to work, and the economic and job opportunities created by new growth in our communities. It is an idea that addresses the questions of how best to plan for and manage growth, when and where new residential and commercial development as well as schools and major highways should be built and located and how to pay for the infrastructure required to serve a growing population.

In its broadest sense, Smart Growth means meeting the underlying demand for housing created by an ever-increasing population and prosperous economy by building a political consensus and employing market-sensitive and innovative land-use planning concepts. It means understanding that suburban job growth and the strong desire to live in single-family homes will continue to encourage growth in suburbia. At the same time, Smart Growth means meeting that housing demand in "smarter ways" by planning for and building to higher densities, preserving meaningful open space and protecting environmentally sensitive areas. The key elements of NAHB's Smart Growth strategy include the following:

Anticipating and planning for economic development and growth in a timely, orderly and predictable manner;

Establishing a long-term comprehensive plan in each local jurisdiction that makes available an ample supply of land for residential, commercial, recreational and industrial uses as well as taking extra care to set aside meaningful open space and to protect environmentally sensitive areas;

Removing barriers to allow innovative land-use planning techniques to be used in building higher density and mixed use developments as well as infill developments in suburban and inner-city neighborhoods;

Planning and constructing new schools, roads, water and sewer treatment facilities and other public infrastructure in a timely manner to keep pace with the current and future demand for housing, and finding a fair and broad-based way to underwrite the costs of infrastructure investment that benefits the entire community;

Achieving a reasonable balance in the land-use planning process by using innovative planning concepts to protect the environment and preserve meaningful open space, improve traffic flow, relieve overcrowded schools and enhance the quality of life for all residents; and

Ensuring that the process for reviewing site-specific land development applications is reasonable, predictable and fair for applicants and contiguous neighbors.

Most important, Smart Growth is understanding the aspirations of Americans—the very people comprehensive growth plans are intended to serve—while protecting the environment and quality of life for all Americans. Where do people want to live? What type of homes do they want for themselves and their children? What can they afford? What types of jobs and economic opportunities do they seek and expect?

Ironically, the concept of Smart Growth has emerged on the 50th anniversary of the nation's 1949 National Housing Act, the landmark bill in which Congress first set forth the national goal of "providing a decent home in a suitable living environment for every American family."

Housing's Record Accomplishments

Since then, the achievements of the housing industry have been nothing short of remarkable. In the past 50 years, home builders have built nearly 75 million new homes and apartment units, or three of every four housing units in the country today. Millions more have been remodeled and rehabilitated. The homeownership rate has increased from 44 percent to a record 66.3 percent today. And, in recent years, a strong economy, low interest rates and improvements in the housing finance system have opened the door to homeownership for millions of minorities and immigrants previously unable to buy a home. The quality of new housing has also improved steadily over the past 50 years, making today's new homes more comfortable, more durable, easier to maintain and much more energy efficient than ever before.

The benefits of this housing growth reach far beyond the housing market. New housing construction has helped lift the nation's economy to new heights, creating millions of jobs in home building–related industries each year. It has expanded the tax base and generated billions of dollars of tax revenues for local governments, and triggered spending for goods and services that accounts for about 4 cents of every dollar spent in the U.S. annually. It has also contributed greatly to individual financial security, allowing America's 69 million home-owning households to accumulate $5 trillion in home equity, which accounts for close to half the net worth of those households.

But the job of housing America is far from complete. The nation's population is projected to grow by about 30 million people over the next 10 years. More than a million new households are being formed annually. America's home builders will have to construct between 1.3 and 1.5 million new housing units each year just to meet the underlying demand for shelter during the next decade. This does not include the additional housing units and support required to meet the housing needs of more than 5 million Americans who still live in substandard housing or pay more than 50 percent of their incomes for rent.

Building a Political Consensus

How well we plan for projected increases in households, changing demographics and lifestyles and an expanding economy will have a major impact on the quality of life in years ahead. When used properly as a planning tool, Smart Growth can help expand homeownership opportunities and allow Americans to obtain the home and lifestyle of their dreams. There are some, however, who want to turn Smart Growth into a tool to stop or slow growth. Such a move would penalize and put at greatest risk those living at the edge of housing affordability—the young, minorities, immigrants and moderate-income families who are just now taking advantage of today's economic prosperity and low interest rates and are entering the homeownership market in record numbers.

It is also worthwhile to note that residential and commercial growth is fluid—meaning that when it is stopped in one place, it will inevitably occur somewhere else. The forces of no growth are, in part, responsible for the leapfrog development patterns of the past. Attacking past development patterns and blaming builders does not recognize the fact that public policy dictates where development occurs. Such political rhetoric is not only wrong and counterproductive but it polarizes the very people who should sit down together and work out solutions on Smart Growth.

Understanding where people want to live and the homes they want to live in is the first step in mapping the patterns of growth for America in the decade ahead. Seeking common ground and building a political consensus must follow. This discussion should start in each local jurisdiction—city, county or township—because the politics of growth are uniquely local and because the authority to determine land use is vested in local government. While general planning principles are useful, the actual planning tools and strategies selected will vary according to local market conditions.

The federal government's role should be to encourage—not mandate—local communities to adopt long-term comprehensive plans that will meet the demand for new housing, public infrastructure and other services in the decade ahead. The concept of purchasing open space should not be used to block the path of development, a move that would exacerbate the leapfrog development patterns of the past.

"Smart Growth" Principles

The National Association of Home Builders endorses the concept of Smart Growth as outlined in this statement. When used appropriately and in concert with market forces, Smart Growth can serve as a blueprint for planning and building an even better America in the years ahead. To assist local communities in developing Smart Growth plans, NAHB supports and encourages implementation of the following concepts:

Meeting the Nation's Housing Needs: As a fundamental part of any "Smart Growth" plan, a community must plan for and accommodate its anticipated growth in economic activity, population and housing demand as well as ongoing changes in demographics and lifestyles. For example, when setting aside meaningful open space, a local community should rezone other land to assure there is an ample supply of land available for residential development. For the nation, annual increases in population mean that America's home builders will have to construct between 1.3 and 1.5 million new housing units per year to meet the underlying demand for shelter. Meeting this demand for shelter and increasing homeownership opportunities are compelling national goals that must be addressed in every community's comprehensive growth plan. It is the responsibility of every community to plan for and embrace the growth that is naturally triggered by economic prosperity.

Providing a Wide Range of Housing Choices: NAHB recognizes the basic right of every American to have a free choice in deciding where and in what kind of home to live. In poll after poll, Americans continue to show a strong preference for single-family homes in a suburban setting. In fact, when asked in a recent survey whether they would prefer a single-family home on an individual lot in an outlying suburban market versus a smaller townhouse located near the urban core and closer to work and mass transit, the vast majority of prospective home buyers chose the detached single-family home. Communities should recognize these basic preferences as part of any comprehensive planning process. NAHB supports planning for growth that allows for a wide range of housing types to suit the needs and income levels of a community's diverse population, while recognizing "smart ways" to manage growth by permitting higher densities, preserving open space and protecting environmentally sensitive areas. And while recent gains in homeownership rates are commendable, the dream of owning a home or simply finding decent, affordable housing is still an ongoing struggle for millions of American families. Any Smart Growth planning process, therefore, should provide for affordable housing at all income levels.

A Comprehensive Process for Planning Growth: NAHB supports comprehensive land-use planning that clearly identifies land to be made available for residential, commercial, recreational and industrial uses as well as land to be set aside as meaningful open space. Such plans should protect environmentally sensitive areas as well as take into account a community's projected economic growth rate, demand for new housing and expanded infrastructure—road, schools and other facilities—required to serve a growing population. Builders, land developers and other industry members should be encouraged to lend their expertise and participate in the design and periodic review of a community's comprehensive planning process.

Planning and Funding Infrastructure Improvements: NAHB encourages local communities to adopt balanced and reliable means to finance and pay for the construction and expansion of roads, schools, water and sewer facilities and other infrastructure required to serve a prosperous community. Planning major infrastructure improvements—particularly transportation—requires cooperation across governmental boundaries to resolve issues. Reducing traffic congestion, relieving overcrowded classrooms and providing other public facilities and services are absolutely essential components of any "Smart Growth" plan. Ensuring that the construction of schools, roads and other infrastructure keeps pace with the anticipated growth in population and economic activity is one of the biggest challenges facing local communities today. Appropriate bodies of government should adopt capital improvement plans (with timing, location and funding elements) designed to fund necessary infrastructure required to support new development. Ensuring that infrastructure is funded equitably and that the cost is shared equitably throughout all segments of the community—existing residents as well as newcomers—is an even greater challenge.

Using Land More Efficiently: NAHB supports higher-density development and innovative land-use policies to encourage mixed-use and pedestrian-friendly developments with access to open space and mass transit. To generate greater public support for this type of development, however, will require a change in thinking by people opposed to higher-density development in their own backyards, by local governments that have erected barriers to higher-density development and are easily influenced by citizen groups opposed to any new growth and by typical housing consumers who continue to favor a single-family home on an individual lot.

Revitalizing Older Suburban and Inner-City Markets: NAHB recognizes that revitalizing older suburban and inner city markets and encouraging infill development is universally accepted as good public policy. But even under the best of conditions, infill development will satisfy only a small percentage of a community's demand for new housing. The joint effort announced on February 4 by Vice President Al Gore, the U.S. Conference of Mayors and NAHB to construct 1 million additional market-rate housing units in the nation's cities and inner-ring of the suburbs over the next 10 years is an achievable goal. But to reach that goal, the Administration and nation's cities will have to work closely with the housing industry to overcome major impediments, such as aging infrastructure that makes redevelopment costly and difficult, and federal liability laws that increase risks for builders involved in the redevelopment of "brownfield" sites. Making cities safe from crime, improving the quality of schools and creating employment opportunities are prerequisites for rebuilding the nation's inner cities and for encouraging people to return to them.

As we prepare to enter a new millennium, our nation faces many challenges. One of the most significant is ensuring that, as our population grows and our economy prospers, growth and development occur in a smart, orderly and predictable fashion. The nation's home builders and the 197,000 members of the National Association of Home Builders are committed to pursuing reasonable and market-driven "Smart Growth" strategies that will meet the nation's housing needs, expand home-ownership opportunities, help revitalize the nation's cities and inner suburbs, and build attractive and livable neighborhoods and communities and an even more prosperous America in the 21st century.

Source: National Association of Home Builders, 1999

6

Directory of Organizations

The number of organizations devoted to the issue of urban sprawl has mushroomed over the last five years. Although many organizations have long been working on urban, environmental, and agricultural issues, much of this recent interest is attributable to the national Smart Growth movement and recent embrace of these goals by the Clinton administration in late 1998. Some of the groups and associations listed below have broad-based interests, ranging far beyond urban development, agricultural lands, and environmental policy issues, while others are more narrowly constricted to dealing with this complex problem. However, all have in common a shared interest in urban sprawl, and have developed specific policy positions, issued reports, sponsored research, or otherwise become involved in the public debate surrounding the issue. The groups listed below are also primarily national in scope. A separate list contains groups active at the state and regional levels. Also listed are federal and state governmental agencies that administer programs intended to combat sprawl and its side effects.

National Advocacy Organizations

Alliance for America
P.O. Box 449
Caroga Lake, New York 12032
(518) 835-6702
allianceam@aol.com
http://www.allianceforamerica.org

The Alliance for America is an umbrella organization representing

145

over 500 diverse groups in all fifty states. These grassroots organizations have come together out of a shared concern for safeguarding constitutionally guaranteed property rights. They believe that the "conservation of natural resources and the natural beauty of the environment is attainable without destroying the lives of the people closest to it." They advocate the passage of legislation that mandates governments at all levels to pay just compensation to property owners if regulations should deprive them of the value of their property. The organization serves as a means for groups across the United States to communicate with one another and provides news and information on property rights issues.

Publications: Bimonthly *Trumpet Call* and newsletter available online.

American Association for Small Property Ownership
P.O. Box 4258
Leesburg, VA 20177
(800) 391-7067
http://www.smallpropertyowner.com/~aaspo

Founded in 1993 the American Association for Small Property Ownership seeks to evaluate the effects of laws, regulations, and institutions as they impact small property owners. It is a public policy and educational organization committed to advancing the principles of free markets, limited government, and private property ownership, and to promoting an approach to government regulation that takes into consideration the interests of the small property owner. It seeks to provide real estate professionals with information related to the effects of public policies, taxation, and government regulation on property ownership and real estate investments.

Publications: Monthly newsletter *The Small Property Owner* available online at http://www.almlc.com/~aaspo.

American Farmland Trust
1200 18th Street, NW, Suite 800
Washington, DC 20036
(202) 331-7300
(202) 659-8339 (fax)
info@farmland.org
http://www.farmland.org

The American Farmland Trust provides information and advocacy to farmers and allied organizations that are dedicated to stopping the loss of productive farmland to urban development. The organization acts as a resource for promoting survival strategies for small farms, assists farmers in adopting farming practices that lead to a healthier environment, and helps facilitate the establishment of land trusts to protect farmlands. The organization has articulated a strong call for growth management to protect farmlands in a report titled *Living on the Edge: The Costs and Risks of Scatter Development*, published in 1998.

Publications: A monthly newsletter, *LandWorks Connection* (accessible online), and numerous other educational materials including books, technical reports, fact sheets, and other publications.

American Land Rights Association

P.O. Box 400
30218 N.E. 82nd Avenue
Battle Ground, WA 98604
(360) 687-3087
(360) 687-2973 (fax)
alra@pacifier.com
http://www.landrights.org

The American Land Rights Association began in 1978 as a grassroots organization known as the National Park Inholders Association. Initially, its mission was to protect private property owners from unwanted land takings by the National Park Service. In 1995 the organization changed its name to the American Land Rights Association to reflect its new role as a national clearinghouse and coalition builder for individuals and sympathetic citizen's groups that oppose restrictive land use designations. Its purpose is to "oppose selfish, single-use, restrictive land-use designations that damage local economies." It is not antipark, but argues that parks and wilderness areas "should be established where they do not damage the socioeconomic fabric of rural America." The organization provides a substantial archive of online resources designed to facilitate grassroots groups. It also provides consulting services, a speakers bureau, and a congressional alert system and maintains a federal land users database and a Land Rights Network fax list.

Publications: Publishes a monthly newsletter called the *Land Rights Advocate* and also issues online press releases through its *Action Alerts*.

American Planning Association
122 South Michigan Avenue, Suite 1600
Chicago, IL 60603
(312) 431-9100
(312) 431-9985 (fax)
http://www.planning.org

The American Planning Association and its professional institute, the American Institute of Certified Planners, are organized to advance the art and science of planning and foster awareness of the importance of planning at the local, regional, state, and national levels among elected officials and the general public. Among the many issues addressed by the organization through considerable research and numerous conferences is urban sprawl, about which it has acted as an advocacy organization in policy development at both the state and federal levels. The association offers a wide variety of publications and resource materials through its Planners Bookstore.

Publications: Many books, research reports, manuals, audio and video tapes, computer software, a monthly magazine called *Planning*, and a quarterly newsletter called *The Commissioner*.

American Road and Transportation Builders Association
1010 Massachusetts Avenue, NW, 6th Floor
Washington, DC 20001
(202) 289-4435
(202) 289-4435 (fax)
artbadc@aol.com
http://www.artba.org

The American Road and Transportation Builders Association is a national organization founded in 1902 to serve as the voice of the transportation construction industry. It works to represent the interests of this industry in Washington, D.C., before all branches of the federal government, while also providing its members with information on the policymaking process to facilitate grassroots advocacy. It works closely with other interest groups, which include the American Highway Users Alliance, National Asphalt Pavement Association, and the Road Information Program to advocate for greater federal spending for public transportation and consumer choice in transportation policy alternatives. In its *Building Better Communities* report (2000), this organization and several of its partner advocacy organizations have taken a strong stance opposing the antisprawl measures proposed by Smart Growth advocates.

Publications: Research reports on road construction, press releases, and member resources that include the *ARTBA Washington Newsline* and *Washington Update*, as well as a monthly newsletter entitled *Federal Environmental & Regulatory Review*.

Brookings Institution
1775 Massachusetts Avenue, NW
Washington, DC 20036
(202) 797-6139
(202) 797-2965 (fax)
brookinfo@brook.edu
http://www.brook.edu/es/urban/urban.htm

The Brookings Institution was founded in 1916 as an independent organization devoted to nonpartisan research, education, and publication in the fields of economics, government, foreign policy, and the social sciences. The Center on Urban and Metropolitan Policy seeks to advance research and understanding to "help build strong neighborhoods, cities, and metropolitan regions." It advocates regional solutions to urban problems, a strong role for private sector actors in development, and solutions that come from communities themselves.

Publications: A wide range of books and research papers.

Center for Neighborhood Technology
2125 W. North Avenue
Chicago, IL 60647
(773) 278-4800
(773) 278-3848 (fax)
info@cnt.org
http://www.cnt.org

The Center for Neighborhood Technology was founded in 1978 to help create self-sufficient neighborhood economies in Chicago. Expanding its scope in 1990, its mission is to promote "public policies, new resources and accountable authority which support sustainable, just and vital urban communities." It seeks to help build prosperous, sustainable communities by linking economic and community development with ecological improvement in communities around the country. The center is involved in public policy advocacy, market development, and community planning. Its Neighborhood Early Warning System provides a database and electronic bulletin board as a means to increase community access to local government information in the Chicago area.

Publications: Numerous reports, monthly *Neighborhood Works* magazine, and a periodic newsletter, *Place Matters*.

Center for the Defense of Free Enterprise
12500 N.E. Tenth Place
Bellevue, WA 98005
(425) 455-5038
(425) 451-3959
website@cdfe.org
http://www.eskimo.com/~rarnold/menu.html

The Center for the Defense of Free Enterprise was founded in 1976 as a nonprofit foundation to protect individual rights in the face of restrictions imposed upon the free enterprise system by government. Its members share a concern about "the rollback of 200 years of individual rights and the multitude of restrictions being imposed on America's free enterprise system by big government—and the lack of understanding of this problem by the American people." It serves the purpose of publishing and disseminating information regarding the principles of the free enterprise system, fosters research and study of issues related to economics and governmental regulation, maintains a legal defense fund, sponsors speakers and conferences, funds youth scholarships, and makes available its publications through the Free Enterprise Press. It also maintains close contacts with a variety of business organizations, grassroots groups, and legislative leaders.

Publications: Numerous books, its *White Papers* investigative reports, research reports, public service announcements, and press releases.

Citistates Group
Farley Peters
650 Fairhaven Rd.
Fairhaven, MD 20779
(301) 855-6482
fpeters@citistates.com
http://www.citistates.com

The Citistates Group is a national network of journalists, speakers, and consultants who are committed to fostering greater public awareness about the advantages of metropolitan regional cooperation. They are united by the belief "that successful metropolitan regions are critical to economic competitiveness and sustainable communities." They provide information resources and guest speakers and sponsor conferences to encourage greater awareness of the need for the many local governments that comprise large metropolitan centers to cooperate with one another to their mutual advantage. They also provide consulting services to facilitate visioning, strategic planning, and leadership training in metropolitan (citistate) regions.

Publications: A research commentary, *Peirce Reports*, is published periodically.

Competitive Enterprise Institute
1001 Connecticut Avenue, NW, Suite 1250
Washington, DC 20036
(202) 331-1010
info@cei.org
http://www.cei.org

The Competitive Enterprise Institute was created in 1984 with a dedication to the principles of free enterprise and limited government. Its members believe that American consumers are best served not by government regulation, but by being allowed to make their own choices in a free market place. Its Center for Private Conservation is dedicated to advancing knowledge and information in support of achieving environmental goals through private efforts rather than governmental controls. The institute sponsors and publishes policy-based research, advocates its views through press releases, and provides a variety of information resources to supporters.

Publications: Publishes a weekly newsletter called *Update*, and provides issue positions online through the release of periodic *On Point Policy Briefs*.

Congress for New Urbanism
Hearst Building
5 Third Street, Suite 500A
San Francisco, CA 94103
(415) 495-2255

(415) 495-1731
cnuinfo@cnu.org
http://www.cnu.org

The Congress for New Urbanism was founded in 1993 to act as an advocate for "the restructuring of public policy and development practices to support the restoration of existing urban centers and towns within coherent metropolitan regions" and to "stand for the reconfiguration of sprawling suburbs into communities of real neighborhoods and diverse districts, the conservation of natural environments, and the preservation of our built legacy." The organization takes its name from the congresses it sponsors, which are annual gatherings that provide architects, planners, developers, elected officials, and community representatives the opportunity to discuss issues related to urban development and revitalization. Currently, nine task forces work on specific issues of importance to urban development, seeking to incorporate the insights of New Urbanist thinking into practical proposals. The central office makes available a wide variety of printed resources to the public.

Publications: *Places: A Forum of Environmental Design*, published three times per year; a bimonthly newsletter, *New Urban News*; and bimonthly *Task Force Reports*.

Conservation Fund
1800 N. Kent Street
Suite 1120
Arlington, VA 22209
(703) 525-6300
http://www.conservationfund.org

The Conservation Fund is a national organization dedicated to conserving land from development pressures. The fund has purchased and protected almost 2 million acres of land since 1985. It also assists local communities, private land owners, and government agencies with a variety of programs that are designed to balance conservation with the need for economic development. Current efforts involve promoting sustainable forestry practices; encouraging ecotourism, greenway development, and battlefield protection; and fostering watershed sensitive design and community visioning in the context of local planning efforts.

Publications: Periodic research reports and press releases available online.

Council for Urban Economic Development

1730 K Street, NW, Suite 700
Washington, DC 20006
(202) 223-4735
(202) 223-4745 (fax)
cued@urbandevelopment.com
http://www.cued.org

The Council for Urban Economic Development has offered services and representation to economic development practitioners and allied urban organizations since 1967. Its members are involved in a range of economic development activities that include real estate development, commercial revitalization, job training, infrastructure finance, community development, export promotion, tourism, industrial development, and business financing. Their mission is to "build a stronger network of support for American urban areas and their people through collaboration with the private development sector, public and private educational institutions, and other organizations concerned with urban policy." This is accomplished by providing technical assistance and through the promotion of federal, state, and local policies that encourage diverse economic development in urban areas.

Publications: Annual reports; training manuals; a quarterly magazine, *Economic Development Commentary*; a biweekly newsletter, *Economic Developments*; a bimonthly newsletter, *Revitalizing Neighborhoods*; and a periodic information briefing, *Washington Update*.

Defenders of Property Rights

1350 Connecticut Avenue, NW, Suite 410
Washington, DC 20036
(202) 822-6770
(202) 822-6774 (fax)
mail@defendersproprights.org
http://www.defendersproprights.org

The Defenders of Property Rights is a public interest legal foundation dedicated to protecting private property rights in the face of unwarranted governmental regulation. It acts as a clearinghouse and general resource base for grassroots activism, media reports, and speakers for various broadcast programs. The website provides a variety of online resources for activists seeking more information and links to other organizations.

Environmental Law Institute
Sustainable Use of Land Program
1616 P Street
Washington, DC 20036
(202) 939-3840
http://www.eli.org

The Environmental Law Institute is an independent research and education center focused on the complex and growing body of law associated with the environment. Its "Sustainable Use of Land" program is an ongoing collaborative effort devoted to promoting the sustainable use of urban, suburban, and rural land at the state and local levels. ELI works in collaboration with partners to formulate and implement options for overcoming barriers to environmentally sustainable land use found in local, state, and federal law. The institute regularly sponsors training sessions, forums, and conferences for its membership.

Publications: A bimonthly case reporting publication titled *ELR— The Environmental Law Reporter;* a bimonthly journal of opinion, *The Environmental Forum;* a bimonthly newsletter, *National Wetlands Newsletter;* and periodic research reports, opinion pieces, and press releases available online.

Growth Management Institute
5406 Trent Street
Chevy Chase, MD 20815
(301) 656-9560
http://www.gmionline.org
dporter@gmionline.org

Established in 1992, the Growth Management Institute encourages "effective and equitable management of growth in human habitats." It seeks to provide a forum for the constructive exchange of ideas and information about urban growth management and ultimately hopes to promote strategies and practices aimed at achieving sustainable urban development and redevelopment that preserves environmental quality. To accomplish its mission, the organization publishes a newsletter, acts as a resource in providing information about current developments in growth management, and sponsors periodic meetings to help the public better understand urban growth issues.

Publications: A quarterly newsletter, *The Growth Management Reporter.*

Heartland Institute
19 South La Salle Street, Suite 903
Chicago, IL 60603
(312) 377-4000
(312) 377-5000 (fax)
http://www.heartland.org
think@heartland.org

The mission of the Heartland Institute is to offer the fastest, most convenient and efficient source of public policy information on key policy issues for the media, advocacy groups, and the general public. Founded in 1984, this independent organization acts as a clearinghouse for research articles and opinions taken from a variety of conservative think tanks and advocacy groups that share a common commitment to free market-based solutions to public problems and a reduction in governmental interference in the lives of citizens. It also publishes information, produces videos and other educational materials, and hosts conferences and seminars. In addition to other issues, its informational resources cover property rights and the environment.

Publications: Include books and periodic policy studies papers, in addition to *Environment News,* a monthly newsletter; *Intellectual Ammunition,* a bimonthly magazine; *Policy Fax* news briefs, which can be ordered at (312) 377-3000; and *Heartlander,* a weekly newsletter, which can be accessed by either e-mail or fax.

International City/County Management Association
777 North Capitol Street, NE, Suite 500
Washington, DC 20002
(202) 962-3685
(202) 962-3500 (fax)
http://www.icma.org

Since 1914 the International City/County Management Association has served as a professional and educational organization for appointed administrators, managers, and other professional staff who serve local governments around the United States. The organization was the prime sponsor of the Smart Growth Network, and also has sought to provide education and assistance to local governments in dealing with sprawl-related policy challenges, including environmental programs, brownfields, and urban redevelopment planning. The organization provides technical assistance, training, and a wide variety of publications for local government professionals and students.

Publications: Books, handbooks, reports, and a comprehensive resource called the *Smart Growth Network Starter Kit.*

Land Tenure Center, University of Wisconsin
University of Wisconsin
1357 University Avenue
Madison, WI 53715
(608) 262-3567
(608) 262-2141 (fax)
ltc-uw@facstaff.wisc.edu
http://www.wisc.edu/ltc

Established in 1962, the University of Wisconsin's Land Tenure Center develops project management for short- and long-term activities, sponsors conferences and panels, and facilitates researchers around the world on natural resource tenure, agrarian reform, and related institutional aspects of rural development and natural resource management. It also oversees a doctorate program in development studies. Although the initial focus was on overseas concerns, the center expanded in 1993 to include a program covering land use issues in North America, including urban sprawl. The center approaches land policy issues from a multidisciplinary perspective, and manages an extensive library collection and series of databases on land-related issues. It is funded in part by the U.S. Agency for International Development and is affiliated with the College of Agricultural and Life Sciences at the University of Wisconsin–Madison.

Publications: Publishes the *Land Tenure Center Newsletter*, a biannual newsletter, along with a wide variety of documents, research papers, and working papers, many of which are accessible online.

Land Trust Alliance
1319 F Street, NW, Suite 501
Washington, DC 20004
(202) 638-4725
(202) 638-4730 (fax)
http://www.lta.org

The Land Trust Alliance promotes voluntary land conservation around the nation. It seeks to strengthen the land trust movement by providing leadership, information, skills, and resources to those interested in conserving land through the formation of land trusts. It maintains three field offices that provide a variety of programs to help land trusts operate in a more effective manner through technical assistance, coordination, grant funding, and legal services across the United States.

Publications: Books, directories, informational brochures, video tapes, two quarterly publications called *LTA Landscape* and *Exchange*, and other informational resources.

Lincoln Institute of Land Policy
113 Brattle Street
Cambridge, MA 02138-2400
(617) 661-3016
(617) 661-7235 (fax)
help@lincolninst.edu
http://www.lincolninst.edu

The Lincoln Institute of Land Policy was established in 1974 to encourage both the study and teaching of land policy, including land economics and taxation in the United States and in foreign countries. Its mission is to explore the fundamental forces affecting land use and development: government strategies for managing change; community and individual rights and responsibilities; taxation and regulation; markets; patterns of human settlement and production; and transportation systems. To accomplish these goals, it offers professional development courses, sponsors national and international conferences, funds research and curriculum development projects, and publishes a wide variety of resources.

Publications: Numerous books (some copublished with other organizations), policy focus reports, working papers, abstracts, and a bimonthly newsletter, *Land Lines*.

Local Government Commission
1414 K Street, Suite 250
Sacramento, CA 95814
(916) 448-1198
(916) 448-8246 (fax)
lgc@lgc.org
http://www.lgc.org

The Local Government Commission is a nonpartisan membership organization composed of elected officials, city and county staff, and others who are "committed to developing and implementing local solutions to problems of state and national significance." Through its Center for Livable Communities, it provides a forum and technical assistance to enhance the ability of local governments and community leaders to "be proactive in their land use and transportation planning, and adopt programs and policies that lead to more livable and resource-efficient land use patterns." These tasks are accomplished through the organization of conferences and training workshops, the dissemination of publications and other resources, and the maintenance of a Land Use Library.

Publications: Numerous informational guidebooks; *Livable Places*, a monthly newsletter; and slides and videos.

National Association of Counties
440 First Street, NW, Suite 800
Washington, DC 20001
(202) 393-6226
(202) 393-2630 (fax)
http://www.naco.org

The National Association of Counties was created in 1935 to ensure that the nation's 3,066 counties are given a voice in state and national affairs. It is a full-service organization that provides extensive advocacy services for its membership, including legislative, research, and technical assistance. The organization recently formed a Joint Center for Sustainable Communities, which is committed to "curbing sprawl, promoting brownfields redevelopment, and encouraging smart growth through greater multijurisdictional cooperation." It represents a partnership with the U.S. Conference of Mayors and the National Association of Counties, and is dedicated to helping devise solutions to the complicated set of issues that uncontrolled sprawl raises.

Publications: *County News*, a biweekly newspaper; a weekly, *Legislative Bulletin*, printed while Congress is in session; the bimonthly *Coast to Coast* newsletter; the *County Environmental Quarterly*, published four times per year; and periodic research reports.

National Association of Home Builders
1201 15th Street, NW
Washington, DC 20005

(202) 822-0200
http://www.nahb.com

The National Association of Home Builders represents people who work in the home-building industry around the United States. The organization primarily exists as an advocacy organization for the industry and is "committed to pursuing reasonable and market-driven Smart Growth strategies that will meet the nation's housing needs, expand homeownership opportunities, help revitalize the nation's cities and inner suburbs, and build attractive and livable neighborhoods." As such, it has been an active participant in policy debates and legislative deliberation surrounding urban development planning. It seeks to achieve its aims by sponsoring conventions and home expositions, conducting research on issues related to the home-building industry through its Research Center, and disseminating this information to members, elected officials at all levels, and the general public. Its voter mobilization efforts are supplemented by a political action committee known as BUILD PAC.

Publications: Periodic research reports, public surveys, and a *Daily News Report* available online.

National Association of Realtors
700 11th Street, NW
Washington, DC 20001
(202) 383-1194
(202) 383-7563 (fax)
http://www.nar.realtor.com
InfoCentral@realtors.org

The National Association of Realtors (NAR) was founded in 1908 and represents 720,000 members in the United States. The organization has a decentralized structure, with its primary focus on 1,700 local associations and boards, and 54 state/territory associations of realtors. Members are involved in all aspects of residential and commercial real estate, including brokers, salespeople, property managers, appraisers, counselors, and other aspects of the industry. The NAR provides a facility for professional development, research and exchange of information among its members and the general public, as well as public advocacy for the "purpose of preserving the free enterprise system and the right to own real property." In this latter capacity, the NAR has been actively engaged in opposing what it sees as overly restrictive regulatory measures that hinder private decisions concerning land use and development. Its political action committee encourages members to volunteer in campaigns, conducts voter education on issues related to home ownership and real estate, and actively supports candidates who support its views. The national association has recently put together a comprehensive resource program to assist both realtors and the general public in understanding how best to manage growth while preserving individual property rights in a publication titled *Meeting the Challenge of Growth: A Blueprint for Realtor Action.* This document is available online.

Publications: Periodic research reports, public surveys, press releases, and a *Realtor Magazine* available online.

National Association of Regional Councils
1700 K Street, NW, Suite 1300
Washington, DC 20006
(202) 457-0710
(202) 296-9352 (fax)
http://www.narc.org
narc@clark.net

The National Association of Regional Councils (NARC) represents the interests of regional councils of government, regional planning and development districts, and a variety of other nongovernmental interests that seek to foster urban cooperation and build regional communities. The organization assists community leaders and citizens in developing regional strategies and solutions to sprawl-related issues that cut across local political boundaries. Its activities include policy advocacy, sponsoring "regional summits" among affiliates, acting as an information resource on regional issues, and encouraging research through its Institute for the Regional Community. The NARC is closely affiliated with the Association of Metropolitan Planning Organizations.

Publications: Handbooks and directories, research briefs and special reports, survey information through the regularly published *Regional Council Survey,* a monthly newspaper called the *Regional Reporter,* and a quarterly journal, *The Regionalist.*

National Center for Public Policy Research
777 N. Capitol Street, NE, Suite 803
Washington, DC, 20002

(202) 371-1400
info@nationalcenter.org
http://www.nationalcenter.org

The National Center for Public Policy Research is a communications and research foundation dedicated to providing free market solutions as they apply to a variety of public policy issues, including land use regulation. Founded in 1982, this organization believes that private property owners are the best stewards of our land and environment, and that a free market, individual liberty, and personal responsibility therefore provide the best focus for public policy action, not burdensome government regulation. It maintains an Environmental Policy Task Force, which serves to "help arm conservatives with tools for the environmental policy debate" by providing a forum for coordinating efforts, interpreting regulatory issues, and chairing monthly meetings, as well as publishing a variety of resources to assist members and supporters.

Publications: Publishes monthly research reports titled *National Policy Analysis* and provides a weekly information source, *Scoop*.

National Conference of State Legislatures
1560 Broadway, Suite 700
Denver, CO 80202
(303) 830-2200
(303) 863-8003 (fax)
http://www.ncsl.org

The National Conference of State Legislatures is a bipartisan organization that seeks to improve the quality and effectiveness of state legislatures, to foster communication and cooperation among legislators, and to ensure that states retain a strong and cohesive voice in the federal system. The organization acts as an information source and advocacy organization for the elected legislators and staffs of state, commonwealth, and territorial governments of the United States. With an increasing number of states adopting Smart Growth measures and federal funds now targeting these goals, the conference has sponsored research in growth management and land conservation issues through its Environment, Energy, and Transportation Program.

Publications: A monthly *State Legislatures* magazine; *LegisBriefs*, a weekly newsletter; and periodic research reports and documents.

National League of Cities
1301 Pennsylvania Avenue, NW
Washington, DC 20004
(202) 626-1763
(202) 626-3043 (fax)
pa@nlc.org
http://www.nlc.org

The National League of Cities was established in 1924 by state municipal leagues around the country that shared a commitment to reform. Today, it represents forty-nine leagues, 1,500 member cities, and more than 18,000 cities and towns through its membership. Its mission is "to strengthen and promote cities as centers of opportunity, leadership, and governance." Through this organization, mayors and council members join together to establish unified policy positions, advocate these policies, and share information that strengthens municipal government throughout the nation.

Publications: Books, policy reports, directories, a weekly newspaper called *The Weekly*, and *Issues and Options*, a bimonthly report.

National Trust for Historic Preservation
1785 Massachusetts Avenue, NW
Washington, DC 20036
(202) 588-6000
http://www.nthp.org

Chartered by Congress in 1949, the National Trust for Historic Preservation is committed to ensuring that historic buildings, neighborhoods, and landscapes are preserved and protected from urban development pressures. The organization has taken a strong stance in favor of growth management planning as a means to limit sprawl and shift investment back to neglected, deteriorating central cities and historic downtown areas. It maintains six regional offices, directly oversees the administration of twenty historic sites, and works with local governments and community groups nationwide to facilitate the acquisition and preservation of historic structures and landscapes from urban development. It acts as a national information resource, sponsors conferences, funds research as well as preservation projects, and engages in public policy advocacy in legislative as well as legal affairs. It also gives out a variety of honor awards to recognize organizations and individuals who are committed to historic preservation.

Publications: Books; reports, including the annual *Most Endangered Historic Places* list; *Preservation*, a bimonthly magazine; *Barn Again!*, a rural land preservation magazine; *Preservation Advocate*, a monthly newsletter on legal and public policy issues; and on-line news updates.

Pacific Research Institute for Public Policy
755 Sansome Street, Suite 450
San Francisco, CA 94111
(415) 989-0833
http://pripp@pacificresearch.org

The Pacific Research Institute for Public Policy promotes the "principles of individual freedom and personal responsibility." The institute believes these principles are best encouraged through policies that emphasize a free economy, private initiative, and limited government. By focusing on public policy issues such as education, the environment, law, economics, and social welfare, the institute strives to foster a better understanding of the principles of a free society among leaders in government, academia, the media, and the business community. It has sponsored research and published articles on free market solutions to urban sprawl.

Publications: Books and policy papers, a monthly newsletter called *Impact*, a periodic policy brief faxed to subscribers called *Action Alert*, and *Capital Ideas*, a weekly fax broadcast.

Reason Public Policy Institute
3415 South Sepulveda Boulevard, Suite 400
Los Angeles, CA 90034
(310) 391-2245
(310) 391-4395 (fax)
http://www.reason.org

The Reason Public Policy Institute was created in 1978 as a national research and educational organization that promotes "public policies based on rationality and freedom as the basic underpinnings of a good society." This is generally interpreted to mean policies based upon individual liberty and responsibility and a free market approach. Current research areas include infrastructure and transportation, urban land use and economic development, environmental quality, and education. The institute's Urban Futures Program is devoted to promoting voluntary, private sector, and market-oriented solutions to urban problems that include urban economic development policy and land use planning at the local, regional, state, and national levels.

Publications: Publishes *Reason*, a monthly magazine, and periodic research papers from its *Policy Studies* series, many of which are available online.

Scenic America
801 Pennsylvania Avenue, SE, Suite 300
Washington, DC 20003
(202) 543-6200
(202) 543-9130 (fax)
webmaster@scenic.org
http://www.scenic.org

Scenic America is active at the federal and state levels in the cause of protecting the scenic heritage of America's natural landscapes. Its mission is to "protect natural beauty and community character." In addition to the organization's traditional support for reducing billboard blight and keeping highways scenic, it has endorsed the Smart Growth agenda as an effective strategy for protecting communities from blight.

Publications: Periodic *Fact Sheets* and a newsletter, *The Grassroots Advocate*, as well as *Viewpoints*, a newsletter published three times per year.

Sierra Club
85 Second Street, 2nd Floor
San Francisco, CA 94105
(415) 977-5500
(415) 977-5799 (fax)
information@sierraclub.org
http://www.sierraclub.org

The Sierra Club was launched in 1892 to protect wilderness areas, promote responsible use of natural resources, and restore the quality of natural and human environments. Since 1986 the Sierra Club has been actively involved in urban issues, advocating an urban environment that is "highly efficient and nonpolluting so as to minimize our impacts upon this planet's resources and environment." It therefore promotes planning policies that conserve open space, protect and enhance the quality of urban life, conserve the urban infrastructure, and ensure the safe disposal of urban wastes. With the publication of its report titled *The Dark Side of the American Dream: The Costs and Consequences of Sub-*

urban Sprawl in 1998, this organization entered the policy debate surrounding urban sprawl. It sponsors and publishes research on sprawl, conducts public awareness campaigns, and acts as an advocacy group in state and national politics.

Publications: Publishes monthly *Sierra* magazine and *The Planet*, a monthly online newsletter.

Smart Growth Network
International City Management Association
Smart Growth Network
777 N. Capitol Street, Suite 500
Washington, DC 20002
(202) 962-3591
infor@smartgrowth.org
http://www.smartgrowth.org

The Smart Growth Network was begun in 1998 under the primary sponsorship of the U.S. Environmental Protection Agency's Urban and Economic Development Division. Its mission is to help "create national, regional, and local coalitions to encourage metropolitan development that is environmentally smart . . . fiscally smart . . . and economically and socially smart." It seeks to overcome past division over growth issues and foster coalitions among real estate developers, planners, government officials, lending institutions, community development organizations, and environmental and community activists, all of whom stand to benefit from working together on sprawl-related issues. The network promotes urban development that protects air and water quality, pays for itself without raising property taxes, and promotes community economic vitality, livability, and resource efficiency. The network seeks to sponsor conferences and publish up-to-date information about land use planning initiatives.

Publications: Two primers, including *Best Development Practices* and *Why Smart Growth*, along with *Getting Smart!*, a bimonthly newsletter, and other materials.

Sprawl Watch Clearinghouse
1100 17th Street, NW, 10th Floor
Washington, DC 20036
(202) 974-5157
(202) 466-2247 (fax)
http://www.sprawlwatch.org

The Sprawl Watch Clearinghouse is an online electronic resource center that provides information, advice, and referrals on issues related to sprawl, smart growth, and livable communities. It seeks to act as a policy advocate by working with grassroots activists, legislators, developers, planners, architects, and others to help revitalize communities and reduce urban sprawl. It is using its website as a clearinghouse for disseminating books, reports, informational websites, and contact information about affiliated organizations to further these ends. Resources presently available involve a variety of topics related to urban growth, including economic development, environment, farmland preservation, historic preservation, politics, race, rural areas, transit, and urban design.

Sprawl-Busters
21 Grinnell Street
Greenfield, MA 01301
(413) 772-6289
info@sprawl-busters.com
http://sprawl-busters.com

Sprawl-Busters was begun by Al Norman, who was part of a citizen-based grassroots organization that successfully prevented national retailer Wal-Mart from locating a store in the small community of Greenfield, Massachusetts, in 1993. This organization exists to help local community coalitions "to design and implement successful campaigns against megastores and other undesirable large-scale developments." Members provide consulting services for activists to assist with strategic planning, field operations, electoral campaigns, technical support, and related activities.

Publications: A monthly *Sprawl-Busters Alert Newsletter,* and *News-Flash!,* which provides periodic news updates online.

Surface Transportation Policy Project
1100 17th Street, NW, 10th Floor
Washington, DC 20036
(202) 466-2636
(202) 466-2247 (fax)
stpp@transact.org
http://www.transact.org/stpp

The goal of the Surface Transportation Policy Project is to ensure that transportation policy and related public investments help to conserve energy, protect environmental and aesthetic quality, strengthen the economy, promote social equity, and make communities more livable. Participants stress that they "emphasize the needs of people, rather than vehicles, in assuring access to jobs, services, and recreational opportunities." This organization has taken a strong position in favor of Smart Growth solutions to urban sprawl.

Publications: *TransAct*, an online information source that includes a bimonthly newsletter called *The Progress*.

Thoreau Institute
P.O. Box 1590
Bandon, OR 97411
(541) 347-1517
http://www.ti.org

The Thoreau Institute has been involved in research and debates surrounding public lands and related environmental issues since its founding in 1975. It has the perspective that "there are no enemies of the environment, only people with different incentives," and therefore works with all sides to forge solutions. The organization is committed to seeking "ways to protect the environment without regulation, bureaucracy, or central control," believing that alternatives such as user fees, markets, and incentives are more effective in issues such as urban sprawl. The activities of this organization include sponsoring research, educational outreach, and consulting.

Publications: Research reports and a quarterly magazine called *Different Drummer*.

Trust for Public Land
116 New Montgomery Street, 4th Floor
San Francisco, CA 94105
(415) 495-4014
http://www.igc.apc.org/tpl

The Trust for Public Land was founded in 1972 to help conserve land for recreation and preserve natural landscapes in urban areas. The organization is committed to the belief that "connecting people to land deepens the public's appreciation of nature and the commitment to protect it." Since 1972 the trust has helped to protect more than a million acres in forty-five states. The organization provides legal and real estate assistance to landowners, community groups, and government agencies to further the creation of urban parks, gardens, greenways, and riverways, to conserve land for protection and recreational uses, and to safeguard historic landmarks and landscapes.

Publications: A semiannual magazine, *Land and People*, and a newsletter, *On the Land*.

Urban Land Institute
1025 Thomas Jefferson Street, NW
Suite 500 West
Washington, DC 20007
(202) 624-7000
(202) 624-7140 (fax)
webmaster@uli.org
http://www.uli.org

Founded in 1936, the Urban Land Institute's mission is to "provide leadership in the responsible use of land to enhance the total environment." It seeks to foster land use and real estate development that revitalizes America's declining urban communities through better urban planning, business reinvestment, brownfield redevelopment, more efficient transportation, regional cooperation, and better growth management.

Publications: Numerous books, research reports, and an online weekly, *Smart Growth News*.

State and Regional Advocacy Organizations

Cascade Policy Institute
813 S.W. Alder, Suite 450
Portland, OR 97205
(503) 242-0900
info@CascadePolicy.org
http://www.CascadePolicy.org

The Cascade Policy Institute is devoted to the research and dissemination of free market policy solutions in the state of Oregon. It has pressed for greater freedom of choice for citizens and less government involvement in education, public transit, taxation, and a variety of other issues. It published an alternative land use plan for the state in 1997 called *The Oregon Growth Plan*, in which it sought "to promote a new paradigm for growth management in Oregon; one that relies on markets, prices, enforcement of property rights, and decentralized decision making."

Publications: Numerous policy reports available online.

Center for Livable Communities
1414 K Street, Suite 250
Sacramento, CA 95814
(916) 448-1198
http://www.lgc.org

The Center for Livable Communities is a nonprofit organization that provides technical assistance to local governments around the state of California interested in adopting policies that lead to a more environmentally sustainable future. The center offers programs, resources, and advice in the areas of transportation, infrastructure, economic and social development, affordable housing, farmland protection, and conservation of wilderness.

Green Environmental Coalition
P.O. Box 266
Yellow Springs, OH 45387
gec@greenlink.org
http://www.greenlink.org/gec

The Green Environmental Coalition was founded in 1991 to focus the efforts of citizens rallying against a hazardous waste burning plant. Since that time it has continued to work for greater environmental accountability from industry and also expanded its efforts to encompass urban sprawl–related issues through the promotion of a new 1,000 Friends of Ohio organization.

Greenbelt Alliance
530 Bush Street, Suite 303
San Francisco, CA 94108
(415) 932-7776
(415) 932-6530
http://www.greenbelt.org

The Greenbelt Alliance is a land conservation organization active in the San Francisco Bay area. Founded in 1958 it is "dedicated to protecting the region's Greenbelt of open space and making our communities better places to live." It has been instrumental in saving more than 600,000 acres of greenbelt lands and helped raise over $450 million in funds to acquire new parklands and other open space. In addition to fund raising and community activism, this organization also acts as an information resource for other groups around the country seeking to preserve open space and fighting urban sprawl. In the past it has sponsored reports on farmland preservation, compact housing, mass transit, open space, at-risk lands, and regional planning for the Bay Area.

New Jersey Future
204 West State Street
Trenton, NJ 08608
(609) 393-0008
(609) 393-1189 (fax)
njfuture@njfuture.org
http://njfuture.org

New Jersey Future was founded in 1987 as a nonpartisan organization seeking to promote "sustainable development and smart growth." It is a citizens' movement that vigorously supports state, regional, and local land use planning. The organization has taken an especially prominent role in espousing the state Development and Redevelopment Plan, which serves as an advisory plan for county and local governments.

Publications: Bimonthly newsletter available online.

1,000 Friends Organizations

In 1975, 1,000 Friends of Oregon was founded as a citizens' grassroots organization committed to supporting then-governor Tom McCall's legislative initiative to institute mandatory growth management planning across the state. Since that time several states have witnessed the rise of "1,000 Friends" movements. Although each is unique and separate, all involve a diverse coalition of businesses, elected officials, interest groups, and citizens who are united by a commitment to educating and empowering citizens about the dangers of sprawl and the need for state and regional land use planning.

1,000 Friends of Florida
P.O. Box 5948
Tallahassee, FL 32314
(850) 222-6277
http://www.teleport.com/~friends

1,000 Friends of Fresno
4781 East Gettysburg
Fresno, California 93726
(209) 291-2261
(209) 291-4991 (fax)
http://www.1000friendsoffresno.org

1,000 Friends of Iowa
104 Southwest 4th Street
Des Moines, IA 50309
(515) 288-5365
(515) 280-3559 (fax)
kfoi@kfoi.org
http://www.kfoi.org

1,000 Friends of Kaui'i County
P.O. Box 698
Kilauea, HI 96754
(808) 828-2166
(808) 828-1329 (fax)
http://www.hawaiian.net/~cbokauai/k1000

1,000 Friends of Maryland
11 1/2 W. Chase Street
Baltimore, MD 21201
(888) 447-6278
http://www.friendsofmd.org

1,000 Friends of Minnesota
370 Selby Avenue, Suite 300
Saint Paul, MN 55102
(651) 312-1000
(651) 312-0012 (fax)
info@1000fomn.org
http://www.1000fomn.org

1,000 Friends of Oregon
300 Willamette Building
534 Southwest Third Avenue
Portland, OR 97294
(503) 497-1000
info@friends.org
http://www.teleport.com/~friends

1,000 Friends of Pennsylvania
1211 Chestnut Street, Suite 900
Philadelphia, PA 19107
(215) 568-2225
(215) 663-0528 (fax)
info@1000Friends.org
http://www.1000friends.org

1,000 Friends of Washington
1305 Fourth Avenue, Suite 303
Seattle, WA 98101
(206) 343-0681
(206) 343-0683 (fax)
friends@eskimo.com
http://www.1000friends.org

1,000 Friends of Wisconsin
16 North Carroll Street, Suite 810
Madison, WI 53703
(608) 259-1000
(608) 259-1621 (fax)
http://www.1000friendsofwisconsin.com

Vermont Forum on Sprawl
110 Main Street
Burlington, VT 05401
(802) 864-6310
(802) 862-4487 (fax)
information@vnrc.org
http://www.vtsprawl.org/index3.htm

The Vermont Forum on Sprawl seeks to assist Vermonters in understanding the detrimental impacts of unplanned sprawl on the state. It advocates solutions that involve more compact land development and greater protection for rural landscapes.

Federal Government Agencies

With the launching of President Bill Clinton's Lands Legacy and Livable Communities initiatives, a number of federal agencies have been given responsibility for modifying existing programs to address the issue of urban sprawl. Those agencies with specific antisprawl mandates are listed below.

U.S. Department of Agriculture
Natural Resources Conservation Service
14 Independence Avenue, SW
Washington, DC 20250
(202) 720-2847
(202) 690-0693 (fax)
http://www.nrcs.usda.gov

Open space protection through farmland conservation easements is one of the most effective means for preserving natural landscapes and limiting the spread of urban sprawl. The Natural Resources Conservation Service of the United States Department of Agriculture oversees the federal Farmland Protection Program. This enables individuals and groups to purchase conservation easements with the assistance of local, state, and federal funds. The federal government provides up to a 50 percent share of the fair market value for land acquired under this program. The USDA also has created a Sustainable Development program that works to improve the profitability, land stewardship and enhancement of small farmers across the nation.

U.S. Department of Energy
Center of Excellence for Sustainable Development
Office of Energy Efficiency and Renewable Energy
Denver Regional Support Office
1617 Cole Boulevard
Golden, CO 80401
(800) 363-3732
(303) 275-4830 (fax)
http://www.sustainable.doe.gov/welcome.htm

One of the core missions of the U.S. Department of Energy is to ensure that the nation has ample supplies of clean and affordable energy resources. To accomplish this goal the department has established a Center of Excellence for Sustainable Development to provide information and support to communities that are seeking to achieve a more sustainable source of energy. This program is fostering awareness about urban sprawl, encouraging local zoning and other ordinances that encourage better energy planning, and providing other educational resources and grant funds.

U.S. Department of Housing and Urban Development
451 7th Street, SW
Washington, DC 20410
(202) 401-0398
http://www.hud.gov/live1.html

In its capacity as the nation's housing and community develop-ment agency, the U.S. Department of Housing and Urban Devel-opment has been a major factor in influencing land use decisions in urban areas. This federal department has embraced the Clin-ton administration's Livable Communities initiative by incorpo-rating its focus into existing programs that foster economic opportunity, enhance the quality of life, and build a stronger sense of community in impoverished inner city communities. Among the most important of these programs are Community Development Block Grants that target brownfield cleanups and Empowerment Zones and Enterprise Communities funds that help refocus development dollars in neglected inner city areas. HUD has also supported more effective use of planning through its partnership in the Growing Smart initiative sponsored by the American Association of Planners.

U.S. Department of the Interior
1849 C Street, NW
Washington, DC 20240
(202) 208-3100
http://www.doi.gov/livability

The Department of the Interior is the nation's leading public lands management agency. As such, it has responsibilities for wildlife protection, natural resources conservation, and promot-ing research, among other things. The department is committed to facilitating local and state efforts to mitigate sprawl through the provision of reliable data, mapping, and planning assistance, especially as it applies to recreation, wildlife habitat, and historic preservation. Among the agencies in the Department of the In-terior are: the U.S. Geological Survey, which is collecting topo-graphic and land use information to document land use change in urban areas, and the U.S. Fish and Wildlife Service, which is working with local governments and communities to help iden-tify and preserve open space that represents critical habitat for endangered or threatened species. As part of its Lands Legacy initiative, the Department of Interior has also made available $150 million for matching grants to state, local, and tribal gov-ernments for the acquisition of land and easements for parks, greenways, outdoor recreation, and wildlife habitat with prior-ity given to projects consistent with statewide smart growth plans.

U.S. Department of Transportation
400 7th Street, SW
Washington, DC 20590
(202) 366-4000
http://tcsp-fhwa.volpe.dot.gov/index.html

The traditional mission of the U.S. Department of Transportation (DOT) is to ensure that America has a "fast, safe, efficient, accessible and convenient transportation system." In response to growing concerns about the link between urban sprawl and federal highway construction, the DOT has launched its Transportation and Community and System Preservation program as a comprehensive research and grant initiative that is designed to "investigate the relationships between transportation and community and system preservation and private-sector-based initiatives." States, local governments, and metropolitan planning agencies are eligible for discretionary grants to plan and implement strategies that improve transportation efficiency; reduce environmental impacts of transportation; reduce the need for future public infrastructure investments; ensure efficient access to jobs, services, and centers of trade; and examine private sector development patterns and investments that support these goals. The department also provides funds to encourage mass transit in local communities.

U.S. Environmental Protection Agency
Development, Community and Environment Division
204 W. State Street
Washington, DC 20460
(202) 260-1849
(202) 260-1812 (fax)
http://www.epa.gov/livability

The Environmental Protection Agency (EPA) is charged with implementing federal laws designed to promote public health by protecting our nation's air, water, and soil from harmful pollution. Since the Livability Agenda was announced by the Clinton administration, the EPA has been assigned significant new responsiblities for responding to challenges presented by urban sprawl through its stewardship of the Better America Bonds program. These bonds are intended to provide state and local communities with the financing necessary to preserve open space, protect water quality, and clean up brownfields in neglected industrial areas. Communities will pay zero interest on a fifteen-year bond through tax credits equal to the amount of interest otherwise paid on these loans. This will supplement the EPA's existing Brownfields Economic Redevelopment Initiative program, which has provided more than $1 billion to clean up and redevelop abandoned properties. The EPA is also working to make its substantial data on environmental quality available to planning and transportation agencies to better facilitate awareness of the consequences of sprawl.

State Agencies

Over a dozen states have adopted their own comprehensive growth management laws designed to address issues raised by urban sprawl. These states have adopted a wide variety of policy instruments to oversee these efforts. Other states continue to rely largely upon local government officials and regional planning agencies to deal with urban development and land use issues. The following list of states provides contact information for those seeking to learn more about antisprawl initiatives at the state government level.

Arizona Land Department
1616 West Adams
Phoenix, AZ 85007
(602) 542-4061
(602) 542-2600 (fax)
http://www.land.state.az.us/

The Arizona Preserve Initiative was passed by the state legislature in 1996 as a means for encouraging the preservation of select parcels of state trust land around urban areas for open space. It permits citizens to petition the state land commissioner to reclassify trust lands for conservation purposes.

California Coastal Commission
45 Fremont Street, Suite 2000
San Francisco, CA 94105
(415) 904-5200
http://ceres.ca.gov/coastalcomm

The California Coastal Act of 1976 places severe restrictions upon any development that takes place within coastal zones of the state, empowering a Coastal Commission to issue permits in these limited areas. Although there is no state mandate in place, many California communities have adopted their own growth management ordinances.

California Environmental Resources Evaluation System
California Resources Agency
1416 Ninth Street, Suite 1211
Sacramento, CA 95814
(916) 653-5656
http://ceres.ca.gov

The California Environmental Resources Evaluation System was established by the state Resources Authority to facilitate access to a variety of electronic data on land use. The program seeks to improve environmental analysis and planning, and maintains resources accessible to local governments and citizens.

Colorado Smart Growth Action Center
Department of Local Affairs
1313 Sherman Street
Room 323
Denver, CO 80203
(303) 866-2353
http://www.state.co.us/smartgrowth

Colorado adopted an incentive-based growth management law in 1970. It directs the state Land Board to establish a long-term stewardship trust of up to 300,000 acres of land. The board is authorized to sell or lease conservation easements on state trust lands. A state Land Use Commission develops a land use planning program for the entire state and possesses additional powers that enable it to issue cease and desist orders regarding any real estate development that constitutes a danger to public health when authorized by the state governor and local county commission. It also may assume planning authority where local governments have deferred to it when a state interest is at stake. In 1995 Governor Roy Romer established a Smart Growth Center in the state government to encourage awareness and collaboration aimed at curbing urban sprawl.

Denver Regional Council of Governments
2480 W. 26th Avenue, Suite 200B
Denver, CO 80211
(303) 455-1000

(303) 480-6790 (fax)

http://www.drcog.org/index.html

In 1997 the Denver metropolitan area adopted Metro Vision 2020 to address sprawl problems in the region. The plan calls for the establishment of a voluntary urban growth boundary and increased support for regional transit.

Connecticut Office of Policy and Management
450 Capitol Avenue
Hartford, CT 06106
(860) 418-6200
(860) 418-6487 (fax)
OPMinfo@po.state.ct.us
http://www.state.ct.us/opm

The Office of Policy and Management has the responsibility to formulate a statewide land use development plan. This plan has only advisory authority for regional and local planning agencies, and encourages local governments to take measures to limit the impact of sprawl. Connecticut also has a farmland preservation program.

Delaware Office of State Planning
Suite 7, 3rd Floor
Thomas Collins Building
540 S. DuPont Highway
Dover, DE 19901
(302) 739-3090
(302) 739-6958 (fax)
http://www.state.de.us/planning

The Land Use Planning Act requires that the Office of State Planning work to coordinate land use decisions made by state, county, and municipal governments. This mission is accomplished through research and analysis of land use, dissemination of information regarding land use planning, and helping county governments develop state-mandated comprehensive plans. In its *Shaping Delaware's Future* report (1997), the office made recommendations in favor of directing state funds and future development into existing communities, urban concentrations, and designated growth areas to combat sprawl. Delaware also has a farmland preservation program.

Florida Division of Community Planning
2555 Shumard Oak Boulevard
Tallahassee, FL 32399
(850) 487-4545
(850) 488-3309 (fax)
http://www.dca.state.fl.us/fdcp

In 1984 the state of Florida passed the State and Regional Planning Act, which mandated the preparation of a statewide comprehensive growth plan, and the preparation of regional plans in each of eleven regions of the state. The following year this law was amended to include each local government, which was henceforth required to prepare comprehensive plans consistent with regional and state growth management plans. As part of these plans, local governments were to devise a plan for the provision of infrastructure. They were also forbidden access to state development permits unless public facilities were concurrently available to meet needs generated by new developments. The state Division of Community Planning and its Bureau of Local Planning oversee these functions.

Georgia Department of Community Affairs
60 Executive Park South
Atlanta, GA 30329
(404) 679-4940
http://www.dca.state.ga.us/planning/index.html

The Georgia Planning Act of 1989 authorized the state Department of Community Affairs to establish rules and procedures for local government and regional agency review of development projects with a regional impact. Regional agencies and local governments jointly consider a list of factors in determining the potential impact of new development on the environment and natural resources of the region, regional economies, housing, and public services.

Hawaii Department of Land and Natural Resources
1151 Punchbowl Street
Honolulu, HI 96813
http://www.hawaii.gov/icsd/dlnr/dlnr.html

The Land Use Law of 1961 classified all land in Hawaii into four districts, which included urban, rural, agricultural, and conservation designations. Regulatory authority over land use in urban areas was then shifted to county governments, while agricultural lands were to be under the shared authority of counties and a state land use commission. Other lands were to be controlled by the Department of Land and Natural Resources. In 1979 a statewide land use plan was mandated for all state agencies, but counties have been largely exempted since 1984.

Maine State Planning Office
184 State Street
Station 38
Augusta, ME 04333
(207) 287-2851
http://www.state.me.us/spo/homepage.htm

The state of Maine passed an act in 1988 mandating that each of the state's municipalities develop a comprehensive plan, using statewide goals as a guide. Because funding has been inadequate, the law primarily serves as a cooperative program between municipalities, regional agencies, and the state. Maine also has a farmland preservation program.

Maryland Office of Planning
Room 1101
301 W. Preston Street
Baltimore, MD 21201
(410) 767-4500
(410) 767-4480 (fax)
http://www.op.state.md.us/oplabout.htm
http://www.op.state.md.us/smartgrowth

The state legislature enacted the Maryland Economic Growth, Resource Protection, and Planning Act in 1992. This established seven guiding "Visions" for future growth in the state, required all local plans to comply with the specific provisions of the act, and required consistency of state and local capital projects with local plans. In 1997 a Smart Growth law was added that bars state funding from subsidizing urban sprawl outside of designated growth areas. Maryland also has the most active farm preservation program in the country.

Massachusetts Office of Environmental Affairs
Division of Conservation Services
100 Cambridge Street
Boston, MA 02202

(617) 727-1552

http://www.magnet.state.ma.us/dcs

Massachusetts has an active farmland preservation program. The Division of Conservation Services provides technical and financial assistance to Massachusetts communities seeking to conserve open space from development or convert it to parkland. It also administers conservation restrictions that are part of the state's farmland protection program.

Metropolitan Council
Mears Park Center
230 E. 5th Street
St. Paul, MN 55101
(651) 602-1000
http://www.metrocouncil.org
data.center@metc.state.mn.us

The Metropolitan Council is a governmental entity that has authority over seven counties and includes some 2.4 million people who comprise the Minneapolis–St. Paul metropolitan region. The council provides a number of services that include operating the region's bus system, wastewater collection and treatment, housing and redevelopment, parks, and land use planning. The council works to overcome problems associated with sprawl by issuing detailed reports on regional growth patterns and devising plans to develop regional transportation, wastewater treatment, aviation, and parks.

Minnesota Planning
658 Cedar Street
St. Paul, MN 55155
(651) 296-3985
minnesota.planning@mnplan.state.mn.us
http://www.mnplan.state.mu.us

Minnesota Planning is a state agency that has the responsibility to conduct research on statewide trends that include land use issues, to maintain a land management information center, and to provide planning assistance to local governments. It has recently undertaken research on sprawl issues.

New Hampshire Office of State Planning
2 Beacon Street
Concord, NH 03301

(603) 271-2155
(603) 271-1728 (fax)
http://www.state.nh.us/osp/ospweb.htm

The Office of State Planning has the responsibility to encourage orderly development of the state and wise management of its resources. It compiles, analyzes, and disseminates information and research; facilitates planning in other state agencies; and provides technical assistance to local communities with planning, growth management, natural resource conservation, and economic development. New Hampshire also has a farmland preservation program.

New Jersey Office of State Planning
Department of Community Affairs
33 West State Street
Trenton, NJ 08625
(609) 292-7156
(609) 292-3292 (fax)
http://www.state.nj.us/osp

New Jersey created a State Planning Commission in 1985 for the purpose of addressing sprawl-related concerns. It is charged with adopting a triennial State Development and Redevelopment Plan that has the purpose of coordinating growth planning, transportation, urban renewal, and resource conservation efforts around the state. More recently this plan has designated growth and preservation areas to facilitate land use planning. The state's twenty-one counties and 566 municipalities were mandated to conduct reviews of their own land use plans and ordinances through a "cross-acceptance" process, but not required to follow the state plan. In 1998 the state constitution was amended to dedicate almost $100 million annually from the state sales tax to purchase land for conservation and recreation purposes. New Jersey also has a farmland conservation program.

North Carolina Office of State Planning
116 West Jones Street
Raleigh, NC 27603
(919) 733-4131
(919) 715-3562 (fax)
http://www.ospl.state.nc.us

The Office of State Planning compiles data on land use information around the state and provides planning assistance to state and local government agencies.

Oregon Department of Land Conservation and Development
1175 Court Street, NE
Salem, OR 97301
(503) 373-0060
http://lcd.state.or.us

Oregon adopted a comprehensive statewide growth management law in 1973. The act sets forth nineteen mandated planning goals to guide municipalities and counties as they plan new growth and development. Among these goals are requirements that urban growth boundaries be established, prime farmland protected, adequate housing provided, and local mass transit planning undertaken. Planning disputes involving developers, property owners, and local and state agencies are heard before the Land Use Board of Appeals.

Pennsylvania Center for Local Government Services
325 Forum Building
Harrisburg, PA 17120
(800) 223-6837
http://www.dced.state.pa.us/PA_Exec/DCED/government/land-use.htm

The Center for Local Government Services was established in 1999 for the purpose of identifying and promoting the best land management practices across the state. It is charged with assisting local governments seeking to implement state land use objectives, encouraging regional cooperation in land use planning, advising state agencies with methods to achieve state land use objectives, and reporting annually on land use trends. Pennsylvania also has a farmland conservation program.

Portland Metro
600 NE Grand Avenue
Portland, OR 97232
(503) 797-1700
(503) 797-1797 (fax)
http://www.metro.dst.or.us

Portland Metro is the nation's only elected regional government, with jurisdiction over a three-county area that includes the city of

Portland. It has substantial responsibility for land-use and transportation planning. It also directly administers a number of regional public facilities such as the Portland Zoo, several stadiums, and parks.

Rhode Island Statewide Planning Program
1 Capitol Hill
Providence, RI 02908
(401) 222-1220
(401) 222-2083
http://www.athena.state.ri.us/planning

The state of Rhode Island adopted a law in 1988 that authorizes the State Planning Council to develop a comprehensive State Guide Plan addressing land use, physical development, environmental concerns, economic development, and conservation. It further mandates that every city and town develop a comprehensive plan that contains nine common elements. Once such a plan is adopted, the local government is required to bring its zoning ordinances into conformance with it. The state has the authority to review these plans and may reject those that do not conform with the requirements of the state guidelines. Local officials may request a review from the Comprehensive Plan Appeals Board. Rhode Island also has a farmland conservation program.

Tennessee Department of Environment and Conservation
401 Church Street
L & C Tower, 21st Floor
Nashville, TN 37243
(888) 891-8332
http://www.state.tn.us/environment/

The Tennessee state legislature adopted a law in 1998 that requires each of the state's ninety-four counties to establish a coordinating committee to develop countywide growth plans. These plans must identify urban growth boundaries for each municipality. Planned growth areas must be large enough to accommodate growth for the next twenty years. Two counties with metropolitan forms of government are exempted from the law.

Vermont Department of Housing and Community Affairs
National Life Building
Planning Office, Drawer 20
Montpelier, VT 05620

(802) 828-3211
(802) 828-2928 (fax)
http://state.vt.dca/housing

In 1970 Vermont adopted a state law mandating that major real
estate developments obtain a permit before proceeding. Nine regional environmental commissions were created to oversee the
process of reviewing and granting approvals. Any decision can
be appealed to the Vermont Environmental Board. In 1988 the
state passed an additional law that establishes statewide planning goals along with state incentives to encourage local communities to draw up plans that conform to these goals. Vermont
also has a farmland conservation program.

Washington Department of Community, Trade,
and Economic Development
906 Columbia Street, SW
P.O. Box 48300
Olympia, WA 98504
(360) 753-7426
(360) 586-3582 (fax)
http://www.wa.gov/cted/growth/index.html

In 1990 the state of Washington approved a growth management
law designed to reduce the detrimental impacts of sprawl. Patterned after Oregon's law, the act provides for thirteen statewide
planning goals. The following year three regional Growth Management Hearing Boards were created to hear appeals brought
by citizens and by the state to ensure that local plans are consistent with statewide goals.

Wisconsin Office of Land Information Services
17 South Fairchild Street, 7th Floor
Madison, WI 53703
http://www.doa.state.wi.us/olis
doaweb@doa.state.wi.us

The Wisconsin Lands Council is charged with the responsibility
of identifying critical land issues and offering solutions to the
governor through periodic reports. The Office of Land Information Services provides staff support for the Wisconsin Land
Council, acts as a clearinghouse for access to land information,
and offers technical assistance to other state agencies and local
governments.

7

Selected Print Resources

Books

Abbott, Carl, Deborah Howe, and Sy Adler, eds. *Planning the Oregon Way: A Twenty-Year Evaluation.* Corvallis, OR: Oregon State University, 1994. 328 pp. ISBN 0-87071-381-7.

Oregon was among the first states to adopt a comprehensive planning system specifically designed to mitigate growth pressures stemming from urban sprawl. Now in place for over thirty years, it has attracted much research attention as well as controversy, both in Oregon and around the rest of the country. This book evaluates the system, assessing its strengths and weaknesses, and offers recommendations for the future.

Arendt, Randall G. *Conservation Design for Subdivisions: A Practical Guide to Creating Open Space Networks.* Washington, DC: Island Press, 1996. 160 pp. ISBN 1-55963-489-8.

The author challenges the notion that new urban development automatically leads to the destruction and loss of natural landscapes and species habitat. Making an argument for balancing conservation with economic needs, he outlines a four-step process for rearranging the density on each development parcel so that no more than half the buildable land becomes house lots and streets. The book includes model zoning and subdivision ordinance provisions, as well as numerous site plans, photographs, and sketches of houses and landscapes. This innovative book is copublished by the American Planning Association, the Natural Lands Trust, and the American Society of Landscape Architects.

Audirac, Ivonne, ed. *Rural Sustainable Development in America.* New York: John Wiley and Sons, 1997. 448 pp. ISBN 0-47115-233-1.

Many rural, farm-based communities are under threat of development by burgeoning growth spilling out from metropolitan areas. This collection of essays examines problems faced by many rural communities, demonstrating that indigenous talents and resources can be used to revitalize agriculture, develop more efficient public services, and explore new opportunities in the development of greenways and recreational industries.

Baldassare, Mark. *Trouble in Paradise: The Suburban Transformation in America.* New York: Columbia University Press, 1986. 251 pp. ISBN 0-23106-014-9.

This book offers a critical analysis of the new suburban communities that evolved since the 1960s across America. The author is particularly concerned with the problems that have accompanied rapid growth and industrialization without needed changes in public values or social structure. He identifies six challenges facing suburbs today: the need for affordable housing; conflicts over growth management; the fragmentation of governmental authority at the local level; public opposition to taxes; rising costs of service delivery; and competing values derived from increasingly diverse communities. The data, analysis, and conclusions are drawn from a study of California suburbs, but the author provides insight that is generally applicable to suburbs around the nation.

Barnett, Jonathan. *The Fractured Metropolis: Improving the New City, Restoring the Old City, Reshaping the Region.* New York: Harper Collins, 1995. 250 pp. ISBN 0-06430-222-9.

This book explores ways of ameliorating the split between older central cities and the metropolitan periphery of new edge cities. Making use of case studies from diverse metropolitan regions around the United States, the author summarizes the effects of sprawl and recommends ways to improve city design and offset urban decay so as to rehabilitate older city centers while benefiting newer suburban areas. He urges planners and politicians to consider regional trends when making local decisions and discusses how choices in the design of suburbs, transportation, utilities, and open spaces can have an impact on historic downtowns and older urban centers. The book is illustrated with numerous maps, photographs, and drawings.

Baxandall, Rosalyn, and Elizabeth Ewen. *Picture Windows: How the Suburbs Happened.* New York: Basic Books, 2000. 320 pp. ISBN 0-46507-045-0.

The authors of this historical work attempt to chronicle the transformation of rural lands into suburban developments accessible to the rising post–World War II middle class. They discuss the hopes and promises that these new housing projects and accompanying shopping centers provided for many people who had grown up in hard times and previously been excluded from home ownership. The authors use interviews of people in several Long Island suburban communities to explore popular stereotypes about what attracted people to live in these communities. They find that many of these images have little to do with actual experiences, especially as they explore the lives of a diverse group of people that include blacks, immigrants, gay, elderly, divorced, and single Americans. Surmising from their interviews as well as diaries, scrapbooks, and other archival sources they conclude that the suburbs remain centers of social and architectural experimentation.

Beatley, Timothy. *Ethical Land Use: Principles of Policy and Planning.* Baltimore, MD: Johns Hopkins University, 1994. 302 pp. ISBN 0-80184-698-6.

Is there an identifiable "land ethic" that balances economic considerations with concerns for beauty, sustainability, conservation, and quality of life? Drawing on a variety of cases that involve urban sprawl, this book offers an exploration of the philosophical dimensions of land use policy based on the underlying premise that such decisions involve ethical choices. The book offers a practical set of principles to guide future land use policy making and planning.

Beatley, Timothy, and Kristy Manning. *The Ecology of Place: Planning for Environment, Economy, and Community.* Washington, DC: Island Press, 1997. 225 pp. ISBN 1-55963-478-2.

Recognizing that the United States lies at a critical juncture in which "the American people have important choices to make about the types of places they wish to inhabit and the kinds of environments they hope to leave their children and grandchildren," the authors seek alternatives to sprawl in which land is consumed sparingly, cities and towns function in harmony, local economies thrive, and cities work together to create communities of enduring value. They identify architecture that celebrates a town's history and personality, and planning designs that foster face-to-face contact among citizens. Their philosophy of community sustainability encourages civic pride, reinforces community heritage, uniqueness, and a sense of place.

Beaumont, Constance E. *How Superstore Sprawl Can Harm Communities.* Washington, DC: National Trust for Historic Preservation, 1994. 120 pp. ISBN 0-89133-392-4.

The author challenges the popular notion that bulk discount stores and chain superstores bring benefits to the community. They document numerous cases in which superstore sprawl development on the periphery of urban areas has devastated historic downtown centers and destroyed a once-cherished sense of community. Other alternatives to superstores are offered as a means for attaining economic growth, jobs, and higher tax revenues. Regulatory guidelines are also offered to local governments seeking to mitigate the worst effects of superstore sprawl.

Beaumont, Constance E. *Smart States, Better Communities.* New York: National Trust for Historic Preservation, 1996. 408 pp. ISBN 0-89133-356-8.

This book describes state policies in place around the country that help citizens preserve community character through historic preservation, community revitalization, and rural greenspaces conservation. A variety of informative case studies explore topics such as transportation alternatives, property rights, and mechanisms for stopping sprawl.

Benfield, F. Kaid, Matthew Raimi, and Donald D. Chen. *Once There Were Greenfields: How Urban Sprawl Is Undermining America's Environment, Economy, and Social Fabric.* Natural Resources Defense Council, 1999. 228 pp. ISBN 1-89334-017-1.

This book meticulously documents the consequences of sprawling growth patterns. The authors describe how this kind of development has contributed to the loss of irreplaceable natural landscapes, the neglect of inner cities, massive traffic congestion, air and water pollution, endangered public health, engendered rising tax rates, and fostered the makings of an energy crisis in the near future. They offer a variety of Smart Growth principles to guide future developments that balance economic progress with environmental protection and social goals.

Blakely, Edward J., and Mary G. Snyder. *Fortress America: Gated Communities in the United States.* Washington, DC: Brookings Institution, 1997. 200 pp. ISBN 0-81571-002-X.

Growing numbers of Americans are retreating to exclusionary gated residential developments in search of physical security and segregated community life. This book explores this phenomenon and how it will impact the future of the United States. Attention is focused on such issues as the privatization of public services, the restriction of public access to community areas, and the fragmentation of social life that this engenders.

Bower, Sidney. *Good Neighborhoods.* New York: Praeger, 1996. 232 pp. ISBN 0-27595-181-2.

This book explores the sociological and aesthetic issues surrounding community and neighborhood life. The author traces the changing image of the ideal residential area through early and contemporary eras, describing how four types of ideal neighborhood have evolved into the present model. Practical suggestions are offered for encouraging healthier residential communities that permit neighbors to coexist peacefully, while accommodating the needs and lifestyles of diverse urban dwellers.

Brandes-Gratz, Roberta, and Norman Mintz. *Cities Back from the Edge.* New York: John Wiley & Sons, 1998. 400 pp. ISBN 0-47114-417-7.

One of the key elements of any strategy for overcoming urban sprawl is to reestablish the primacy of traditional central cities. The authors demonstrate that this is presently occurring in a number of major urban centers around the country. They illustrate how resurgent cities are able to recreate thriving, vibrant downtowns that offer desirable alternatives to malls, big-box superstore realtors, and suburban housing. They identify common elements of success, offering guidelines for future planners.

Buchsbaum, Peter A., and Larry J. Smith, eds. *State and Regional Comprehensive Planning: Implementing New Methods for Growth Management.* Chicago: American Bar Association, 1993. 260 pp. ISBN 0-89707-904-3.

Bringing state-level agencies into land use planning decisions has been advocated by many groups frustrated by the inability or unwillingness of local boards to aggressively stand up to the forces of urban sprawl. To date a dozen states have actually adopted such legislation, which has taken a variety of forms across the country. Many other states are considering similar measures. This book offers a collection of essays by some of the nation's leading land use lawyers and academics, each of whom offers insight into different aspects of this issue. Three of the essays offer general observations, commenting on the political forces at work, debates over state involvement, and future trends. Other contributors analyze growth management issues and initiatives in nine states, as well as one Canadian province.

Burby, Raymond J., and Peter J. May. *Making Governments Plan: State Experiments in Managing Land Use.* Baltimore, MD: Johns Hopkins University Press, 1997. 200 pp. ISBN 0-80185-623-X.

Many of the most pressing issues associated with urban sprawl cross local government jurisdictional boundaries, suggesting that state-level policy action is necessary. To date, over a dozen states have adopted comprehensive land use management programs, and almost thirty others have more narrowly conceived regulatory programs mandating state involvement in local planning. This book offers an intensive overview of state involvement in planning and growth management in local communities, with case studies drawn from a number of the most important experiments, including Florida and Oregon. It also provides an extensive analysis of program design and implementation with recommendations for future state planning and growth management programs.

Burrough, Peter, and Rachel McDonnell, eds. *Principles of Geographic Information Systems.* London: Oxford University, 1998. 333 pp. ISBN 0-19823-366-3.

Land use decision makers are increasingly drawing upon massive computerized geographic information system (GIS) databases. This book introduces the theory behind GIS and its practical applications, showing how these systems collect, store, and analyze spatial data. It covers the fundamentals of coding data, database management, and linkages with ground survey and remote-sensing equipment, much of which is accomplished on the Internet.

Callies, David L. *Preserving Paradise: Why Regulation Won't Work.* Honolulu, HI: University of Hawaii Press. 120 pp. ISBN 0-82481-576-9.

Hawaii was the first state in the nation to adopt state-level growth management laws to help preserve its agricultural economy and natural habitat, and combat encroaching urban sprawl. To date it remains more involved in land use issues than any other state, with strict regulations and development restrictions administered by powerful state- and county-level agencies. The author, a leading authority on land use law in Hawaii, explores the many regulatory bottlenecks and outright abuses associated with these laws, especially in light of current court rulings regarding regulatory takings. Finding that present mechanisms in state laws are inadequate for preserving open space, wetlands, coastal resources, and other public amenities, he makes a strong case in favor of alternatives that include a greater role for government in purchasing development rights, sponsoring incentives for more affordable housing, and working with nonprofit conservation groups and land trusts.

Calthorpe, Peter. *The Next American Metropolis.* Princeton, NJ: Princeton Architectural Press, 1993. 175 pp. ISBN 1-87827-168-7.

One of the most outspoken advocates of the New Urbanist school of architectural design, Calthorpe demonstrates how many of the social, economic, and environmental crises faced by America's growing metropolitan areas are linked to sprawl patterns of growth. The author challenges fellow architects and real estate developers to reorient their projects in ways that mitigate these serious problems. Case studies are utilized to support a series of guidelines for future development.

Carlson, Daniel. *At Road's End: Transportation and Land Use Choices for Communities.* Washington, DC: The Surface Transportation Policy Project and Island Press, 1995. 168 pp. ISBN 1-55963-338-7.

This book examines federal transportation policy, tracing how new interstate highways have encouraged the destruction of traditional neighborhoods, destroyed wetlands, and subsidized sprawl development over the past forty years. It also chronicles the controversies that these programs have generated, and shows how recent changes in federal policy under the 1991 Intermodal

Surface Transportation and Efficiency Act have been designed to mitigate some these problems. The author demonstrates how new coalitions of environmentalists, developers, and community leaders have worked together with federal authorities to fashion transportation alternatives that facilitate better regional coopera- tion and growth management goals. Using data from seven case studies he provides a thorough analysis of transportation designs and demonstrates how these can impinge upon land use choices and larger quality-of-life questions.

Catlin, Robert A. *Land Use Planning, Environmental Protection, and Growth Management: The Florida Experience.* Chelsea, MI: Ann Arbor Press, 1997. 262 pp. ISBN 1-57504-042-5.

Since the end of World War II, Florida has been forced to devise policies to deal with the most explosive, rapid, and persistent urban growth in the United States. The author contends that much of this growth has been accompanied by all of the worst implications of sprawl. The book helps readers understand why and how state policy shifted from a completely unfettered lais- sez-faire approach to one of the most rigidly devised growth management strategies in the nation in the 1980s. Detailed cov- erage of policy debates and program implementation is provided for both state environmental initiatives of the 1970s, as well as growth management legislation of the 1980s and 1990s. This is followed by a series of well-reasoned recommendations to im- prove the planning and development processes at both state and local levels.

Daniels, Tom. *When City and Country Collide: Managing Growth in the Metropolitan Fringe.* Washington, DC: Island Press, 1998. 420 pp. ISBN 1-55963-597-5.

This book examines the decline of farming and rural small-town economies as the fringe of urban development encroaches fur- ther into the countryside. It reviews past growth management techniques and why many of these have proven to be ineffective. The author presents a series of planning and design principles that encourage more compact urban development, as well as farmland protection mechanisms that enable these rural commu- nities to survive into the future.

De Grove, John M., and Deborah A. Miness, eds. *The New Fron- tier for Land Policy: Planning and Growth Management in the*

States. Cambridge, MA: Lincoln Institute of Land Policy, 1992. 176 pp. ISBN 1-55844-121-2.

This book provides a comprehensive overview of the politics surrounding growth management legislation as it has been adopted and implemented by seven states: Florida, New Jersey, Maine, Vermont, Rhode Island, Georgia, and Washington. The contributors to this edited volume help illustrate the many different strategies presently being pursued at the state level and demonstrate both the limitations and possibilities that state-level intervention can have for controlling urban sprawl.

De Long, James V. *Property Matters: How Property Rights Are Under Assault and Why You Should Care.* New York: Free Press, 1997. 390 pp. ISBN 0-68487-437-7.

This book argues that government agencies at all levels routinely usurp the private property rights of citizens through land use regulations, environmental laws, historic preservation rules, and other means. Although acknowledging the value of preserving irreplaceable resources, the author argues that it is not the law, but rather the overbearing implementation of vague regulations that denies individuals their right to just compensation for lost property. He decries city and regional planning as a failure, "intellectually corrupt," and inherently biased against economic growth. He calls for reforms to the legal system, which at present unjustly imposes the costs of litigation on struggling property owners, and alternatives to government-mandated planning. The book is abundantly illustrated with brief case studies that show how individuals have been adversely affected by the laws and regulations described by the author.

Diamond, Henry L., and Patrick F. Noonan, eds. *Land Use in America.* Washington, DC: Island Press and the Lincoln Institute of Land Policy, 1996. 351 pp. ISBN 1-55963-464-2.

The editors of this book offer a broad overview of major land use issues of the past twenty-five years, chronicling the patterns and social impacts that have accompanied the urban transformation of America. This text is also designed to explore policy alternatives that promote environmental conservation, foster community values, and allow for greater fiscal sustainability into the future. It includes twelve essays from leading voices in the debate, including politicians, government officials, and activists.

Dodge, William R. *Regional Excellence: Governing Together to Compete Globally and Flourish Locally.* Washington, DC: National League of Cities, 1996. 417 pp. ISBN 1-88615-224-1.

The author, who is president of the National Association of Regional Councils and a leading advocate for regionalism, documents past efforts to foster regional cooperation among the many diverse governments that make up America's sprawling, fragmented metropolitan centers. A detailed look at several case studies illustrates just how politically complicated such arrangements can be, as well as the benefits attained when coalitions are able to foster effective regional governance.

Downs, Anthony. *New Visions for Metropolitan America.* Washington, DC: Brookings Institution, 1995. 256 pp. ISBN 0-81571-925-6.

This work provides a succinct analysis of the problems plaguing American urban areas: increased traffic congestion, air pollution, decline in affordable housing, and growing demands on taxpayers to pay for the extension of public services to cover new urban development. This is followed by a review of a number of competing policy alternatives that promise to provide a more equitable and less costly guide to future urban development.

Duany, Andres, Elizabeth Plater-Zyberk, and Jeff Speck. *Suburban Nation: The Rise of Sprawl and the Decline of the American Dream.* San Francisco, CA: North Point Press, 2000. 256 pp. ISBN 0-86547-557-1.

Three leading town planners share their opinions based on decades of experience designing new neighborhoods and inner city revitalization projects. This book provides important background analysis of the factors that shape sprawling urban development patterns along with a critical commentary of why New Urbanists find this kind of design so objectionable. Missing from these designs, they argue, is any attempt at fostering a sense of community, as well as concerns about environmental preservation and energy efficiency. Their prescription, gained from years of experimentation in dozens of projects around the country, is a neotraditional design that emphasizes pedestrian-friendly public space, easy access to mass transit, and architectural models that bring neighborhoods together in a unified whole.

Echeverria, John, and Raymond B. Eby, eds. *Let the People Judge: Wise Use and the Private Property Rights Movement.* Washington, DC: Island Press, 1995. 369 pp. ISBN 1-55963-276-3.

The Wise Use movement first organized in the Western states to fight tougher regulatory policies on federal lands. The movement has expanded in recent years to include property rights activists around the country dedicated to fighting planning mandates and other governmental regulations that are designed to combat urban sprawl. This book reviews the legal debate surrounding the takings issue, addresses the "jobs versus environment" debate, and explores the interests that have organized to support the property rights movement.

Endicott, Eve, ed. *Land Conservation through Public-Private Partnerships.* Washington, DC: Island Press, 1993. 364 pp. ISBN 1-55963-176-7.

This book provides a detailed examination of public-private partnerships that can help local governments set aside land for parks, gardens, and other uses that protect natural landscapes. It features case studies authored by participants in a variety of settings. Each case study offers practical guidelines for establishing partnerships and how to manage them successfully.

Engwicht, David. *Reclaiming Our Cities and Towns: Better Living with Less Traffic.* Gabriola Island, BC (Canada): New Society Publishers, 1993. 190 pp. ISBN 0-86571-283-2.

The author cites the detrimental impact that more traffic and automobile dependence have had on the quality of life in America's urban centers. He advocates alternatives to automobile-dependent travel, such as public transportation, new road designs, cycling, and designing roads that are more friendly to pedestrian traffic. The book includes sample bylaws and charters that cities and towns can enact to accomplish these goals.

Ewing, Reid. *Best Development Practices: Doing the Right Thing and Making Money at the Same Time.* Chicago: American Planning Association, 1996. 180 pp. ISBN 1-88482-910-4.

A leading practitioner and academic in urban planning in Florida, Ewing challenges the conventional wisdom that high-quality development costs too much money. Drawing upon case examples of some of today's most acclaimed developments, a total of forty-three "best practices" are identified for land use, transportation, environment, and housing in this practical manual designed for urban planners and architects. Case studies show how these practices make good business sense for developers, while also helping to combat the side effects of sprawl, including reducing automobile dependence, increasing the supply of affordable housing, preserving open spaces, and other important public purposes. The book is richly illustrated with photographs, charts, and sketches.

Garreau, Joel. *Edge City: Life on the New Frontier.* New York: Doubleday, 1991. 548 pp. ISBN 0-38542-434-5.

This book offers one of the most highly regarded and articulate statements on the issue of urban sprawl development in the past decade. The author chronicles the origins and development of urban residential and commercial centers on the periphery of older core cities, which he labels "edge cities." Regarding the emerging dominance of these new cities as one of the salient developments of the twentieth century, he states, "Americans decided to change just about all our routines of working, playing, and living. We created vast new urban job centers in places that only thirty years before had been residential suburbs or even corn stubble." He attributes much of the present decline of traditional downtown urban centers to public policies that subsidize and foster these new developments on the urban periphery, and also ponders the social implications connected with the new suburban communities as they have developed in metropolitan regions from Boston to Detroit, Phoenix, Dallas, and San Francisco.

Garvin, Alexander. *The American City: What Works and What Doesn't.* New York: McGraw-Hill, 1995. 640 pp. ISBN 0-07022-919-8.

This book presents a "multidisciplinary review of the many attempts to fix the American city." It explains the logic behind a wide range of municipal improvement strategies, examines classic cases of their application, and develops a framework for predicting successful project design based on six key elements. The author suggests that the key to revitalizing America's declining central cities lies in a combination of private sector initiatives, community action, and broad-based government policy. Some 250 programs and projects from 100 cities around the United States provide fertile subjects for the author's analysis, which highlights both successes and failures at urban revitalization. The book is fully illustrated throughout.

Garvin, Alexander, and Gayle Berens. *Urban Parks and Open Space.* Washington, DC: Urban Land Institute, 1997. 217 pp. ISBN 0-87420-809-2.

One method for revitalizing central-city areas is to convert derelict and neglected lots into thriving new parks. The authors cite numerous cases from around the United States where successful linear parks, community gardens, and similar efforts to create natural open-space landscapes have contributed to healthier residential neighborhoods, and fostered tourism, economic development, and other benefits in once-declining downtowns and waterfronts. The book includes practical information on financing, design, management, program development, and public-private partnerships.

Girling, Cynthia L., and Kenneth I. Helphand. *Yard, Street, Park: The Design of Suburban Open Space.* New York: John Wiley & Sons, 1994. 256 pp. ISBN 0-47117-844-6.

The authors seek to demonstrate how well-designed open space can improve suburban residential neighborhoods and protect them from the unwanted side effects of uncontrolled sprawl development. They describe how communities across the country are making use of open space networks that link neighborhood backyards with local and regional parks and greenways.

Gruen, Nina J. *Housing in Suburban Employment Centers.* Washington, DC: Urban Land Institute, 1994. 100 pp. ISBN 0-87420-765-7.

Prevailing development patterns have pushed an increasing percentage of employment opportunities out of traditional central cities and into newly emerging edge cities on the periphery. This book calls upon planners, businesses, real estate developers, and local government officials to work together in promoting higher-density housing so as to make more efficient use of finite suburban land resources. This will serve the related goals of controlling unwanted sprawl into the countryside, while also reducing commuting times and pollution, and making affordable housing more available. Four case studies are included to demonstrate the feasibility of higher-density housing in suburban locales.

Hommann, Mary. *City Planning in America: Between Promise and Despair.* Westport, CT: Praeger, 1993. 151 pp. ISBN 0-27594-473-5.

The author, a trained city planning professional with many years of experiences, shares her perspective on the role of planning in the development of American cities. She is critical of current practices that largely relegate planning to an advisory role subordinate to prevailing political processes that are too often driven by moneyed interests. The book provides a critical overview of the urban development of America's metropolitan areas and much insight into the intensely political nature of planning. Suggestions are offered based on the relative success of European planning.

Jackson, Kenneth T. *Crabgrass Frontier: The Suburbanization of the United States.* London: Oxford University, 1985. 396 pp. ISBN 0-19503-610-7.

The author offers a thorough exploration of American and European history to trace the origins of suburban-style development in the United States. This book also chronicles the post-World War II rise of suburbs that accompanied the steady decline of America's major urban areas. The book explores why citizens choose to relocate, as well as assesses the social, political, and economic effects of this trend.

Jacobs, Harvey M., ed. *Who Owns America? Social Conflict over Property Rights.* Madison, WI: University of Wisconsin, 1998. 268 pp. ISBN 0-29915-994-9.

This is a collection of critical perspectives on the property rights debate from eighteen contributors, each of whom represents leading voices around the nation in land use law, history, anthropology, economics, sociology, and environmental studies. It examines the legal and political evolution of land use rights, while also surveying current controversies over public regulation of private land, public land management, and the roles culture and ethnic values play in land use.

Katz, Peter, and Vincent Scully. *The New Urbanism: Toward an Architecture of Community.* New York: McGraw-Hill, 1994. 245 pp. ISBN 0-07033-889-2.

This fully illustrated book introduces the fundamental goals and design components of the New Urbanist movement. Numerous examples are cited from acclaimed projects such as Seaside, Florida, and Laguna West, California. For each project, the author analyzes the needs and conditions of the local community, and then demonstrates how the traditional village concept was planned and constructed to fulfill these goals.

Kay, Jane Holtz. *Asphalt Nation: How the Automobile Took Over America and How We Can Take It Back.* New York: Crown Publishers, 1997. 440 pp. ISBN 0-52021-620-2.

America's love affair with the automobile has been one of the major stimulants toward ongoing urban sprawl, as well as highway congestion and air pollution. The author calls for policies that will reverse the national dependency on automobiles. Citing successful efforts already underway across the country, an articulate argument is made that calls upon politicians, businesses, architects, and planners to end the destructive cycle.

Klein, Richard D. *Everyone Wins! A Citizens' Guide to Development.* Chicago: American Planning Association, 1990. 142 pp. ISBN 0-91828-663-8.

This book is a practical guide for community groups facing problems related to land use development pressures. The author seeks to identify solutions that do not prohibit development, but rather channel it into the most beneficial outcomes for the community as a whole. He shows how to identify goals and look for solutions, explains the development process and its legal ramifications, and gives tips on how to research an issue, organize a group, and generate support in the community.

Kunstler, James H. *The Geography of Nowhere: The Rise and Decline of America's Man-Made Landscape.* New York: Simon and Schuster, 1993. 304 pp. ISBN 0-67188-825-0.

This is one of the most influential works in recent years exposing the deep sociological problems associated with urban sprawl, along with more traditional planning concerns. It offers a stinging critique of trends leading to the rise of new suburbs and demise of traditional core cities. The author argues that this trend has had a detrimental impact on society, contributing to the erosion of community bonds and commitment. Examples are provided from a number of cities that include Detroit, Los Angeles, and Portland.

Kunstler, James H. *Home from Nowhere: Remaking Our Everyday World for the Twenty-First Century.* New York: Simon and Schuster, 1996. 318 pp. ISBN 0-68483-737-4.

In an upbeat follow-up to his earlier volume the author explores the growing movement across America to restore the quality of life and vitality of neighborhoods and communities. He offers case studies from around the country that reflect the New Urbanist emphasis on building traditional village centers.

Langdon, Philip. *A Better Place to Live: Reshaping the American Suburb.* Amherst, MA: University of Massachusetts, 1994. 270 pp. ISBN 1-55849-106-6.

The author makes a strong case for the adoption of suburban design principles associated with the New Urbanist school. He demonstrates how neighborhood-based developments that incorporate more compact town centers, wider ranges of housing choices, and walkable streets can bring about an entirely new way of life that fosters community values and cohesion. Numerous case studies are utilized to demonstrate how such neotraditional designs have been incorporated into several recent developments around the country.

Leccesse, Michael, and Kathleen McCormick, eds. *Charter of the New Urbanism.* New York: McGraw-Hill, 2000. 160 pp. ISBN 0-07135-553-7.

Over the course of the 1990s, the San-Francisco-based Congress for the New Urbanism has positioned itself as a leading source of innovation among architects and urban designers who share a common dislike for conventional urban patterns of development that foster sprawl. Their designs seek to encourage the creation of close-knit neighborhoods, energy efficiency, and environmental conservation through neotraditional patterns that fall back on principles of an earlier era. Contributors such as Andres Duany, Peter Calthorpe, and Liz Moule explain how these designs can be utilized in a variety of different projects that range from large-scale housing complexes to single streets and buildings. Developments include both new towns as well as renewal schemes for older neighborhoods. Case studies are included to help the reader better understand how these principles can be applied in a diverse number of settings.

Lewis, Paul G. *Shaping Suburbia: How Political Institutions Organize Urban Development.* Pittsburgh, PA: University of Pittsburgh Press, 1996. ISBN 0-82293-938-X.

This book explores the various political and economic forces influencing the development of American metropolitan areas. The author challenges prevailing views that dismiss the importance of local and regional political institutions in the suburbs as irrelevant. Case studies derived from an examination of suburban politics in Denver, Colorado, and Portland, Oregon, are used to illustrate how influential local institutions—however fragmented and disunited—can alter the growth dynamics of both urban regions.

Little, Charles E. *Hope for the Land.* New Brunswick, NJ: Rutgers University Press, 1992. 228 pp. ISBN 0-81351-802-4.

When America's natural landscapes and land resources are destroyed, communities are lost and lives diminished. The author, a prominent Washington activist associated with land conservation and environmental causes, argues that the land is the basis for community, drawing evidence for this thesis from the experience of many people interviewed in the book who rely upon the land and its resources for their well-being. Decrying current and past government land policy with many observations from around the country, the author offers a "land ethic" that can serve as the basis for future land use policy.

Marzulla, Nancie G., and Roger J. Marzulla. *Property Matters: Understanding Government Takings and Environmental Regulation.* Rockville, MD: Government Institute, 1997. ISBN 0-86587-554-6.

This is a highly readable handbook for those seeking to better understand the basic legal arguments being made by property rights advocates who allege that uncompensated takings occur through the enforcement of federal and state government land regulations. The book offers a wide range of analysis that covers both theoretical principles and more specific applications involving wetlands, endangered species, the federal Superfund law, mining, and land use zoning. The authors also offer an agenda of legislative solutions to rectify deficiencies in state laws that deny proper rights of property owners. Both authors have extensive legal and land management experience and are also associated with the national Defenders of Property Rights public interest legal organization.

Meltz, Robert, Dwight H. Merriam, and Richard M. Frank. *The Takings Issue: Constitutional Limits on Land-Use Control and Environmental Regulation.* Washington, DC: Island Press, 1995. 525 pp. ISBN 1-55963-380-8.

As challenges to environmental and land use controls by landowners and the property rights movement have become more frequent, the concept of takings has become increasingly important to local officials, planners, and the courts. This volume is an objective and authoritative introduction to the issues surrounding regulatory takings at the local, state, and federal levels. It addresses procedural hurdles involved in court cases, definitions of what constitutes a taking, planning and zoning issues, and remedies available to landowners and others seeking redress. The authors, all lawyers with considerable expertise in this field, provide comprehensive analyses of current legal interpretations and government enactments, and speculate about future directions—all in a clear and accessible format that makes this book valuable for nonlawyers as well as legal specialists.

Mitchell, John H. *Trespassing: An Inquiry into the Private Ownership of Land.* Reading, MA: Addison-Wesley, 1998. 295 pp. ISBN 0-20144-214-0.

This book traces the history of property ownership back into the earliest years of European settlement in America, demonstrating how concepts of land have evolved over the past four centuries. This book provides a solid context for current debates and controversies surrounding private property and the public interest.

Moe, Richard, and Carter Wilkie. *Changing Places: Rebuilding Community in the Age of Sprawl.* New York: Henry Holt, 1997. 288 pp. ISBN 0-80504-368-3.

This book offers an overview of the costs and consequences of urban sprawl, providing numerous case studies and other statistical information to support the authors' arguments. It also offers a comprehensive blueprint for alternatives to sprawl. In particular the authors stress that historic preservation of older urban areas can be utilized as an effective strategy for making central cities livable again.

Nelessen, Anton C. *Visions for a New American Dream.* Chicago: American Planning Association, 1994. 374 pp. ISBN 1-88482-900-7.

This book is an attempt to provide urban and regional planners with a practical blueprint for designing urban communities that avoid the pitfalls of sprawl. An accomplished architect and urban planner, the author draws on a number of case studies from New Jersey as the basis for outlining in detail a seven-step planning process and ten design principles that promise to create one of several different alternative communities that foster social interaction and environmental sustainability. Special attention is given to techniques aimed at creating a common community vision among rival interests found in any locality. It is fully illustrated with photographs, architectural sketches, and charts.

Newman, Peter, and Jeffrey Kenworthy. *Sustainability and Cities: Overcoming Automobile Dependence.* Washington, DC: Island Press, 1999. 464 pp. ISBN 1-55963-660-2.

The authors make the case that the essential character of a city's land use is shaped and guided by prevailing transportation grids and patterns. They provide a survey of global cities on the basis of a range of sustainability factors and indicators, showing how many urban centers are creatively overcoming transportation challenges without greater reliance on automobiles. Only by reducing dependence on automobiles will cities of the future be able successfully to combat rising social and economic problems, and promote truly sustainable development into the future.

Nivola, Pietro S. *Laws of the Landscape: How Policies Shape Cities in Europe and America.* Washington, DC: Brookings Institution, 1999. 126 pp. ISBN 0-81576-081-7.

Do we have anything to learn from the experience of European urban growth planning? This book addresses the issues of American urban development and sprawl from a comparative perspective, noting that many other industrial societies struggle with similar growth patterns. Most importantly, the author explores why policies designed to control suburban growth have actually helped induce greater sprawl in the United States, but not in Europe. He offers a critical analysis of traditional Smart Growth–inspired controls in light of policies in Europe, where more compact forms of development have long been fostered by government planners. He concludes with a series of recommendations based on both the successes and failures of European experience that include implications for tax reform, transportation policy, crime policy, education, small business development, fiscal policy, energy policy, and immigration.

Norwood, Ken, and Kathleen Smith. *Rebuilding Community in America: Housing for Ecological Living, Personal Empowerment, and the New Extended Family.* Berkeley, CA: Shared Living Resource Center, 1995. 406 pp. ISBN 0-96413-462-4.

This book calls upon architects, real estate developers, and planners to return a sense of community to America's suburban neighborhoods. It explores various types of housing that foster the ideals of community, including village clusters and cohousing. The authors offer design models, techniques, and practical suggestions for creating sustainable communities that conserve resources. The book includes case studies of both real and fictional communities.

Orfield, Myron. *Metropolitics.* Washington, DC: Brookings Institution, 1997. 245 pp. ISBN 0-81576-639-4.

Many serious problems and inefficiencies arise when adjacent local governments—divided into rich and poor, suburban and agricultural, incorporated and unincorporated—fail to work together on common problems. The author makes a strong case that only through regional cooperation can issues like infrastructural maintenance, mass transportation, education, and affordable housing be addressed fully. Extensive data and examples drawn from the successes associated with the Minneapolis–St. Paul metropolitan regional government are included.

Peirce, Neal, Curtis Johnson, and John S. Hall. *Citistates: How Urban America Can Prosper in a Competitive World.* Santa Ana, CA: Seven Locks Press. 1993. 359 pp. ISBN 0-92976-534-6.

The very nature of sprawl defies policy prescriptions confined to individual local government jurisdictions. The authors of this book examine contemporary urban challenges and see a rising age of the citistate, which includes not just a center city, but an entire metropolitan region working together to solve common problems. They explore the potential that regional cooperation could bring to many complicated interjurisdictional problems that include urban sprawl. The book includes six case studies from Phoenix, Seattle, Baltimore, Dallas, St. Paul, and Owens-boro, Kentucky. These analyses examine each region's special problems and suggest potential solutions that tap into regional resources, building up to an eight-point formula for success.

Pindell, Terry. *A Good Place to Live: America's Last Migration.* New York: Henry Holt, 1995. 432 pp. ISBN 0-80505-024-8.

Stating that the "true story of America is an unfinished quest for place and community," the author explores the American penchant for migration through history: from the Old World to the New, from settled areas to the frontier, rural areas to big cities, and ultimately the most current manifestation of this trend—the massive movement to suburbs. Citing pollution, crime, and a lost sense of community, thousands of Americans are leaving suburban life in search of a more traditional, small town environment. The author believes that such migrants are really seeking a sense of community and values they associate with this setting. Drawing vignettes from fourteen communities around the United States and Canada, he illustrates how these aspirations are fulfilled in a variety of rural, small town locales. The book underscores the culture malaise associated with much of America's urban sprawl development.

Plotkin, Sidney. *Keep Out: The Struggle for Land Use Control.* Berkeley, CA: University of California Press, 1987. 360 pp. ISBN 0-52005-806-2.

In this incisive book, the author explores the contradictions surrounding land use laws and policy issues in the United States, intoning that "we demand rights to roam free, but we reserve rights to set our land apart and keep others at bay." The book traces the increasing business disaffection with the scattered powers of urban and metropolitan land use control through the 1950s and 1960s that often thwarted corporate and state plans. He also examines the involvement of environmental organizations and inner-city activists in the 1970s who demanded changes in the status quo, and chronicles the ultimate triumph of local actors in preventing comprehensive land use reform from being implemented at the state and federal levels.

Porter, Douglas R. *Managing Growth in America's Communities.* Washington, DC: Island Press, 1997. 311 pp. ISBN 1-55963-442-1.

This book surveys the regulatory and programmatic mechanisms that have been employed around the country to better manage urban sprawl. Examples are provided from dozens of communities, as well as state and regional approaches, along with evaluations of the relative success and failure of these efforts. Brief profiles present overviews of problems, techniques implemented, outcomes, and contact information for conducting further research. Also included are informational sidebars written by leading experts in growth management and planning.

Porter, Douglas R., ed. *State and Regional Initiatives for Managing Development.* Washington, DC: Urban Land Institute, 1992. 259 pp. ISBN 0-87420-731-2.

Should states and regional governmental entities have some say in the location and character of major land development projects that will affect the economic and social well-being of tens of thousands of citizens, or should this remain an entirely local-level issue? This book explores this question in considerable detail, showing that although regional interests clearly are present, in many states decision making remains among local officials. Case studies provided by a variety of knowledgeable contributors offer an appreciation for the great variation that exists around the country in regional and state-level growth management programs.

Real Estate Research Corporation. *The Costs of Sprawl: Environmental and Economic Costs of Alternative Residential Development Patterns at the Urban Fringe.* 3 Volumes. Washington, DC: U.S. Government Printing Office, 1974.

This pioneering three-volume study was among the first comprehensive efforts to research the phenomenon of urban sprawl in the United States. The research and analysis seeks to quantify the financial costs to individuals, communities, and society at large as a result of sprawling metropolitan development patterns. The study is particularly concerned with the effects of leapfrog development, in which developers seek land beyond settled communities to avoid land use controls. It details the wasteful nature of this practice in use of land as well as the inefficiencies created in the provision of public services. The study also explores alternative development patterns that would be less costly.

Roseland, Mark. *Toward Sustainable Communities: Resources for Citizens and Their Governments.* Gabriola Island, BC

(Canada): New Society Publishers, 1998. 256 pp. ISBN 0-86571-374-X.

The author offers suggestions and innovative solutions to a wide range of municipal and neighborhood problems that are compounded by uncontrolled sprawl and development. Topics include such pressing needs as public transportation, traffic congestion, land use and housing, water and sewage provision, waste reduction and recycling, economic development, and better governance. Each chapter contains specific tools for achieving the goal of sustainable community, plus essential contacts and references.

Rusk, David. *Cities without Suburbs.* Baltimore, MD: Johns Hopkins University Press, 1993. 147 pp. ISBN 0-94387-550-1.

The former mayor of Albuquerque, New Mexico, and now a nationally recognized consultant, the author chronicles the destructive impact that sprawling suburban development has had on many of America's "inelastic" central cities over the past forty years. He argues that the ongoing decline of inner-city communities will continue as long as these urban areas are socially and economically isolated from the financial vitality and economic growth engines contained in the periphery. As a solution, the author presents an extensive argument in favor of the creation of regionwide metropolitan governments that can bridge these gaps and benefit all.

Rusk, David. *Inside Game/Outside Game: Winning Strategies for Saving Urban America.* Washington, DC: Brookings Institution Press, 1999. 384 pp. ISBN 0-81577-650-0.

In this book Rusk follows up on his earlier work with policy recommendations for declining cities that cannot seem to break out of poverty. Surrounded by sprawling suburban growth, rising concentrations of poverty within city neighborhoods, and growing fiscal strain, these cities must call upon an "outside game" that involves entire metropolitan regions. Key elements for Rusk's recommendations include regional growth management, fair-share affordable housing programs, as well as regional tax base sharing. His most important recommendation is a mandatory mixed-income housing policy for all new residential construction. His analysis cites cases where such measures have been implemented through a variety of political alliances that include business associations, faith-based coalitions, and state-level political support. Illustrations are drawn from case studies in Portland (Oregon), Montgomery County (Maryland), Dayton (Ohio), and Minneapolis–St. Paul (Minnesota).

Sadie, Moshe, and Wendy Kahn. *The City after the Automobile.* Boulder, CO: Westview, 1998. 200 pp. ISBN 0-81333-545-0.

The authors highlight the connection between automobile-dependent transportation and the growth of scattered, low-density urban and commercial sprawl. Citing growing public dissatisfaction with traffic congestion, inadequate parking, automobile maintenance costs, and eroding pedestrian life, they offer a future vision based on rapid, automated, and efficient transportation systems. A number of new technologies are discussed that greatly expand the boundaries of traditional dialogue on this subject.

Schneekloth, Linda H., and Robert G. Shibley. *Placemaking: The Art and Practice of Building Communities.* New York: John Wiley & Sons, 1995. 263 pp. ISBN 0-87420-851-3.

The authors decry the demise of older downtowns, the blight and neglect of inner cities, and the sterility of newer suburban commercial and residential development on the periphery. All promoted what they describe as a disconnection between people and the built environment that surrounds them, thereby fostering a host of social ills. This book advocates "placemaking," a practice that helps both citizens and planners work together to create places that support economic development and social harmony in communities.

Sexton, Richard, and Ray Oldenburg. *Parallel Utopias: The Quest for Community.* San Francisco: Chronicle Books, 1995. 195 pp. ISBN 0-81180-547-6.

A devastating critique is offered of sprawling real estate developments that are designed to cater to automobile-dependent transportation on the periphery of America's cities. The authors suggest that alternatives are possible that still provide urban convenience to residents and actually enhance the quality of life through greater communion with nature. Examples from two communities in California and Florida are offered, along with lavish illustrations and photographs.

Shaw, Jane S., and Ronald D. Utt, eds. *A Guide to Smart Growth: Shattering Myths, Providing Solutions.* Washington, DC: Heritage Foundation, 2000. 166 pp. ISBN 0-89195-088-5.

Two conservative scholars offer an edited collection of essays that examine the issue of urban sprawl and Smart Growth proposals advocated by many liberal organizations. The various authors provide a critical evaluation of the causes of sprawl, as well as the policy implications of proposals such as growth boundaries, subsidized mass transit, higher-density development, and the like. Full chapters are devoted to issues such as zoning law reform and traffic congestion. The book also offers a reevaluation of the supposed success of Smart Growth initiatives in Portland, Oregon, and Atlanta, Georgia, illustrating where these policies have gone awry, and what needs to be done to correct them.

Sies, Mary Corbin, and Christopher Silver. *Planning the Twentieth-Century American City.* Baltimore, MD: Johns Hopkins University Press, 1996. 594 pp. ISBN 0-80185-164-5.

The authors explore how the built environment of the modern American city was developed over the previous one hundred years. They illustrate how rational planning strategies have often given way to social, political, economic, ideological, bureaucratic, and environmental forces. The book provides detailed background and context information that is necessary for truly understanding the present dilemmas faced by America's growing metropolitan areas.

Simons, Robert A. *Turning Brownfields into Greenbacks.* Washington, DC: Urban Land Institute, 1998. 181 pp. ISBN 0-87420851-3.

One major stimulus encouraging sprawl is serious environmental contamination found in abandoned or underutilized industrial lands. With the use of subsidies, incentives, and other inducements, developers can be attracted back to central cities to foster new economic opportunities. The author describes how city governments can navigate federal and state regulations, secure financing and loan guarantees, reduce liability, and undertake remediation of polluted sites. Illustrations are contained in thirteen case studies, each of which provides practical models and strategies for success.

Smith, Herbert H. *Planning America's Communities: Paradise Found? Paradise Lost?* Chicago: American Planning Association, 1991. 262 pp. ISBN 0-91828-671-9.

The author, an experienced planning professional, offers a report card on the successes and failures of planning in the United States. He examines fifteen cities around the country, focusing on how state and federal governments affect planning, the performance of professional planners, and the involvement of public officials and citizens in the process. Other variables considered in this analysis involve the impact of local economies, taxation, and the courts. This book greatly assists general audiences in learning how planning fits into public policy and where it is leading the country.

Stokes, Samuel N., A. Elizabeth Watson, and Shelley S. Mastran. *Saving America's Countryside.* 2d ed. Baltimore, MD: John Hopkins University Press, 1997. 496 pp. ISBN 0-80185-547-0.

This book illustrates how citizens and activist groups can successfully protect natural, scenic, and agricultural landscapes of rural communities from encroaching urban sprawl. It provides step-by-step instructions for organizing a community, inventorying resources, setting up land trusts, passing local land protection ordinances, and obtaining outside funding. Examples from across the United States demonstrate how rural communities are able successfully to preserve valuable natural resources.

Teaford, Jon C. *Post-Suburbia: Government and Politics in the Edge Cities.* Baltimore, MD: Johns Hopkins University Press, 1997. 210 pp. ISBN 0-80185-450-4.

The author explores the political dimensions of the new "edge cities" that have developed on the periphery of major metropolitan areas. It discusses the adaptation of county units of government to the ideals and demands of residents who have come to the metropolitan fringe for opportunity and fulfillment—a desire for low taxes, high-quality schools, locally available shopping, and new roads to ease commuting times. Six case studies are used to illustrate these newly emerging political patterns, including Suffolk and Nassau Counties in New York; Oakland County, Michigan; DuPage County, Illinois; Saint Louis County, Missouri; and Orange County, California.

Thomas, G. Scott. *The United States of Suburbia: How the Suburbs Took Control of America and What They Plan to Do with It.* Amherst, NY: Prometheus Books, 1998. 290 pp. ISBN 1-57392-243-9.

This book chronicles the dramatic shift in political power from central cities to suburbs that has taken place over the previous four decades. The author provides population data, as well as detailed analyses of socioeconomic and political trends to support his contention that the distinctive values and outlook of suburban residents will dominate politics into the future.

Tiner, Ralph W. *In Search of Swampland: A Wetland Sourcebook and Field Guide.* Rutgers, NJ: Rutgers University Press, 1998. 380 pp. ISBN 0-81352-506-3.

Environmental regulations require all new urban development to be in harmony with the preservation of sensitive wetlands. This has triggered many controversies and court battles in areas experiencing growth pressures and sprawl development patterns. This book serves as a much-needed field guide to wetlands ecology and identification. Richly illustrated and including full, nontechnical explanations, it examines the primary causes of wetland degradation and loss and suggests specific techniques to save these fragile and threatened areas.

Van Vliet, William, ed. *Affordable Housing and Urban Redevelopment in the United States.* Thousand Oaks, CA: Sage Publications, 1997. 288 pp. ISBN 0-80397-050-1.

A number of American cities have successfully met the challenges of providing affordable housing and redeveloping urban areas in spite of reduced federal funding and ongoing suburban sprawl. Nine informative case studies illustrate lessons learned from flourishing projects in Chicago, New York, Boston, Cleveland, Baltimore, and Los Angeles. Successes are attributable to several key elements that include joint venture projects, neighborhood coalition building, innovative financing mechanisms, nonprofit activity, community participation, and successful planning design.

Varady, David P., and Jeffrey A. Raffel. *Selling Cities.* New York: State University of New York Press, 1995. 367 pp. ISBN 0-79142-558-4.

Much of the urban sprawl phenomenon is attributable to the on-going flight of high- and middle-income citizens out of the older central cities and into the periphery. The authors maintain that the key to revitalizing America's central cities lies in attracting and retaining middle-class homeowners through the revitalization of urban schools and more widespread availability of affordable housing. They analyze case studies of cities that have established magnet schools, tax abatements, low-rate mortgage programs, and other instruments to lure the middle class away from the distant suburbs and back to the city.

Weitz, Jerry. *Sprawl Busting: State Programs to Guide Growth.* Chicago: American Planning Association Press, 1999. 376 pp. ISBN 1-88482-928-7.

As public concern over the effects of sprawl grows, planners, developers, and public officials alike are talking about the potential merits of Smart Growth laws. Can we learn from the experience of state laws that have already been in place for decades? This book provides a thorough review of four statewide growth management programs in Oregon, Georgia, Washington, and Florida. For those seeking to advocate growth management elsewhere, the author provides lessons on how to craft legislation, set up administrative structures, and build political support among local and county governments for state-mandated land use planning.

Wentling, James. *Designing a Place Called Home: Reordering the Suburbs.* New York: John Wiley & Sons, 1995. 290 pp. ISBN 0-47129-389-X.

How can architects and planners make new homes and suburban communities more responsive to humanistic needs, particularly in light of constant pressures to keep housing prices down? This book provides an architect's opinions on the design flaws associated with suburban production homes that make up all but a fraction of America's new housing stock in sprawling suburban areas. He argues that suburban architects and developers have been unduly influenced by the automobile at the expense of pedestrian traffic, thus neglecting features that would foster community values. Alternative planning and housing designs are offered that promise to integrate architecture with community, enhance environmental preservation, and halt the worst effects of sprawl. This book is well illustrated with architectural plans, layouts, and photographs.

Wilson, Alex. *Green Development: Integrating Ecology and Real Estate.* New York: John Wiley & Sons, 1998. 528 pp. ISBN 0-47118-878-6.

Real estate developers have traditionally been at odds with environmentalists and community groups in pushing for acceptance of their sprawl-inducing projects. This book suggests that such conflicts are not inevitable, citing numerous development practices that restore habitats, revitalize communities, and still earn profits. Over one hundred cases and projects are included to illustrate how environmentally friendly development can enhance community values and mitigate the worst side effects of sprawl.

Yandle, Bruce, ed. *Land Rights: The 1990s' Property Rights Rebellion.* Lanham, MD: Rowman and Littlefield, 1995. 333 pp. ISBN 0-84768-029-0.

This edited text provides extensive insight into the legal and political arguments of the property rights movement. Contributors offer well-researched essays that provide background on environmental protection laws, reviews of several key cases dealing with regulatory takings, and speculation on the future of this debate among rival groups, both in the courts and the arena of electoral politics.

Zovanyi, Gabor. *Growth Management for a Sustainable Future: Ecological Sustainability as the New Growth Management Focus for the 21st Century.* Westport, CT: Praeger, 1998. 221 pp. ISBN 0-27596-135-4.

The author traces the origins of growth management movements around the country over the past thirty years, assessing why these efforts have been so ineffective at stemming environmentally harmful growth. He evaluates local and state growth management controls, the involvement of professional planners, and the courts, finding that each has worked to accommodate growth in ways that only worsen political conflict while failing to combat environmentally harmful outcomes. He concludes that the principle of ecological sustainability must become the primary focus of future growth management efforts. Only when new developments are downsized and redesigned to accommodate ecological sustainability will growth management truly meet its lofty goals.

Reports and Monographs

American Farmland Trust. *Farming on the Edge.* Washington, DC: American Farmland Trust, 1997. 80 pp.

This report offers a summary of the views and positions of America's leading farm preservation organization. It vividly demonstrates how urban sprawl development is leading to the loss of irreplaceable, fertile agricultural lands as well as threatening an entire sector of the United States economy. The twenty most threatened agricultural regions in the nation are identified and analyzed. The report includes information on the Geographic Information Systems methodology used to analyze land patterns and extensive discussion of issues surrounding farmland loss, as well as research and policy recommendations.

Bank of America. *Beyond Sprawl: New Patterns of Growth to Fit the New California.* San Francisco: Bank of America, 1995. 53 pp.

This report was sponsored by a diverse coalition that included the California Resources Agency, Bank of America, the Greenbelt Alliance, and the Low Income Housing Fund, and reflects an emerging consensus in the key state of California about the dangers of sprawl development. The report details how traditional land development patterns in this state have led to mostly unplanned patterns of sprawl, rising pollution, loss of prime agricultural lands, and threats to environmentally sensitive areas. Interestingly, the report links these problems to a higher cost of doing business in the state, losses in worker productivity, and underutilized investments in older urban communities. Rather than recommending limitations on future growth, the report issues a "call for California to be smarter about how it grows—to invent ways we can create compact and efficient growth patterns that are responsive to the needs of people at all income levels, and also help maintain California's quality of life and economic competitiveness." This report was deeply influential in the formation of the Smart Growth movement that has dominated the debates surrounding urban sprawl in recent years.

Bauer, David, Taylor Bowlden, Bill Buff, Christian Klein, Loren Sweatt, Jay Hansen, Paul Haaland, Frank Moretti, and Bill Outlaw. *Building Better Communities: A Toolkit for Quality Growth.* Washington, DC: The Quality Growth Coalition, 1999. 81 pp.

What is the best way to deal with worsening road congestion, pollution, and loss of open space associated with urban sprawl? Should America's longstanding habit of continually expanding its highway and road system be dramatically changed? Sponsored by a coalition of groups that include the American Highway Users Alliance and the American Road and Transportation Builders Association, this monograph offers what its writers describe as "common sense solutions that will work" to balance these concerns with the ongoing need to expand and improve the national transportation system, promote economic growth, and honor the rights of citizens to be free to choose their own means of travel. It provides background information, case studies, and policy recommendations for alternatives to the Smart Growth agenda.

Beaumont, Constance. *Challenging Sprawl: Organizational Responses to a National Problem.* Washington, DC: National Trust for Historic Preservation, 1999. 112 pp.

Debates over urban development were once dominated by environmental groups arguing with real estate developers. This is no longer the case though, according to the author of this report. She documents the many different voices of the growing movement against sprawl, demonstrating that the new consensus over development represented by the Smart Growth movement includes not only environmental groups, but also business executives, religious leaders, politicians from both major political parties, academics, and governmental officials from all levels.

Bollier, David. *How Smart Growth Can Stop Sprawl: A Briefing Guide for Funders.* Washington, DC: Essential Books, 1998. 69 pp.

This report is designed to alert private foundations of the causes and dangers that urban sprawl poses for the United States if present trends continue. It provides a concise overview of the subject of urban sprawl. It describes how government subsidies encourage urban disinvestment, automobile dependence, racial polarization and residential segregation, environmental harm, and a loss of community life. It then reviews many different strategies that offer hope for revitalizing older communities and arresting urban sprawl.

Burgess, Patricia. *Revisiting "Sprawl": Lessons from the Past.* Cleveland, OH: Maxine Goodman Levin College of Urban Affairs at Cleveland State University, 1998. 41 pp.

The recent debate surrounding urban sprawl is not the first time in American history that concerns have been expressed about metropolitan and regional development patterns. This monograph examines the current controversies over land use zoning, urban growth patterns, and environmental conservation in light of past eras when these issues attracted widespread public attention and policy action. The author concludes with several lessons from the past that present-day participants would be wise to consider.

Cox, Wendell. *The President's New Sprawl Initiative: A Program in Search of a Problem.* Heritage Foundation Backgrounder Report No. 1263. Washington, DC: Thomas A. Roe Institute for Economic Policy Studies, 1999. 11 pp.

This report from the ideologically conservative Heritage Foundation offers one of the most comprehensive rebuttals to date of both President Bill Clinton's Livable Communities Initiative and the host of critics of urban sprawl. The author contends that many of the claims of antisprawl planning advocates are unfounded regarding the loss of open space. They also challenge the assumption that the general public is largely discontent with urban living and looking for alternatives. Further, the report counters that New Urbanist-inspired proposals that call for higher-density, compact development and greater reliance on mass transit would only worsen environmental problems.

Edgens, Jefferson, Gerard C. Mildner, and Samuel R. Staley. *A Line in the Land: Urban Growth Boundaries, Smart Growth, and Housing Affordability.* Policy Study No. 263. Washington, DC: Reason Public Policy Institute, 2000. 54 pp.

More than 100 cities and countries have adopted some form of growth boundary to curb sprawl and protect open space from development. This study examines several representative case studies of growth boundaries that include Portland, Oregon; Boulder County, Colorado; and Lancaster County, Pennsylvania, to test whether such mechanisms actually accomplish the goals intended. The report concludes that growth boundaries have not achieved their supporters' objectives, mainly due to contrary public preferences and market forces. Further, they argue that growth boundaries have negative side-effects that force up housing and land prices that reduce housing affordability.

Hirschhorn, Joel. *Growing Pains: Quality of Life in the New Economy.* Washington, DC: National Governors' Association, 2000. 68 pp.

This report was compiled at the request of the nation's governors to provide an assessment of the impact that a decade of rapid economic growth has had on the quality of life in America's urban centers and the potential dangers this holds for future economic prosperity. This monograph provides a concise summary of relevant data on topics such as traffic congestion, environmental quality, loss of open space, and attendant costs to state government. It also provides an overview of growth management programs in place across the country and the problems with fragmented planning administered by local governments. The author offers a strong recommendation in favor of enhanced planning and better coordination to manage growth pressures as a means for warding off future costs.

Holcombe, Randall G. *Florida's Growth Management Experiment.* Tallahassee, FL: James Madison Institute, 1994. 14 pp.

This policy study summarizes the main controversies surrounding Florida's landmark 1985 statewide growth management legislation that was aimed at controlling sprawl across the state. The study shows that regulations encouraging more compact urban development, comprehensive planning, and other growth controls have been relatively ineffective, while at the same time increasing development and housing costs for Floridians.

Maine State Planning Office. *The Cost of Sprawl.* Augusta, ME: Executive Department, 1997. 20 pp.

This report charts the path of urban development in Maine from 1960 to 1990. It indicates that although the state population has not increased dramatically, the extent of developed urban land has markedly increased in a sprawl-like pattern. The study contends that this kind of development has had several detrimental consequences for the state, including increased local and state taxes, overextended public services, and higher rates of pollution and resource depletion. It has left older cities and town centers saddled with declining populations and underused infrastructures. The report concludes with a call for greater investment in town and city centers and the promotion of regional planning solutions.

Morandi, Larry, and Phyllis Myers. *New Directions in Growth Management: Incentives for Land Conservation.* Washington, DC: National Association of State Legislators, 1998. 23 pp. ISBN 1-55516-770-5.

Interest is growing in voluntary approaches to harmonizing development needs and conservation of critical land resources. Such approaches envision a larger, more flexible role for state and local governments to balance growth and conservation. The authors respond to these new directions by providing information about recently enacted state and local measures that encourage voluntary, community-driven, and incentive-based techniques; how and where these are being proposed and applied; and the outcomes of these initiatives.

National Association of Home Builders. *Statement of Policy on Smart Growth.* Washington, DC: NAHB, 1999. 23 pp.

The National Association of Home Builders represents the home-building profession in the United States. As such, it has a great deal to say regarding Smart Growth policy initiatives that are designed to place some restrictions on real estate development. The report reaffirms the NAHB's support for orderly and predictable development through the greater use of long-term comprehensive planning and reaffirms the need for open space environmental conservation. However, it firmly rejects proposals that would restrict free markets, discourage consumer choice, or unfairly place the cost of infrastructure on developers.

National Association of Realtors. *Meeting the Challenge of Growth: A Blueprint for Realtor Action.* Washington, DC: National Association of Realtors, 2000. 24 pp.

This report is both a guidebook for members of the National Association of Realtors and an informational resource for the general public regarding antisprawl measures either adopted or being considered for legislative enactment by state and local governments across the United States. The report advises against heavy-handed regulation that "may distort real estate markets, limit choice and make homes less affordable." It cites the results of its own extensive national consumer survey that indicates most Americans are wary of more regulatory controls on land use, preferring local control over land use decisions and the use of incentives and marketplace forces to help manage growth.

Office of the President of the United States. *Building Livable Communities: A Report from the Clinton-Gore Administration.* Available online at http://www.livablecommunities.gov/ report2k.htm. 1999. 22 pp.

This report provides a detailed summary of the federal initiatives launched under President Bill Clinton's Livable Communities program. Its aim is to "provide communities with tools, information, and resources that they can use to enhance their quality of life, ensure their economic competitiveness, and build a stronger sense of community." Based on the findings of the Community Empowerment Board and the President's Council on Sustainable Development, the Livable Communities program pulls together resources from more than a dozen federal agencies that influence patterns of urban growth by helping to ease traffic congestion, preserve farmland and other open spaces, and revitalize declining urban neighborhoods. These initiatives were included in the president's fiscal 2000 budget proposals.

O'Toole, Randal. *The Vanishing Automobile and Other Urban Myths.* Oak Grove, OR: Thoreau Institute, 1996. 64 pp.

This monograph appeared as a special issue of *Different Drummer,* the quarterly journal of the Thoreau Institute. It offers a critical assessment of growth management policies in Oregon. The author contends that present laws, as well as new proposals pushing for light rail systems, greater housing densities, and further extensions of urban growth boundaries, are objectionable because they only invite more involvement from state government into the private lives of citizens. Further, it is argued that these proposals will, in the end, only exacerbate sprawl by inadvertently encouraging leapfrog development into the more distant rural countryside. The report offers a set of alternative proposals that rely on incentives rather than planning dictates to deter sprawl and cut back pollution.

Planners Advisory Service. *Performance Standards for Growth Management.* Chicago: American Planning Association, 1996. 45 pp.

Increasing numbers of communities are adopting performance standards to control the effects of proposed developments and limit sprawl. This report from the American Planning Association explores the effectiveness of such measures in stopping sprawl, as well as problems that often arise when land developers must adhere to such rules. Six essays develop a variety of useful ideas and suggestions on point systems, threshold standards, adequate public facility ordinances, and other performance standards to guide local planners and politicians. The report also examines key legal issues related to performance standards, and is fully illustrated with charts and diagrams.

Planners Advisory Service. *The Principles of Smart Development.* Chicago: American Planning Association, 1998. 80 pp.

This report prepared by the American Planning Association is designed for communities facing the challenge of accommodating urban growth pressures in a way that fosters economic development. Five principles are identified as being critical for citizens to consider, each of which is given substantial analysis and tips for implementation. Case studies effectively demonstrate how each of these principles can be useful in solving real-world development dilemmas faced by communities around the United States.

Planners Advisory Service. *Staying Inside the Lines: Urban Growth Boundaries.* Chicago: American Planning Association, 1992. 30 pp.

The American Planning Association has published this report to educate the general public about the advantages of urban growth boundaries as a means for minimizing the impact of urban growth pressures. It explains exactly how urban growth boundaries can concentrate new development within mapped areas to ensure efficient delivery of public services, preserve more open land, protect farmland, and prevent costly side effects of sprawl. The report defines different types of urban growth areas, discusses the criteria for mapping boundaries, and tells how to make the boundaries workable through zoning regulations. It features case studies from four states that have adopted growth boundaries to illustrate how these principles work in practice.

Staley, Samuel. *The Sprawling of America: In Defense of the Dynamic City.* Policy Study No. 251. Los Angeles, CA: Reason Public Policy Institute, 1999. 60 pp.

The author, a leading conservative economist, offers a critical evaluation of state growth management programs that have been designed to protect farmland and open space from sprawl. He offers a thorough review of the debates on these issues along with some of his own original research on land use patterns in the United States. He concludes that low-density development and suburbanization do not significantly threaten the quality of life for most people, and makes a case in favor of relying on real estate markets rather than comprehensive planning to bring about the best outcomes for society.

Staley, Samuel, and Lynn Scarlett. *Market-Oriented Planning: Principles and Tools.* Policy Study No. 236. Los Angeles, CA: Reason Public Policy Institute, 1997. 40 pp.

This report offers a critical analysis of current urban planning practices in the United States. It argues that the vagaries of the rezoning process and uncertainties associated with local and/or state review create unnecessary costs and delays, inhibiting investment in land over time. The authors also find that the permitting process is so time consuming that developers have much less time to devote to more important issues like planning. They conclude that urban planning and land use regulation would better meet public expectations and preferences if market forces were given a greater role to play. Several specific recommendations are included to support market-oriented planning reforms.

United States Environmental Protection Agency. *EPA's Framework for Community-Based Environmental Protection.* Washington, DC: Office of Reinvention, 1999. 26 pp.

This report reflects a growing consensus in the federal Environmental Protection Agency that ongoing problems with pollution, environmental degradation, and urban sprawl cannot be addressed effectively through traditional, top-down, command-and-control approaches to regulatory enforcement. Rather, the agency is reorienting its programs toward a more localized and inclusive strategy that involves stakeholders coming together to identify concerns, set priorities, and implement comprehensive solutions. This new approach is intended to be grounded at the community level, and reflect local values, perceptions, and priorities. It also is designed to foster awareness among communities that national environmental problems are connected to local land use development decisions and planning.

United States General Accounting Office. *Community Development: Extent of Federal Influence on "Urban Sprawl" Is Unclear.* Washington, DC: GAO Resources, Community and Economic Development Division, April 1999. 85 pp.

This report was prepared by the General Accounting Office in response to a request by the U.S. Senate to research the origins of urban sprawl, explore to what degree federal programs have an effect on this phenomenon, and make recommendations for federal policy. It acknowledges that a great deal of anecdotal evidence exists tying federal government policies with the influences of urban sprawl through specific programs, taxation, and regulation. However, the report does not recognize existing quantitative research as conclusive, and therefore does not uniformly endorse such claims. Rather, it states that "the level of federal influence is difficult to determine."

Wisconsin Strategic Growth Task Force. *Land Use Issues Facing Wisconsin.* Volume 1. Madison, Wisconsin. December 1995. 61 pp.

This report offers an extensive overview of land development patterns in Wisconsin. It explores the role of state agencies and local governments in land use, reviews property rights concerns, and the necessity for informed local land decisions. It recommends that the state define a land use "vision," allow and encourage tax-base sharing tools among neighboring communities, discourage local governments from adopting minimum standards for infrastructure and home building, and promotes land use planning by all levels of government.

Young, Dwight. *Alternatives to Sprawl.* Cambridge, MA: Lincoln Institute of Land Policy, 1995. 32 pp. ISBN 0-81579-687-0.

This report from the Lincoln Institute of Land Policy explores alternatives to the prevailing pattern of low-density housing and the sprawl patterns of development that result. Extensive use of graphics and charts help to illustrate some of the most promising methods now being utilized around the country.

8

Selected Nonprint Resources

Videocassettes

The Air We Breathe

Type:	Videocassette
Length:	48 minutes
Date:	1996
Cost:	$150.00
Source:	Bullfrog Films
	P.O. Box 149
	Oley, PA 19547
	(800) 543-3764
	http://www.bullfrogfilms.com

This documentary production calls attention to the serious public hazards created by air pollution, and closely links these problems to prevailing suburban development patterns. Filmed in several major urban centers in Canada and the United States, this film explores how "political choices and sociocultural forces" have led to a worsening crisis in air quality, including the overriding dependence on automobile transportation and urban sprawl development. Through the testimony of scientists, activists, and urban planners, the film also seeks to outline solutions that include alternative fuels, zero-emission vehicles, and integrated public transit options. Case studies are offered of steps some cities are taking to combat air pollution.

Back against the Wall

Type:	Videocassette
Length:	18 minutes
Date:	1997
Cost:	$10.00

Source: Vermont Natural Resources Council
9 Bailey Avenue
Montpelier, VT 05602
(802) 223-2328

Created by the Preservation Trust of Vermont, this film reviews the impacts of superstore development on vulnerable local economies, urban patterns, and the social fabric. The video calls upon communities to plan for their future development as a strategy for fighting the forces of urban sprawl.

Beyond Sprawl
Type: Videocassette
Length: 15 minutes
Date: 1997
Cost: $42.00
Source: Planners Book Service
American Planning Association
122 S. Michigan Avenue
Suite 1600
Chicago, IL 60603
(312) 786-6344
(312) 431-9985 (fax)
BookService@planning.org
http://www.planning.org

This video, produced by the Chesapeake Bay Local Government Advisory Committee, highlights six strategies that have been utilized in the Chesapeake Bay watershed region to combat sprawl by protecting natural resources, preserving farmland, and revitalizing rural and small-town economies. Featured in the video are urban growth boundaries, infill development, transit-oriented development, transfer of development rights, rural clustering, and traditional neighborhood development. Each technique is clearly explained with live action and graphics to facilitate the adoption of these methods in other parts of the country.

Brownfields Redevelopment
Type: Videocassette
Length: 17 minutes
Date: 1998
Cost: $9.95
Source: International City Management Association
777 North Capitol Street, NE

Suite #500
Washington, DC 20002
(202) 962-3680
(202) 962-3565 (fax)
http://bookstore.icma.org

This video is designed to educate local government officials and citizens about the possibilities for revitalizing declining urban areas through the redevelopment of polluted industrial sites. A case study of New Orleans shows how cities can successfully use brownfields redevelopment to spur new opportunities in economically depressed low-income neighborhoods that have long been neglected. Through the use of specific examples, viewers learn how New Orleans created a consortium of stakeholders and used local government to promote justice and opportunity. Narrated by Ellis Marsalis.

Challenge of Change
Type: Videocassette
Length: 15 minutes
Date: 1990
Cost: $25.25
Source: Planners Book Service
               American Planning Association
               122 S. Michigan Avenue
               Suite 1600
               Chicago, IL 60603
               (312) 786-6344
               (312) 431-9985 (fax)
               BookService@planning.org
               http://www.planning.org

This is a documentary-style video developed by the American Institute of Certified Planners that focuses on how urban planning works and why it can provide long-term benefits to communities. Illustrations are drawn from four case studies. Planners in Oakland County, Michigan, helped the people of a sprawling residential area known as Lodi develop a new community commercial and governmental center while also preserving natural landscapes. Planning in Austin, Texas, helped protect the city water supply from urban growth pressures that were encouraging erosion and pollution. San Diego used a long-range transportation plan to develop a light rail system. And in Boston, community planners encouraged city officials to use linkage fees on new development projects to provide funding for the refurbishment of buildings that had been incorporated into an affordable housing project.

Community as a Learning Resource
Type: Videocassette and curriculum materials
Length: 45 minutes
Date: 1994
Cost: $69.00
Source: Planners Book Service
           American Planning Association
           122 S. Michigan Avenue, Suite 1600
           Chicago, IL 60603
           (312) 786-6344
           (312) 431-9985 (fax)
           BookService@planning.org
           http://www.planning.org

This package developed by leading planner Ramona K. Mullahey is designed to teach young adults about the increasing importance of planning in American communities. Students are made aware of the problems that arise in communities when proper planning is neglected, including traffic congestion, air pollution, and a lack of affordable housing. The curriculum guide is full of ideas and hands-on exercises to help educators teach about the built environment and planning. The exercises can be customized to a range of skill and age levels. The video highlights instructional resources on community planning and development.

Conserving Rural Character and Open Space through Innovative Land Use Techniques
Type: Videocassette slide show
Length: 60 minutes
Date: 1989
Cost: $125.00
Source: Planners Book Service
           American Planning Association
           122 S. Michigan Avenue, Suite 1600
           Chicago, IL 60603
           (312) 786-6344
           (312) 431-9985 (fax)
           BookService@planning.org
           http://www.planning.org

Leading planner and land preservation activist Randell Arendt has traveled the country showing his slide presentation and popularizing the notion of balancing conservation ideals with land development. This videocassette contains the entire slide show. It provides a review of innovative land use planning techniques that are designed to protect and preserve open space from encroaching urban sprawl. It focuses on how to use open-space zoning to conserve rural landscapes, control roadside commercial development, provide affordable housing, and restrict lakefront/riverfront development.

Costs of Sprawl
Type: Videocassette
Length: 180 minutes
Date: 1996
Cost: $59.95
Source: Planners Book Service
American Planning Association
122 S. Michigan Avenue, Suite 1600
Chicago, IL 60603
(312) 786-6344
(312) 431-9985 (fax)
BookService@planning.org
http://www.planning.org

A panel of leading experts discusses the far-reaching costs of residential and commercial developments that lead to sprawl. Explanations are provided for how sprawl affects transportation, financial resources, land use, social equity, natural landscapes, and the overall quality of life for suburban dwellers. It was developed by the Planning Commissioner Service of the American Planning Association.

Dilemmas of Development
Type: Videocassette and curriculum materials
Length: 20 minutes
Date: 1990
Cost: $55.00
Source: Planners Book Service
American Planning Association
122 S. Michigan Avenue, Suite 1600
Chicago, IL 60603
(312) 786-6344

(312) 431-9985 (fax)
BookService@planning.org
http://www.planning.org

Developed by the Urban Land Institute, this set of instructional materials provides the tools to create an entire high school social studies curriculum on planning and land development. It includes extensive materials that introduce students to planning theory, design concepts, and the tools of land use regulation. Materials include a variety of instructional aids, site maps, and text, in addition to video. It is designed to highlight the tradeoffs implicit in any land use policy decision.

Farmland Forever
Type: Videocassette
Length: 17 minutes
Date: 1991
Cost: $20.00
Source: American Farmland Trust
            1200 18th Street, NW, Suite 800
            Washington, DC 20036
            (800) 370-4879
            (413) 586-9332 (fax)
            info@farmland.org
            http://www.farmland.org

This documentary video shares the stories of many farmers facing difficulties due to encroaching urban development pressures. It also demonstrates how profitable farming can be sustained through the selling of conservation easements. Filmed on both coasts, the video dispels myths about these programs—for example, that farmers who sell easements are not eligible for credit or that they don't apply to certain types of farming. Produced for America's leading agricultural preservation advocates by Florentine Films, it provides a valuable resource for any person seeking more information about conservation easement programs.

Land Use and Building the American Community
Type: Videocassette
Length: 60 minutes
Date: 1996
Cost: $75.00
Source: Planners Book Service

American Planning Association
122 S. Michigan Avenue, Suite 1600
Chicago, IL 60603
(312) 786-6344
(312) 431-9985 (fax)
BookService@planning.org
http://www.planning.org

This video is a primer on New Urbanism planning and design techniques from Peter Calthorpe, one of the leading voices and practitioners in the movement. The video chronicles how planners have helped to create more livable, functional communities across the country through the creation of economically diverse housing with easy access to work, play, and school. Published under the auspices of the Rocky Mountain Land Use Institute.

Mega-Cities: Innovation for Urban Life
Type: Videocassette
Length: 28 minutes
Date: 1997
Cost: $39.95
Source: Video Project
                  5332 College Avenue, Suite 101
                  Oakland, CA 94618
                  (510) 655-9050
                  (510) 655-9115 (fax)
                  videoproject@igc.apc.org
                  http://www.videoproject.org

This video illustrates nine creative solutions for urban problems put forth by the Planning Group of the Los Angeles Mega-Cities Project. The subjects of study are twenty-three mega-cities around the world that contain ten million or more people each, all of which face similar problems trying to create economic opportunity, control urban congestion, and contain sprawl. The video demonstrates the potential of urban leadership programs that teach neighborhood activists to replicate successful planning projects in their own communities.

New Urbanism: Market, Myth, and Reality
Type: Videocassette
Length: 75 minutes
Date: 1997
Cost: $75.00

Source: Planners Book Service
American Planning Association
122 S. Michigan Avenue, Suite 1600
Chicago, IL 60603
(312) 786-6344
(312) 431-9985 (fax)
BookService@planning.org
http://www.planning.org

The New Urbanist vision for America's communities has been embraced by many mainstream planners and designers. But advocates and detractors are still engaged in an ongoing debate over whether this concept can truly accomplish all that it promises. This video examines these arguments in light of the experiences of several New Urbanist projects from around the country. Developed by Benjamin Herman and James Constantine of the Rocky Mountain Land Use Institute.

Planning Education Kids Style
Type: Videocassette and curriculum materials
Length: 18 minutes
Date: 1994
Cost: $35.00
Source: Planners Book Service
American Planning Association
122 S. Michigan Avenue, Suite 1600
Chicago, IL 60603
(312) 786-6344
(312) 431-9985 (fax)
BookService@planning.org
http://www.planning.org

This resource was designed for middle school–aged children and includes instructional materials to assist teachers in putting together an introduction to planning and urban design concepts. Hands-on classroom activities allow students to put these ideas into practice by designing buildings and urban layouts. The video offers an example of how one school used this model curriculum. Produced by Nancy Benziger Brown of the American Planning Association, Tennessee Chapter.

Rethinking Suburban Sprawl
Type: Videocassette
Length: 60 minutes

Date: 1996
Cost: $20.00
Source: DPZ Architects and Town Planners
            1023 S.W. 25th Avenue
            Miami, FL 33135
            (305) 644-1023

This film offers a critical commentary on urban development patterns and architectural designs that have evolved since 1945. Narrated by Andres Duany, one of the leading proponents and practitioners of New Urbanist design, it offers a series of recommendations to restore the fabric of community and promote civility in our urban landscapes.

Road to the Future

Type: Videocassette
Length: 58 minutes
Date: 1997
Cost: $89.95
Source: Films for the Humanities and Sciences
            P.O. Box 2053
            Princeton, NJ 08543
            custserv@films.com
            http://www.films.com

This program is from the award-winning "Coming and Going" series that covers the ways in which travel and transportation have influenced the way people in the United States live. Its scope reaches back into past history, studies current trends, and covers projections about the future. In this episode transportation is linked to the growth and development of four major cities. Los Angeles offers an example of the link between sprawling urban development and unfettered ribbons of superhighways, and the problems that this has created. Chicago has invested enormous resources in mass transit, only to discover that many commuters are bypassing it as they travel from one "edge city" suburb to another. The relative wealth of investment and opportunities in suburban Tyson's Corner, Virginia, is contrasted with poverty-stricken Washington, D.C., located just a few miles away. Finally, Portland, Oregon, offers an example of how urban planning can bring about successful integration of transportation and the urban environment.

Smart Growth
Type: Videocassette
Length: 15 minutes
Date: 1998
Cost: $6.50
Source: International City/County Management Association
           777 North Capitol Street, NE, Suite 500
           Washington, DC 20002
           (202) 962-3685
           (202) 962-3500 (fax)
           http://www.icma.org

The purpose of this video is to educate citizens and public officials about the causes and consequences of urban sprawl and the
benefits of Smart Growth principles. A variety of cases are cited
from around the country to illustrate how Smart Growth can
achieve benefits for all parties involved. This is a production of
the Smart Growth Network, a cooperative partnership of a variety of planning agencies, businesses, and organizations nationwide that are seeking to develop a consensus on future urban
development. Included among the network's sponsors is the U.S.
Environmental Protection Agency's Urban and Economic Development Division.

Suburban Open Space Planning and Design
Type: Videocassette
Length: 135 minutes
Date: 1995
Cost: $59.95
Source: Planners Book Service
           American Planning Association
           122 S. Michigan Avenue
           Suite 1600
           Chicago, IL 60603
           (312) 786-6344
           (312) 431-9985 (fax)
           BookService@planning.org
           http://www.planning.org

This video reviews the spatial development of American suburbs
and explains how open planning strategies can make these communities more livable. It provides detailed explanations of a wide
range of approaches that planners can utilize to achieve good suburban design. Produced by the American Planning Association.

Taking Charge
Type: Video slide presentation and 287-page instructional
            manual
Length: 28 minutes
Date: 1996
Cost: $60.00
Source: Planners Book Service
            American Planning Association
            122 S. Michigan Avenue, Suite 1600
            Chicago, IL 60603
            (312) 786-6344
            (312) 431-9985 (fax)
            BookService@planning.org
            http://www.planning.org

This video package is intended to educate people about how to protect their communities from urban development pressures. The manual explains how to establish a community vision and create a growth management plan that is compatible with that vision. The video slide presentation shows concrete examples of techniques that communities across the United States have used to preserve historic buildings and scenic settings that are compatible with the need to develop land resources. Produced by the Mountains to Greenway Trust.

Traditional Town Planning Techniques
Type: Videocassette
Length: 240 minutes
Date: 1997
Cost: $432.00 for the series
Source: The Earthbeat Institute
            Route 10, Box 87-E
            Santa Fe, NM 87501
            (505) 471-4039
            althouse@nets.com

This set of videos provides a total of sixteen fifteen-minute lectures on the merits of traditional town planning design. Recorded in Seaside, Florida, one of the nation's leading examples of this form of design, the videos provide information on urban planning techniques, market analysis, pricing, financing, retailing, architectural design, and traffic patterns. Speakers range from experts in New Urbanist design, such as Andres Duany, to the mayor of Charleston, South Carolina, real estate experts, and traffic engineers.

Transportation Management and Edge Cities
Type: Videocassette
Length: 90 minutes
Date: 1994
Cost: $59.95
Source: Planners Book Service
American Planning Association
122 S. Michigan Avenue, Suite 1600
Chicago, IL 60603
(312) 786-6344
(312) 431-9985 (fax)
BookService@planning.org
http://www.planning.org

The ongoing process of urban sprawl growth has left America with a new type of urban agglomeration known as "edge cities" located on the periphery of major metropolitan areas. This video describes how automobile-dependent transportation systems greatly impact the relative quality of life for residents of edge cities. It also offers suggestions for alternative, less consumptive forms of transportation that can be encouraged and developed by planners. Produced by the American Planning Association.

Understanding Urban Sprawl
Type: Videocassette
Length: 47 minutes
Date: 1999
Cost: $129.00 (purchase), $75.00 (rental)
Source: Films for the Humanities and Sciences
P.O. Box 2053
Princeton, NJ 08543
(800) 257-5126
(609) 275-3767 (fax)
http://www.films.com

In this program, scientist and environmentalist Dr. David Suzuki examines the social, economic, and environmental implications of low-density sprawl development that spreads out from the edges of cities. The program argues that for decades suburban housing has carried the promise of paradise, but the need for continuous infrastructure development and the intensification of sprawl-related ecological issues, which are eroding health and the quality of life, are making the true impact of suburbia painfully clear. Case studies used in this program demonstrate that this phenomenon is not restricted to the United States. In addition to a report on Los Angeles, Mexico City and Vancouver, British Columbia, are also featured. Portland, Oregon, is show-cased as a model of what can be done when administrators, businesses, and homeowners commit themselves to slowing sprawl and reestablishing the amenities that make for a healthy community.

Why Plan? A Primer for the Concerned Citizen
Type: Videocassette
Length: 30 minutes
Date: 1988
Cost: $90.00
Source: Planners Book Service
             American Planning Association
             122 S. Michigan Avenue, Suite 1600
             Chicago, IL 60603
             (312) 786-6344
             (312) 431-9985 (fax)
             BookService@planning.org
             http://www.planning.org

Produced by the Municipal Video Project, this video explains the importance of community planning, who and what is involved in the planning process, and the consequences of unplanned, sprawl development. It includes a brief history of planning in the United States and comments from a noted land use attorney, several planning officials, and the executive director of the League of California Cities. This video is ideal for new commissioners, council members, service clubs, and civic groups seeking to know more about the subject of planning.

Software

Serving Maps on the Internet
Type: Computerized textbook and learning tool; materials include 130-page paperback and CD-ROM.
Date/Version: 1998
System(s):   IBM PC compatible with a 33 Mhz 486 processor, 8 MB RAM, SVGA video or Macintosh System 7 or better

Cost: $24.95
Source: Planners Book Service
               American Planning Association
               122 S. Michigan Avenue, Suite 1600
               Chicago, IL 60603
               (312) 786-6344
               (312) 431-9985 (fax)
               BookService@planning.org
               http://www.planning.org

Geographic Information Systems (GIS) are increasingly being used by planners, businesses, and governments to obtain much-needed information on urban trends and spatial growth patterns, including studying the impact of sprawl. Huge databases are now accessible via the World Wide Web that transmit this information instantly across the globe. Professional planner Christian Harder of the Environmental Systems Research Institute has assembled this helpful resource to introduce new users to the benefits of GIS. It provides twelve case studies that illustrate how organizations use web-based GIS to improve community services and plan for the future. It serves as a useful introduction to the many different ways that this technology can facilitate the collection and analysis of information.

SimCity 3000
Type: PC simulation game
Date/Version: 1998
System(s):   IBM PC, Pentium 166 or higher, 48MB RAM,
                 8MB Video Card, 6X CD-ROM
Cost: $49.95 (SimCity 3000), $29.95 (SimCity 2000)
Source: Electronic Arts
                 P.O. Box 9025
                 Redwood City, CA 94063
                 (650) 628-4311
                 (650) 628-5999 (fax)
                 http://www.ea.com

For ages twelve and up, this game is designed for home entertainment, but offers both children and adults a great deal of practical knowledge about urban planning and the complex issues surrounding sprawling development in America's cities. The game permits players to tinker endlessly with a city entirely of their own making, zoning residential neighborhoods, building parks, locating businesses, laying out utility lines, digging subway tunnels, and forming other key elements of a large metropolis. Players have the option to create their own city from scratch, or to start with a prebuilt metropolis. The great value in the game is the way in which the computer confronts the would-be designer with the consequences of his or her development decisions. Everything from property tax protesters to traffic congestion and response times to house fires is covered in this excellent simulation. Players also have the benefit of accessing advisors who represent different economic, social, and political interests in the city, thus exposing them to other dimensions of the real urban world. The newest version, SimCity 3000, has improved graphics as well as a vastly expanded scope that permits city designers to develop approximately 100 square miles of land. New features are available via the Maxis website at http://www.Simcity.com.

Spreadsheet Models for Urban and Regional Analysis

Type:	Spreadsheet tutorial; materials include 451-page text plus 3 and 1/2 inch diskette.
Date/Version:	1992
System(s):	IBM PC compatible, 386 processor, 8 MB RAM, Lotus 1-2-3 software, SVGA video card
Cost:	$44.95
Source:	Planners Book Service
	American Planning Association
	122 S. Michigan Avenue, Suite 1600
	Chicago, IL 60603
	(312) 786-6344
	(312) 431-9985 (fax)
	BookService@planning.org
	http://www.planning.org

Three experienced planners, Richard E. Klosterman, Richard K. Brail, and Earl G. Brossard of the Center for Urban Policy Research have put together a helpful introductory package for those interested in learning more about how to use spreadsheet programs in urban planning. As planners are being called upon to develop better means for dealing with urban sprawl, computer-based models are increasingly being utilized. This resource is designed to introduce spreadsheet models for demographic forecasting, economic analysis, environmental modeling, planning, and decision making. It features nineteen spreadsheet models with dozens of applications and contains advice on how to use the models, collect and enter data, interpret findings, and develop applications.

Glossary

adequate public facility ordinance   A growth management tool used by urban planners. Such ordinances require real estate developers to ensure that adequate public facilities, such as electricity, water, sewerage, and roads, are in place in a new development before it will be accepted by the community.

American Institute of Certified Planners   An organization for qualified professional planners affiliated with the American Planning Association. To become a member requires passing an examination after having demonstrated some practical experience working as a planning professional.

Better America Bonds   Federal funds made available to states and local communities to preserve and enhance open space, protect water quality, and clean up and redevelop urban brownfields. Communities pay zero interest on the bonds, and the principal is due within fifteen years. The program was launched under President Bill Clinton's "Livability Agenda" and is administered through several federal agencies. It is designed to encourage regional approaches that reflect collaborative land use planning among neighboring communities.

brownfields   Abandoned, idled, or underutilized industrial land that cannot be redeveloped due to serious environmental contamination. The presence of brownfields is a significant reason why commercial and industrial development has failed to materialize in many economically depressed inner-city communities in the United States.

central business district   A designation given by planners to the innermost core of an urban area that historically existed as the commercial and political center of the community. Such historic downtowns are the traditional focus for retail, commercial, and office land uses in cities. Today these zones have undergone considerable decline due to suburban and regional shopping centers and office parks that have siphoned investment, business activity, and consumer attention away from them.

citistate   A metropolitan region consisting of one or more historic central cities surrounded by cities and towns that have a shared identification; function as a single zone for trade, commerce, and communication; and share social, economic, and environmental interdependence.

civic art   A term used by New Urbanists to refer to the effort made to embellish public buildings and places with architecture and design features that help define and celebrate the community.

cluster zoning   A method of zoning in which development restrictions are waived in other more suitable areas in order to encourage more compact, higher-density land use. Such zoning is used in an effort to protect vulnerable open space from development.

community   A collection of people who share a common sense of identity and knowledge about the place in which they reside. In its strongest sense, it implies regular interaction among people, accountability, and a sense of shared commitment to civic ideals.

compact development   Exists where buildings are situated within close proximity to one another, and may apply to either residential housing, commercial developments, or a mixture of both. This kind of development is often preferred by planners and environmentalists because it enables people to get around by walking, uses less land, and can foster a greater sense of community.

comprehensive plan   A plan prepared by the citizens of a community to guide current and future land use development in their locality. These plans commonly incorporate elements such as economic goals, environmental protection, health, public safety, traffic circulation, and fiscal stability. All states have enabling legislation permitting local governments to create comprehensive plans, although these plans have only an advisory status in most.

concurrency   A growth management technique that disallows new real estate development unless adequate road, utility, and other publicly funded service infrastructure is already present or funded so that it will be completed at the same time as the development.

conservation easement   An agreement between a landowner and an outside party to restrict the future development of that land to certain specified uses (such as farmland or in an undeveloped state) in return for compensation. Such easements can be negotiated and paid for by government or by private, nonprofit trusts seeking to preserve open space and scenic landscapes.

density   In the context of urban planning refers to the number of buildings per mile or acre. Higher density leads to more compact development on less land, while lower density contributes to sprawling development on greater amounts of land.

Department of Housing and Urban Development   A federal agency established in 1965 through the consolidation of housing and urban development programs and agencies. This agency administers the various housing laws passed by Congress that provide federal assistance for states and local communities to realize urban renewal plans, including the provision of water and sewer services, affordable housing, planning assistance, open space acquisition, and a variety of other urban-related issues.

development impact assessment   A formal study that uses a variety of measures to determine whether a proposed land use will impose acceptable costs and burdens upon a community. Areas usually addressed in these assessments are fiscal, traffic, public facility, and special impacts such as air quality, noise, and exposure to other hazards.

edge cities   Large suburban communities located on the periphery of metropolitan areas that have evolved into growth points and function independently of the traditional central city of the region. These cities have attracted the highest share of business investment, new residential housing, and commercial development over the past twenty-five years, often to the detriment of central cities that cannot compete with the low taxes, cheap undeveloped land, and close proximity to low-density residential neighborhoods.

eminent domain   The power of government to acquire land and property for public use for which the owner must receive just compensation, as specified by the U.S. Constitution.

exclusionary zoning   Land use rules that make the construction of affordable housing difficult if not altogether impossible to achieve by imposing regulatory costs that are unjustified from the standpoint of conventional health or safety considerations. Exclusionary techniques include imposing unreasonably large minimum lot sizes, prohibitions on multifamily dwellings and mobile homes, and other measures that keep low-income citizens from residing in the community.

exurb   Rural areas located miles outside of defined metropolitan regions and suburbs. Many of these unincorporated areas have been undergoing rapid urban growth as new highway interchanges are built that enable commuters to reach them in a day's journey to and from work.

Geographic Information Systems (GIS)   Comprises a variety of software and hardware computer systems that relate and display geographic (spatial) data. Information can be incorporated into these databases from a wide variety of sources and typically includes geologic, ecological, land use, demographic, transportation, economic development, and other factors. The capacity of GIS to quickly overlay new information on top of existing data and to display it in diverse graphic presentation formats has enabled land use planners, business developers, governmental officials, and many others to make more rational decisions regarding present and future land use.

greenbelt   An integrated system of open land that surrounds a metropolitan region that is protected from urban and incompatible rural development. Greenbelts can consist of a variety of lands including parks, natural preserves, state forests, and protected farmlands.

growth management   Attempts by communities to regulate the amount, timing, location, and character of current and future land development. Communities undertake growth management planning to avoid experiencing tax increases that result from new housing and commercial development, mitigate traffic congestion, and prevent other socially unacceptable burdens created by urban sprawl.

historic district   A collection of buildings, structures, and associated objects and land that possess a recognized historic value. If authorized by state statute and enacted by a local ordinance, a historic district or landmark commission is empowered to restrict or control changes to exterior architectural features visible from public ways. Such districts are eligible for state and federal funds to facilitate preservation.

home rule   An optional method for organizing and empowering municipal governments that grants such communities substantial autonomy to draft, adopt, and amend their own charters. Home rule enables many local governments to resist attempts by regional and/or state planning agencies to influence local land use decisions.

impact fees   A fee levied on real estate developers by local governments for each project they undertake. These fees are designed to mitigate the otherwise onerous impact of expanded public facilities and infrastructure that are necessary when new homes or businesses are located within a community.

infill development   Real estate investment that occurs in a depressed urban area that has suffered from a lack of business and job opportunities. This type of urban revitalization is often cited by planners and activists as a preferred alternative to the ongoing commercial and residential development of open spaces located at the periphery of metropolitan regions.

inholding   A privately held tract of land that is completely surrounded by public parklands. Landowners under such circumstances complain of unfair regulatory burdens placed upon them by state and federal officials.

land trusts   Nonprofit voluntary organizations that work with landowners to protect natural, scenic, and agricultural lands threatened by urban development. Land trusts use a variety of tools to conserve open space, including acquisition of conservation easements that permanently restrict land use, outright purchases of land for conservation, and the facilitation of estate planning.

leapfrog development   A situation that occurs when real estate developers and home builders bypass established suburban communities that have imposed strong growth controls and development restrictions and locate their projects in ever more distant unincorporated areas. This urban growth pattern perpetuates the problem of urban sprawl.

master plan *See* **comprehensive plan**

metropolitan government Exists where a regional government agency has been granted limited powers over constituent local governments in a large metropolitan area. Metropolitan governments exercise substantial authority over land use decision making in only a few communities in the United States. The most significant of these are Portland, Oregon, and Minneapolis, Minnesota.

New Urbanism A school of design founded on the conviction that the built spaces of an area deeply influence the quality of community life, and therefore planners and architects have the responsibility to construct socially diverse, aesthetically pleasing environments for their fellow citizens. New Urbanists argue that a more compact neighborhood design, with dense housing clustered around mixed-use commercial zones, a reliance on mass transit, preservation of open space, and inspiring neotraditional civic architecture fosters values that reaffirm community spirit and oneness.

NIMBY An acronym for "Not In My Backyard," representing an attitude that commonly finds expression among home owners who find a proposed change to existing land use to be objectionable due to the detrimental impact they perceive it to have on their own property values and quality of life.

open space Land that lacks any substantial buildings or residential uses and therefore imposes few burdens upon a community to underwrite the cost of public services. Such land is either left in its natural state as a preserve, set aside for passive recreational use purposes as a public park, or is utilized for some agricultural purpose such as cultivation or grazing that does not greatly alter the existing natural landscape.

performance zoning Local codes that stipulate what real estate developers and builders may or may not do in terms of end results. This is an alternative to detailed, exacting regulations that tend to bog the process down in red tape and often fail to accomplish larger community goals.

planned unit development Land use regulations that permit relaxation of the zoning standards for a specific district so as to provide flexibility in the placement of buildings in exchange for an overall development plan for the property. Under an approved plan of this type, the local community has in effect entrusted a real estate developer with the task of developing a substantial tract of land in a responsible and beneficial manner.

planning board An appointed or elected body of citizens who exercise authority over the orderly use and development of land within a local government jurisdiction. Responsibilities include overseeing the implementation and enforcement of zoning bylaws and developing long-range land use plans.

property rights In the context of land use issues, refers to the exclusive right to possess, use, and dispose of land (i.e., real property) that any owner enjoys, as recognized by common law and upheld in the courts of the United States.

purchase of development rights An arrangement whereby a farmer voluntarily sells the development rights of farmland to a state government, receiving compensation for the development restrictions (conservation easement) placed on the land thereafter. The goal of these programs is to keep land in agricultural and open space use. Under these agreements, the farmer retains title to the land and can sell or pass along the land to others, although the development restrictions remain. It is assumed that the money received by the farmer will be used to buy down debt, reinvest in equipment, or for other purposes that help keep the farm financially viable.

regionalism The belief that the many communities that presently constitute large cities and their surrounding metropolitan areas are best able to address shared problems through regional governmental cooperation, rather than independently derived, disjointed policies. Regionalism can work through formal organizations such as a council of governments, or on a more informal basis through cooperative agreements and contracts negotiated among neighboring communities. Proponents suggest that such arrangements offer the possibility of overcoming racial disparities and resource inequities, shaping more balanced growth, and promoting sustainable economic development.

regulatory taking The loss of market value that occurs when a piece of real estate is affected by development restrictions imposed by environmental regulations. Restrictions are likened to the loss of land due to an eminent domain taking by government. Property rights proponents maintain that such "takings" are unconstitutional under the terms of the Fifth Amendment to the U.S. Constitution, unless just compensation is offered by the government.

right-to-farm laws State laws that provide farmers with legally defensible protection from nuisance lawsuits for standard farming practices. Such laws arose in response to burdens placed on farmers by people who built residences and shops on land adjacent to farmland and then complained about the noise, spray drift, odors, slow-moving machinery, and other features of farming that detracted from their enjoyment of their own property.

scatter development *See* **sprawl**

site plan review   Takes place when a community vests its planning and/or zoning agency with the responsibility of granting building permits based on a review of new land development, taking into consideration building safety, layout of utilities, internal circulation, adequacy of parking, and buffering from adjacent land uses. This is the principle tool that most local governments possess for regulating land use.

Smart Growth   A strategy that seeks to overcome the historic deadlock between progrowth and antigrowth forces. Advocates hope to achieve economic development while recognizing the need for communities to better the quality of life of existing residents, to preserve open space, and to contain costly fiscal burdens associated with rapid, unplanned commercial and residential development. Smart Growth presupposes that carefully planned development derived through inclusive processes of consensus building is the best way for communities to grow.

smart roads   A proposal to issue electronic devices known as transponders (or smart tags) that compute mileage charges for drivers for use of roads by the mile. The charge for mileage would be higher for trips during daily rush hours as an inducement to drivers to either commute at less congested times or share the cost of a ride with another person.

sprawl   Refers to both the outward spread of commercial, industrial, and residential development into open spaces located on the fringes of urban centers and the detrimental side effects that this kind of development pattern imposes upon citizens. Negative effects of sprawl include the loss of productive agricultural lands and other natural landscapes, increasing tax burdens associated with the need to underwrite the expansion of urban services to newly developed areas, rising traffic congestion on existing road networks, overcrowded public schools, and a general loss of community identity in the midst of automobile-dependent, low-density subdivision housing.

stakeholders   The people and organizations who share an interest in the present and future development of a community. Stakeholders interested in land use decisions typically include individual residents and landowners, civic and religious organizations, business associations, environmental and conservation groups, and governmental agencies at all levels.

strip development   Consists of commercial buildings of all types located along a heavily traveled road or highway corridor for a relatively long distance. Such developments are faulted by planners for being wasteful of open space, creating significant traffic congestion, and for being mostly accessible only by automobile. They exist in stark contrast to compact commercial development, such as shopping malls, in which a variety of store buildings are located close together within easy walking distance and make better use of limited space.

subdivision The process by which a tract of land is split into smaller parcels, lots, or building sites so that the parcels may eventually be sold and developed. Regulation of subdivision by agents of local governments serves the purpose of controlling the process so that substantial changes to existing land are compatible with the wishes of the larger community.

suburb An urban community that is located outside of the environs of an older city. Suburbs have a separate political jurisdiction, tax base, school system, and other services from that of the traditional city center. Suburbs also often possess a different racial and ethnic composition from the center city.

sustainable communities Communities that are able to accommodate the needs of present-day economic development while preserving non-renewable resources and ensuring that the future quality of life for residents is not compromised.

sustainable development Urban growth that meets the economic needs of living generations without spoiling assets for the generations that follow.

traditional neighborhood development An urban architectural design in which the basic unit of planning is the neighborhood district, which is limited in size, with a well-defined edge and focused community center. The design reflects a deliberate attempt to foster community interaction through a network of interlinking street patterns, gathering points, and shopping districts that are arranged within walking distance of densely arranged homes.

traffic calming A variety of measures designed to slow down the speed of motor vehicles. Originally, devices such as speed bumps, traffic circles, and directional barriers were advocated so as to ensure the safety of bicycles and pedestrians on city streets. More recently, calming devices have been proposed for major highway commuting corridors to impede the flow of traffic, thereby encouraging motorists to consider alternative means of transportation such as buses and rail lines.

transferable development rights A program in which development rights for land previously designated as appropriate for urban and commercial uses may be sold to real estate developers, providing a financial incentive for landowners to remain in farming. The developers then have clearance by the community to use these development rights in other specified areas previously designated for high-density urban and commercial land use.

transit-oriented development Exists where regional urban plans call for new housing or commercial development that will accommodate mass transit by bus or train. Transit-oriented development usually involves such elements as high housing density, concentration of commercial activities in a compact center, and pedestrian amenities that facilitate movement to and from transit stops. This kind of planning reflects a policy of limiting private automobile use, thereby fostering a decline in local traffic congestion and air pollution.

urban growth boundary Lines that are mapped out by planners as a means to contain sprawling urban development that is encroaching upon greenspaces located beyond city limits. They mandate that all development must be concentrated in land area within a boundary, usually with allowances for greater density and mixed use.

urban land As defined by the United States Census Bureau, an urbanized area must have a population of at least 2,500 people per square mile, and adjacent areas must have a density of 1,000 people per square mile.

urban renewal Any type of coordinated effort that combines public subsidies with private sector investment capital to revitalize a deteriorating and economically depressed urban area.

urban service area A defined area where water, sewer, roads, and other public services will be extended by government to facilitate urban residential and commercial development. The purpose of these areas is to limit development to the confines of such zones and thus prevent sprawl growth into the countryside.

visioning A collective effort on the part of public officials, business executives, and other community leaders from all of the local governments that comprise a metropolitan region to formulate a shared vision for the region that encourages cooperation toward commonly held goals. Among the priorities of these efforts is typically an attempt to rein in the forces of sprawl development.

Wise Use A political ideology and citizen's movement that has organized to oppose governmental land use regulations and restrictions that indirectly result in the loss of property values for landowners and businesses. Central to this view is the belief that any such regulation constitutes a governmental "taking" and therefore must be compensated for the fair market value that has been lost as required by the U.S. Constitution.

zoning Refers to rules governing land use in a community. Such rules are designed to control the type of use, building height, minimum lot sizes, building setbacks, parking, signage, landscaping, and other structural features of interest to citizens, and are adopted through the democratic process under the authority of a zoning ordinance.

zoning board of appeals An appointed body of citizens who share responsibility for overseeing the enforcement of a local government zoning code. The primary activity of such boards is to hear requests for waivers (variances) from citizens who feel that a particular provision of the code is imposing unnecessary hardship or practical difficulties upon them.

Index

251

Donald C. Williams is associate professor of government at Western New England College, Springfield, Massachusetts.